NEW MER

General Editors:
William C. Carroll, Boston University
Brian Gibbons, University of Münster
Tiffany Stern, University College, Oxford

The interior of a Restoration theatre
by C. Walter Hodges

NEW MERMAIDS

The Alchemist
All for Love
Arden of Faversham
Arms and the Man
Bartholmew Fair
The Beaux' Stratagem
The Beggar's Opera
The Changeling
A Chaste Maid in Cheapside
The Country Wife
The Critic
Doctor Faustus
The Duchess of Malfi
The Dutch Courtesan
Eastward Ho!
Edward the Second
Elizabethan and Jacobean Tragedies
Epicoene or The Silent Woman
Every Man In His Humour
Gammer Gurton's Needle
An Ideal Husband
The Importance of Being Earnest
The Jew of Malta
The Knight of the Burning Pestle
Lady Windermere's Fan
London Assurance
Love for Love
Major Barbara
The Malcontent
The Man of Mode
Marriage A-La-Mode
Mrs Warren's Profession

A New Way to Pay Old Debts
The Old Wife's Tale
The Playboy of the Western World
The Provoked Wife
Pygmalion
The Recruiting Officer
The Relapse
The Revenger's Tragedy
The Rivals
The Roaring Girl
The Rover
Saint Joan
The School for Scandal
She Stoops to Conquer
The Shoemaker's Holiday
The Spanish Tragedy
Tamburlaine
The Tamer Tamed
Three Late Medieval Morality Plays
    Mankind
    Everyman
    Mundus et Infans
'Tis Pity She's a Whore
The Tragedy of Mariam
Volpone
The Way of the World
The White Devil
The Witch
The Witch of Edmonton
A Woman Killed with Kindness
A Woman of No Importance
Women Beware Women

NEW MERMAIDS

SIR GEORGE ETHEREGE

THE MAN OF MODE

Edited by John Barnard, Professor Emeritus,
University of Leeds

BLOOMSBURY
LONDON · NEW DELHI · NEW YORK · SYDNEY

Bloomsbury Methuen Drama

An imprint of Bloomsbury Publishing Plc

50 Bedford Square
London
WC1B 3DP
UK

1385 Broadway
New York
NY 10018
USA

www.bloomsbury.com

First New Mermaid edition 1979 © 1979 Ernest Benn Limited
Second edition with revised introduction published 2007
Reprinted by Bloomsbury Methuen Drama 2010, 2011, 2012, 2013, 2014

© A & C Black Publishers Limited 2007

British Library Cataloguing-in-Publication Data
A catalogue record for this book is available from the British Library.

ISBN: PB: 978-0-7136-8193-2

Library of Congress Cataloging-in-Publication Data
A catalog record for this book is available from the Library of Congress.

Typeset by RefineCatch Ltd, Bungay, Suffolk
Printed and bound in Great Britain

CONTENTS

ACKNOWLEDGEMENTS

In preparing this edition my greatest debt has been to the play's earlier editors. H. F. B. Brett-Smith's learned annotation and careful handling of textual difficulties helped at crucial points. John Conaghan's Fountainwell text, which contains the fullest bibliographical examination yet published of *The Man of Mode*'s first edition, was helpful in preparing both text and commentary. In modernizing, A. W. Verity's edition gave help on some occasions. The sane, informed, and careful scholarship of W. B. Carnochan's Regents Restoration edition was constantly of use.

With real generosity, Professor Harold Brooks allowed the use of unpublished information from his edition of Oldham – so enabling Dorimant's reference to an elephant, which has defeated previous editors, to be revealed as a topical allusion. Paul Levy gave gastronomic advice. Mr. Philip Wilby of the University of Leeds very kindly created modern versions of Dr Staggins's contemporary setting of Dorimant's song ('When first Amintas') and of Sir Car Scroope's song, and did so at very short notice.

Mr David Masson of the Brotherton Collection, the University of Leeds, was uniformly patient and obliging, as were the staff of the Bodleian Library, Mr Robert Kenedy of the Victoria and Albert Museum, and Dr R. A. Sayce, Librarian of Worcester College, Oxford. For her advice on the Introduction I am deeply indebted to Hermione Lee of the University of York. Both the General Editor of this volume, Dr Brian Gibbons, and my publisher, John Collis, generously gave minute attention to the text and Introduction, saving me from slips and errors of various kinds. I must also thank Paddy Rowe and Sara Broadbent for their care and expertise with an often difficult task in preparing the typescript.

Denton   J. B.
October 1978

Note to Revised Edition

The text of this revised edition remains virtually unaltered (though Paul Hammond's edition of Dryden has persuaded me to revert to the reading of the first quarto in the Epilogue, l. 6): minor corrections and a few additions have been made to the commentary. In line with the new format for the series, a brief account of the play and a plot summary have been added. The main change to the Introduction is that while *The Man of Mode* is still not a regular part of the repertory, it is no longer necessary, as it was in 1979, to lament the play's virtual disappearance from the stage, as the section on *The Man of Mode*'s recent performance history makes clear. I am grateful to Rachel Pilbeam of the Out of Joint Theatre Company and Eleanor Manwell of the Orange Tree Theatre for information and for advice. Professor Martin Banham gave me information about the 1987 Workshop Theatre's production at the School of English, University of Leeds, and put me in touch with James Frieze, now at Liverpool John Moores University, who provided me with photographs and other information. Amanda Worthy of the Open University Library kindly sent me a copy of the television camera script for the OU/BBC's selection from *The Man of Mode* first screened in August 1981. In addition, my thanks are due to C. W. Sheppard, Brotherton Collection, University of Leeds, and to Professor W. R. Owens, Open University.

Oxford   J.B.
March 2007

INTRODUCTION

About the play

The Man of Mode, or, Sir Fopling Flutter, Etherege's finest play and a classic of Restoration drama, is a brilliant and hard-edged courtship comedy. Its sharply observed depiction of fashionable seventeenth-century London society presents a social and sexual battleground whose tensions and moral confusions are as relevant now as then. From the beginning, Etherege's comedy attracted contradictory responses. Is its self-gratifying rake-hero, whose sexual conquests seem to be as much, or more, about his reputation a libertine as anything else, to be admired? Or is his amoral, cynical opportunism, with its exploitation of the sexual double standard, exposed and undercut by the play's bleak honesty? Does the 'wild' and witty heroine succeed in conquering his aversion to love and marriage, and the play's conclusion celebrate the victory of youth over a repressive elder generation?

Stage performances (like critics) can, and have, interpreted *The Man of Mode* very differently. The play has many themes. It draws distinctions between wit and affectation, between style and substance, and between French and English fashions and 'modes'. It insists on the need to distinguish between appearance and reality, sexual gratification and mutual love, and sexual freedom and sexual licence. The play describes the conflict between generations and between town and country, and shows how the masks provided by social manners, with their changing linguistic codes, can be used to manipulate others or to disguise the characters' innermost motives and feelings. This is especially true of the sexual sparring between men and women, which can be amusing, liberating, or dangerous. All these themes are examined through the play's scintillating dialogue, as analytical as it is pointed.

The ideas in *The Man of Mode* are explored through a large and socially varied cast of characters. These include an off-stage whore, tradesmen and tradeswomen, servants and maids, members of the controlling parental generation belonging to the 'last age' and up from the country, and the younger generation. These are the as yet unmarried young men and women, represented by a pair of idealistic young lovers, single women belonging to the *demi-monde* but accepted as part of fashionable society, a rich and beautiful young heiress newly arrived in London, and libertine young men, who include the rake-hero, Dorimant, and the outrageous Sir Fopling Flutter, newly arrived from Paris. Sir Fopling's name, unlike Dorimant's, appears in the title, and the way in which he is cast and acted are crucial factors in staging the play. Sir Fopling, the would-be man of mode, is mocked in comparison with Dorimant, but the two characters can be seen as commenting upon one another.

Summary of the plot

There are two linked main plots. Dorimant, a fashionable man about town and notorious womaniser, rids himself of one mistress, Mrs Loveit, with the aid of her friend, Bellinda. In the process Dorimant seduces Bellinda, while simultaneously pursuing a young heiress, Harriet Woodvill, who has just come up to Town for the first time. He appears to fall in love with Harriet, but she holds him off. Even after he has proposed marriage, she demands that he follow her to that 'sad place', the country, where she may or may not accept him. Interwoven with this plot is that of Young Bellair, expected by his father and Lady Woodvill to marry Harriet, her daughter. However, Young Bellair loves Emilia, and she him: with the help of Emilia's aunt, Lady Townley, Old Bellair's plans are circumvented, largely because the old man, foolishly, falls for Emilia. Recognising his stupidity, Old Bellair blesses his son's marriage, and the older generation accepts Dorimant as Harriet's suitor. More loosely tied to the action is the foolish would-be wit, Sir Fopling Flutter, whose affected Parisian style and manners are ridiculed by the other wits. Mrs Loveit mistakenly believes that her pretended flirtation with Sir Fopling, the mock 'man of mode', will regain Dorimant's attentions by making him jealous, in which she comes close to success. At the conclusion, Mrs Loveit is rejected from the play's social world, though it finds room for Sir Fopling. The comedy ends with a dance celebrating the forthcoming wedding of Young Bellair and Emilia. However, the seriousness of Dorimant's commitment to Harriet remains to be tested by his visit to meet her, and her family, in the country.

The play

The Man of Mode is a finely balanced and brilliantly executed comedy of the sexes. Its psychological insight is allied to a complex and open exploration of the patterns and social proscriptions which, self-consciously and unconsciously, govern courtship. The conventions may differ from those of Shakespearean comedy or modern life, but the basic patterns (and human reasons for those patterns) remain constant. Courtship rituals are also games which are exploratory, allowing the lovers to discern the nature of their partner before full commitment. As such they are at once defensive and offensive, creating room for both advance and retreat, and giving time for discrimination between the merely sexual and more lasting attractions. The norm from which the lovers depart is inevitably supplied by their society, though usually the younger generation seeks its own pattern of conventions distinct from that of their parents. *The Man of Mode* is about the enjoyable, dangerous, necessary, and finally serious games which people play in the most crucial area in which personal fulfilment and instinctual drives have to be accommodated within a social framework – courtship and marriage. While it exhibits the tolerance and gaiety of comedy, *The Man of Mode* is not an entirely comforting or comfortable play. Its affirmation is balanced by an ironic scepticism.

A direct claim for the success and importance of Etherege's final comedy is necessary because interpretations vary so widely as to call any pretensions it may have to coherence or value into serious doubt. For Bonamy Dobrée, Etherege's three plays were 'pure works of art directed to no end but themselves' and are entirely unmotivated 'by any moral stimulus'. *The Man of Mode* has also been characterized as a 'delightfully satiric entertainment', as 'an uncompromisingly tough and realistic play', as a bleak and bitter comedy which exposes Dorimant's 'life of isolation', and as an expression of Dorimant's 'Hobbesian aggressiveness, competitiveness, and desire for power and "glory" . . . an egoistic assertion of self through control of others.'[1] This list by no means exhausts the possible interpretations, but is enough to suggest that the comedy's ambiguities arise either from the ingenuity of critics uneasily trying to answer L. C. Knights's case against Restoration comedy ('trivial, gross, and dull') or from the play's intrinsic resistance to the imposition of a single reading. If the latter, *The Man of Mode*'s refusal to lie comfortably within neatly woven analyses argues its claim to classic status in Frank Kermode's sense – that is, a work in which the multiplicity of what is signified is in excess of the signifier.

Realism and Comedy
Part of the reason for the startling critical disparity is the comedy's own richness, but a too-frequent contributory factor is a misunderstanding of

---

1 Bonamy Dobrée, *Restoration Comedy*, 1924, p. 60; Robert D. Hume, *The Development of English Drama in the Late Seventeenth Century*, 1976, p. 97; Paul C. Davies, 'The State of Nature and the State of War: A Reconsideration of *The Man of Mode*', *University of Toronto Quarterly*, 39 (1969), 53–62; Jocelyn Powell, 'George Etherege and the Form of a Comedy', *Restoration Theatre, Stratford-upon-Avon Studies 6*, ed. J. R. Brown and Bernard Harris, 1965, p. 61; Dale Underwood, *Etherege and the Seventeenth Century Comedy of Manners*, 1957, p. 73. For L. C. Knight's classic attack, see 'Restoration Comedy: The Reality and the Myth', *Explorations*, 1946, pp. 131–49.

how realistic comedy works, a misunderstanding of how such comedies, while needing to capture the texture of a given society from a specific viewpoint, can nevertheless transcend their period. There is a further associated unwillingness to admit the ways in which comedy's strongly formulaic patterns can present a serious examination of moral issues while appearing to collapse these problems into the inevitable happy ending. In the case of *The Man of Mode*, the episodic plot with its inclusion of Sir Fopling, who is not strictly necessary but gives his name to the play and rivals Dorimant in his appeal to the audience, provides an additional difficulty.

The question of the delicate relationship between 'realism' and comedy's bearing on actual life can be conveniently focussed on Sir Fopling, Dorimant, Mrs Loveit and Bellinda. J. H. Wilson argues that Etherege's

> ... idealised portraits are recognisable as the patterns of mannered, aristocratic society. Here is no question of realism; Etherege seized upon and embodied in his play not the real, day by day life of Whitehall, but the life which Whitehall was pleased to imagine it led. Individual items may be factual, but the total picture is a comic illusion.[2]

But comic illusion does not exclude realism since 'realism' itself is a literary convention. What matters is not that *The Man of Mode* is selective, but that its enlarging and simplifying of contemporary life is an interpretative act, which reveals the conflicting values implicit in the tensions present in the audience's own experience. The early evidence shows that the original audience was only too eager to recognize its own world in the play.[3] Sir Fopling, that is, offers the Aristotelian pleasure of imitation (as do the marvellous genre portraits of the Shoemaker and the Orange-woman). Laughter springs from instant recognizability, and from Etherege's precise observation of linguistic and social mannerisms. But the laughter at Sir Fopling also has its source in the audience's anxieties, as Dryden was well aware:

> Yet every man is safe from what he feared,
> For no one fool is hunted from the herd.

> (Epilogue, 33–4)

---

2 *The Court Wits*, 1948, p. 164. Robert D. Hume cites this passage with enthusiasm (op. cit., p. 91).
3 For contemporary attempts to identify characters in Etherege's comedy with their real life models, see 'Early Stage History and Reception' below, pp. xlix–l and n. 59.

Sir Fopling acts as a scapegoat for the audience's unadmitted fear that it too may easily mistake form for substance, an anxiety particularly alive in a period striving for a new style of sophistication. Dryden's efforts as critic and writer to establish 'correct' literary standards, Sprat and the Royal Society's efforts to create a concise and plain English, the life-style of Charles II's court, and Wren's classicism, all owe something to an emulation of European civilization and culture. Curtis D. Cecil's study of the language of Restoration comedy makes clear the way in which the refinement of English prose style and the aspiration towards refined conversation were stimulated by European standards and, in particular, by the example of France.[4] A firm indicator of contemporary aspirations is apparent in the number of handbooks, frequently translated from the French, on manners and conversation published during these years. To the extent which French culture provided a standard, it also threatened cultural imperialism – the incidence in the play of words recently taken from the French is a lexical index of that influence. Hence the need to establish an English sophistication, one distinct from that of the French in particular. Sir Fopling's inanities come from an unthinking acceptance of French fashion and attitudes only equalled by his ignorance. Dorimant's style, on the other hand, looks to France but is distinctly English. It is very striking that when Sir Fopling reveals his ignorance by confusing the Comte de Bussy with Chapman's stage-hero (IV.i, 219–23), the on-stage laughter assumes that everyone, including the women, knows Bussy's *Histoire Amoureuse des Gaulles*, a witty, gossiping account of *liaisons* in aristocratic French society, as well as the names of famous French gallants and their valets. If this is a joke against Sir Fopling, it must also have been a joke which cut uncomfortably close for many in the audience: a knowledge of French gossip and current publications might be assumed in Charles II's Court, but hardly in the public theatre. This point is surely implied by Dryden's comment that 'Sir Fopling is a fool so nicely writ, / The ladies would mistake him for a wit ...' (Epilogue, 7–8).

Taking Sir Fopling and Dorimant together it is evident that the audience is asked to split its knowledge of itself between the two. Sir Fopling exorcises the fear that gallants may too often resemble his idiocies, while encouraging a covert admiration for the fearlessness of Dorimant's manipulation of the new style in manners. The simplicity of that division

4   ' "Une Espèce d'Éloquence Abrégée": The Idealised Speech of Restoration Comedy', *Études anglaises*, 19 (1966), 15–25, 'Libertine and *Précieux* Elements in Restoration Comedy', *Essays in Criticism*, 9 (1959), 239–51, and 'Raillery in Restoration Comedy', *Huntington Library Quarterly*, 29 (1965–66), 147–59.

Royal Shakespeare Company, Aldwych Theatre, 1971: (from left) Lady Bellair (Elizabeth Tyrell), Old Bellair (David Waller), Dorimant (Alan Howard), Sir Fopling Flutter (John Wood), Harriet (Helen Mirren), Medley (Julian Glover), and Emilia (Isla Blair). Photograph by Reg Wilson © Royal Shakespeare Company.

is, however, qualified by the suggestion that Dorimant, as much as Sir Fopling, may be no more than a man of mode. They are linked too in another way. Medley comments on his 'natural indulgence for fools' (III.ii, 129). The audience's attitude to Sir Fopling is at once aggressive and tolerant, even affectionate. Aggression is there because Sir Fopling embodies anxieties, warmth because his monomania makes him indestructible. His complacency means that he is all essential self, and to a degree the invulnerability of his two-dimensional selfhood is enviable. The audience's natural indulgence for fools has a surprising relationship to its natural indulgence for the rake.

Both characters, then, give a significant reflection of contemporary mores in the London of the 1670s, a reflection which assumes the desirability of polished manners. That it reflects an aspiration rather than a fact is self-evident. Dorimant's 'genteel' and civil behaviour eschews brawls and whores: the lives of Rochester and Etherege clearly did not, as the affray with the watch at Epsom in June 1676 demonstrates.[5] Nor does the play show any of the main characters pursuing a career at Court or elsewhere. It is also striking that although *The Man of Mode* clearly implies the existence of a *demi-monde*, it mutes its appearance. Mrs Loveit, says Dorimant, is a 'person of quality' (III.ii, 219) as well as being the 'most noted coquette in town' (IV.i, 195). Both she and Bellinda move naturally in Lady Townley's world. On the other hand, when Dorimant directs suspicion away from Bellinda by pretending that she is mercenary, he reminds the audience of the existence of kept women and whores in the town. Nell Gwynn was only the most obvious example of a woman who had succeeded in Charles's London. Moll Kirke, Maid of Honour to the Duchess of York, had a well publicized affair first with the Duke of Monmouth and then with the Earl of Mulgrave in 1674–6. She was then rumoured to have married Lord Mordaunt, a noted fop, but in fact ended as the wife of Sir Thomas Vernon in 1677.[6] Mrs Loveit's flirtation with Sir Fopling reflects a possible resolution to her ambiguous position in a world which is harsh to a woman whose reputation is threatened. Dorimant tells her that she has a moderate 'stock of reputation left yet' (V.i, 139–40). She must choose how best to use that stock. *The Man of Mode* needs to treat this area with dramatic tact. It might be said to glamorize the promiscuity of the town by passing over the figures of Mrs Loveit and Bellinda, but the audience also knew that in their society experienced women might attain considerable status and even power. That ambiguity is one which the play chooses not to explore, because it is finally a comedy of courtship. The audience's experience of actuality is brought to bear on the comic world, and tests its resolution. 'Realism' is inevitably selective. The morality of art does not lie in the creation of a system acceptable to a moral philosopher, but in its truth to the inconsistencies and contradictions of life portrayed within a specific social context, whose values may be radically confused. The moral conflicts of *The Man of Mode* are those of its period: by revealing the shape of these conflicts accurately, Etherege's play attains truthfulness to human experience.

5   For a contemporary account see 'The Author', pp. lii–iii below.
6   See J. M. Auffret, '*The Man of Mode* and *The Plain Dealer*: Common Origin and Parallels', *Études anglaises*, 19 (1966), 209–22 (at 215–16).

Dorimant and the Moral Issue

However, it is the moral issue which has dominated (and obfuscated) discussion even since the argument between Steele and John Dennis in 1722.[7] Dorimant's character is the crux, as a brief summary of his role shows. The rake-hero is introduced in his dressing-room preparing for action in his chosen arena – the Mall and London's private houses. Surrounded by tradespeople, his friends, and his servant, he reveals how he plans to cast off one mistress, Mrs Loveit, in favour of her closest friend Bellinda. Moreover, he intends, with Bellinda's active help, to trick Mrs Loveit into rejecting him. In the course of Act I he learns of the arrival in London of a beautiful young heiress, Harriet, and at the end of the Act he is shown sending money to a town whore. Despite some near-setbacks, Dorimant does succeed in seducing Bellinda, does cast off Mrs Loveit, and ends the comedy having certainly won Harriet's heart, and almost certainly her hand, without entirely foreclosing the possibility of continued relationships with both Bellinda and Mrs Loveit. The bare bones of the plot show Dorimant's kinship with Don Juan, another seventeenth-century creation who stands as a naturalist and rationalist antagonist to the *précieux* idealizing of Courtly Love. (Just as Machiavelli's semi-mythic status reflects the emotional and intellectual crisis consequent upon the discovery of *realpolitik* in the late sixteenth and seventeenth centuries, and Faustus testifies to the scientific assault on the boundaries of God-given knowledge, so Don Juan is a response to a related crisis in sexual attitudes.) Not surprisingly the play's imagery persistently aligns Dorimant with the Devil – for Lady Woodvill he is 'prince of all the devils in the town' (III.iii, 106–7).[8] But if Dorimant is allied to Don Juan and hence to the libertine and sceptical strain in seventeenth-century culture, whose most obvious contemporary exemplar was Etherege's fellow-wit, Lord Rochester, *The Man of Mode* is not an exploration of the myth's most radical consequences. Unlike Mozart's heroically fated figure he does not face the Commendatore and end in Hell; nor does Etherege's comedy allow Dorimant's delight in controlling others to become the utter ruthlessness of the Vicomte de Valmont and Marquise de Merteuil in *Les liaisons dangereuses* (1782). Dorimant inhabits a more youthful and less extreme world which is predominantly comic in tone, and which, moreover, superimposes the Rake Reformed pattern onto that of the libertine trickster.

7 Further, see 'Early Stage History and Reception' below, pp. l–li.
8 See too I, 105, II.ii, 15, V.ii, 221.

It is the combination of the two patterns which upsets the moralists. Is the scheming intriguer who attains true love and the favours of his mistresses no more than a promiscuous cynic endorsed by the play? Is the gaiety merely heartless? Jeremy Collier is the first in the long line of critics who have thought so. His complaint was that Restoration comedy presented 'Vice under Characters of advantage'. In his reading, 'A finish'd Libertine seldom fails of making his fortune upon the *Stage* . . . there is great Care taken to furnish him with Breeding and Address: He is presently put into a Post of Honour, and an Equipage of Sense: and if he does the worst, he is pretty sure of speaking the best Things; I mean the most lively and entertaining.'[9] Drama ought not to reward sexual misdoing with marriage to the heroine. But it is the claims to gentility, to being a pattern of 'politeness' (that is, of gentlemanly conduct), which really sticks in the throat of the moralist. Dean Lockier exactly caught the paradox which most incensed the play's critics when he called Dorimant a 'genteel rake of wit'.[10] To the accusation of sinfulness is added that of social snobbery. Not only does Dorimant belong to a stylish (and idle) upper middle class, but, with the play's endorsement, he takes for granted the superiority of sophisticated stylishness to the dull morality of the Dissenting clergyman.

All of this is there: it is not the facts which are at issue but the attitude the audience should take to Dorimant. The critical question is in what way does (or should) the audience identify with Dorimant? A direct moral questioning of the comedy in Collier's manner is fundamentally wrongheaded because it does not recognize the particular way in which comedy is serious. The same is in the end true of Dale Underwood's very good book, *Etherege and the Seventeenth-Century Comedy of Manners*. Underwood's sympathetic scholarly investigation of the Libertine, Hobbesian, and Epicurean attitudes which lie behind the play gives essential background from the history of ideas for an understanding of the play, but in his hands *The Man of Mode* is less a play than an expression of a philosophical argument. The effect of Underwood's scholarship is to leave us where we began, with a singularly unpleasant human being on our hands.

What is necessary is to take the comedy out of the study and onto the stage, and to ask about the audience's reaction. Harriet Hawkins rightly points out that any critical response must take account of the fact that 'audiences have often delighted in characters whose behaviour and

9 *Dissuasive from the Playhouse*, 1703, p. 4.
10 Joseph Spence, *Observations, Anecdotes, and Characters of Books and Men*, ed. James M. Osborn, 2 vols., 1966, No. 678 (1–6 September 1730).

attitudes shock them, in characters who have the pride, energy, intelligence, cunning, or power to overleap moral fences and to invert traditional values.'[11] The dramatist pleases the audience, and it is the critic who perceives the moral headaches (and who must, to quote Beckett, provide their own aspirins). After making this point, Hawkins goes on, I think, to betray her own insight. Finding that the 'righteous solemnity' of critics like Jocelyn Powell and Underwood distorts the comic emphasis of Etherege's play, she sees the comedy as much gayer, and much less serious:

> The games people play in Etherege's comedy are timeless (if trivial) ones, and like [Ovid's] *Art of Love, The Man of Mode* is still amusing and relevant enough on its own terms ... For the light comic spirit pervading the play allows us to look at the social spectacles that it mirrors and magnifies and see them as – spectacles. The primary purpose of this comedy seems to be neither immoral nor moral, but rather spectacular ... a glittering, amusing, and witty dramatic spectacle.[12]

This passage is guilty of some confusion. Comedy, like all art, resembles a game in that it causes nothing to happen: it is for free. It differs from the social games played in everyday life, which are for real – if they are merely 'trivial', then so much the worse for our relationships with others. But if in one sense the audience is uninvolved because only watching a 'spectacle', it is also, in a way not easily attained in real life, involved. Since we watch for free, we are free to see ourselves (or other possible selves freed from the normal restrictions imposed upon or adopted by the individual) in the characters and actions enacted on the stage. The realistic texture of Restoration comedy makes it easy to overlook the way in which all drama triggers a psychodrama within the individual members of the audience – indeed, within the audience as a whole. The audience within a public theatre can rarely be so homogenous as to be unaware of the divisions within its own society, and it is clear that the response to *The Man of Mode* on the part of the servants and tradespeople in the upper gallery differed from that of the middle-class woman in the boxes, and that both differed from the reactions of those in the pit. An audience is dynamically implicated in what happens on the stage. It cannot merely watch, but must judge and choose between the characters and their

11 *Likenesses of Truth in Elizabethan and Restoration Comedy*, 1972, p. 81.
12 Ibid., pp. 93–4.

deeds. Further, it is the dramatist who provides the frame of reference, using the prologue, the characters, and the epilogue to establish a preferred viewpoint. Hence, the audience must discriminate between the characters depicted, and do so within standards set up by the play's dominant concepts. *The Man of Mode* is written from the point of view of the group of wits and rakes like Rochester and Sedley, and clearly favours Dorimant (and there is no doubt that Dorimant would at least be stimulating, while Sir Fopling would quickly become tedious). At the same time, the Epilogue, most probably spoken by the actress playing Harriet, strategically switches the audience's attention away from Dorimant, focussing instead on Sir Fopling's inanities.[13]

Comedy deals with topics close to its audience, and is aggressive and violent towards its butts to an extent not usually permissible in society. It is correspondingly over-generous to its victors. Its characteristic targets are anxieties or constrictions which the audience normally accepts out of necessity without altogether liking them. One function of comedy (and of humour) is undoubtedly to release aggression and anxiety, especially the anxiety and aggression surrounding sexuality, which supplies its own forms of embarrassment and unease for each successive generation. The rake hero gains the audience's support because he acts out that side of his audience's psyche which is in real life either denied, or compromised, by the ties or obligations of society. Since comedy in this form often gives the appearance of subversiveness while actually supporting more conservative values (Dorimant is after all bound for marriage with Harriet), it could be reduced to a sociological function – a safe release for feelings otherwise dangerous to society's stability. Aristotle's belief that comedy originated from the ancient Greek phallic songs, along with the Roman institution of Saturnalia, indicate that the genre's roots lie in the deliberate inversion of social values and hierarchies for a set time-limit, and in the vitality and disruptiveness of human sexuality.

A truer, and less anthropologically reductive, account of comedy needs to insist that its confusions and inversions reflect the audience's knowledge that life itself does not fit obediently into any moral patterns. Even a set of strongly held and coherent moral beliefs cannot ensure proper behaviour, especially within personal relationships, a main subject of this play. There is even an inherent ridiculousness in the continued pursuit of what must be betrayed by experience, yet too open an admission of that

---

13 Further on these aspects of the play and Etherege's use of topical allusions to the same end, see John Barnard, 'Point of View in *The Man of Mode*', *Essays in Criticism*, 34 (1984), 285–308.

truth would incapacitate the individual from action, or lead swiftly to
cynicism.

A Society in Flux

The moral issue inevitably focuses attention on Dorimant. Yet the case
for *The Man of Mode* must be drawn from the whole play: it is the
contrast with other attitudes and characters, along with the interplay
between themes, which defines Dorimant's vitality and ambiguity. And
the play as a whole reflects the strains and tensions of a society in flux
over attitudes to gentility, marriage, and sexual behaviour. Judging from
the varying responses to Dorimant within the comedy, he is as ambiguous for the characters within the play as for later critics. The most obvious conflict is that between generations. Lady Woodvill, an 'antiquated
beauty' and 'a great admirer of the forms and civilities of the last age',
still hankers after the *précieux* modes of courtesy of the Court of Charles
I and Henrietta Maria. In her view Dorimant 'delights in nothing but
rapes and riots' (III.iii, 107). She has, of course, seriously misjudged
Dorimant. His style is not carousing and whoring, though the four Bullies who insult Mrs Loveit and Sir Fopling in III.iii show that this kind of
violently aggressive anti-feminist manhood was certainly to be found in
London – the play would like to suggest that its practitioners were drawn
from inferior levels of society with City rather than Court connections.
Manners have changed: Dorimant, despite his Danish serenade of Mrs
Loveit (II.i, 116), belongs to a far more dangerous category – the genteel
rake, who pursues his women not in whorehouses but in private houses
(III.ii, 98–9). Placing gentlewomen at risk adds both a new seriousness
and a new danger to the game. Both the wits and the upholders of
conservative values, Lady Woodvill and Old Bellair, agree that there has
been a significant change in manners. What the wits enjoy, and their
'gravities' (III.i, 110) resent, are the 'freedoms of the present' (I, 117).
The most obvious freedom is the practice of keeping a mistress:
Dorimant claims that even judges have set an example in countenancing
this, 'the crying sin o' the nation' (I, 144–6) – Lady Woodvill's
naivety prevents her from perceiving the true cause of a judge's attentions to her own daughter, Harriet (I, 139–46). It is an age in which a
pretty face and discreet promiscuity will help a woman climb the social
ladder – 'she may come to keep her coach and pay parish duties, if the
good humour of the age continue', and so become, in Medley's words,
one 'of the number of ladies kept by public-spirited men for the good of
the whole town' (IV.ii, 74–7). And *The Man of Mode*, no doubt with
licence, suggests that the practice was common to all classes of town life.

Unsurprisingly then, Lady Woodvill asserts 'Lewdness is the business now; love was the business in my time' (IV.i, 14). The kind of love she has in mind is that of protesting lovers, suffering the flames of unrequited love at the hands of an unyielding mistress, a mode recorded, ironically enough, in Waller's poetry, so often quoted by Dorimant. Courtly love is only possible with a hierarchical society, and Lady Woodvill despairs of the confusions of rank in contemporary society. Playing the character of Mr Courtage, a man made of the 'forms and commonplaces, sucked out of the remaining lees of the last age', Dorimant agrees: 'Forms and ceremonies, the only things that uphold quality and greatness, are now shamefully laid aside and neglected'. Social barriers are crumbling – 'All people mingle nowadays' (IV.i, 8–12). When Old Bellair censures the modern gallants for their disrespect, Lady Woodvill bursts out, 'Quality was then considered, and not rallied by every fleering fellow . . . 'Tis good breeding now to be civil to none but players and Exchange women. They are treated by 'em as much above their condition as others are below theirs' (III.i, 119–24).

As a Royalist and conservative, Lord Clarendon's analysis of post-Civil War England shares Lady Woodvill's concerns,[14] and Act I of *The Man of Mode* bears out the sense of social confusion from the beginning. Dorimant's easy bantering of Foggy Nan and the Shoemaker may depend upon Dorimant's conviction of his social superiority, but it plainly signals an undue familiarity with tradesmen and Exchange women, based on mutual interests – Dorimant's ability to pay and, on both sides, a love of the game. Not only are social distinctions sapped from within by the failure of the rake-hero to behave decorously towards inferiors, but the urban working class has been corrupted by the wits' life style and morals. According to the Shoemaker, apprentices have abandoned their 'harmless' traditional ballads in favour of the wits' scurrilous 'damned lampoons' (I, 249). The Shoemaker himself has attained a dubious sophistication in his marriage – ' 'Zbud, there's never a man i' the town lives more like a gentleman with his wife than I do. I never mind her motions; she never inquires into mine. We speak to one another civilly, hate one another heartily, and because 'tis vulgar to lie and soak together, we have each of us our several settle-bed' (I, 271–5).

The corruption of the lower orders through the imitation of their social betters, and the aspiration to gentility on the part of the servants of

---

14 See *The Continuation of the Life of Edward, Earl of Clarendon*, printed with *The Life*, 1759, II, pp. 21–2. Cited by Christopher Hill, *Puritanism and Revolution*, 1958, which still provides valuable background to the period (see especially chapters 6, 9, and 14).

the fashionable, are as marked in Etherege's London as in Fielding's. Although seen a good deal more benignly, *The Man of Mode* reflects the extent to which city life and its attendant anonymity led to freedom and a rejection of accepted roles and traditional values. Foggy Nan recognizes the Shoemaker as an enemy: although she does not mind what gentlemen say, she despises him as a 'foul-mouthed rogue' and a 'dirty fellow' precisely because he apes the modish libertine values of Dorimant. He is a 'heathen' and an 'atheist'. Medley chides him – 'You have brought the envy of the world upon you by living above yourself. Whoring and swearing are vices too genteel for a shoemaker' (I, 239–41). But in this upside-down world, the Shoemaker gives as good as he gets: ' 'Zbud, I think you men of quality will grow as unreasonable as the women: you would engross the sins o' the nation. Poor folks can no sooner be wicked but they're railed at by their betters' (I, 242–5). The whole concept of gentility is called into question (and the large number of courtesy books published in these years indicates that the concern was not restricted to the comedies).[15]

The ambiguities of Dorimant's London cannot, however, be resolved by any appeal to established values. Lady Woodvill's outmoded ideas of gallantry and subordination offer no viable alternative. They cannot because they ignore the facts of society and because, in the persons of Lady Woodvill and Old Bellair, they are inconsistent and hypocritical. The real grounds for Lady Woodvill's hatred of the 'depraved appetite of this vicious age' are that her beauty is no longer admired: the younger generation 'tastes nothing but green fruit and loathes it when 'tis kindly ripened' (IV.i, 41–2). 'Kindly', which can also mean fully ripened according to its nature, is a witty reminder of the vitality which manners seek to control, and which Lady Woodvill denies. A similarly muddled and self-congratulatory note is evident in Lady Woodvill's companion in foolish age, Old Bellair. He objects to 'idle town flirts' because they do not bring the 'blessing of a good estate' (II.i, 60–2): indeed, the young people have gone so far as to get 'an ill habit of preferring beauty, no matter where they find it' (III.i, 125–6). For the parental generation marriage is a mercenary and social affair: sons and daughters should be governed by their wishes. Moreover, Old Bellair is deeply antipathetic to women as anything but sex objects. The conclusion of the *bachique* in

15 For instance, *The Art of Making Love: or, Rules for the Conduct of Ladies and Gallants in their Amours . . .*, 1676, which is largely taken from the French of Boulanger, and *Art of Complaisance or the Means to oblige in Conversation . . .*, 1673, which W. L. Ustick notes is in the main based on Eustache de Refuge's *Traité de la Cour*, 1618 (*Review of English Studies*, 5 (1929), 149–53). See also II.i, 124, 129 and notes.

Workshop Theatre, University of Leeds, 1987: End of Act I with (from left) Dorimant (David Pope), Handy (Guy Hemphill), Young Bellair (Keith Mkandla), and Medley (Simon Audley). Photograph by Chris Jowett.

which he joins is indicative of his sexual ethos – 'Wine and beauty by turns great souls should inspire; / Present all together – and now, boys, give fire!' (IV.i, 390–1). There is no room for mutual feeling in his idea of courtship. Harriet protests when Old Bellair urges upon her the proposed match with his son, 'You expect we should fall to and love as gamecocks fight, as soon as we are set together. Adod, you're unreasonable!' (III.i, 167–9). Old Bellair's own comic attempts at courting the young and attractive Emilia are coarse and anti-verbal. When praising Emilia's dancing he can only say the opposite of what he means – '. . . go, bid her dance no more. It don't become her, it don't become her. Tell her I say so. (*Aside.*) Adod, I love her' (IV.i, 5–7). His boorishness, his assumption of total authority over his son, and his pursuit of financial advantage over personal happiness where his son's marriage is concerned, all give the lie to any claims his generation can make for superiority: both he and Lady Woodvill are 'unreasonable'. Lady Woodvill's assertion, 'Well, this is not the women's age, let 'em think what they will' (IV.i, 13) is exactly wrong. The new freedoms may bring more danger, but they also offer more choice and the chance of self-determination. As P. F. Vernon has argued, the comedy of Wycherley and Etherege is not hostile to the institution of marriage itself, but it is opposed to marriages of convenience. He aptly cites H. J. Habakkuk's work on patterns of marriage in the period to demonstrate that following the Interregnum and its sequestrations, alliances for dynastic and financial reasons posed a serious problem in the upper classes.[16] Wycherley's concern is evident from the title of one of his poems, 'An Heroic Epistle, To the Most Honourable Match-Maker, a Bawd, call'd J. C. –; proving Free Love more Honourable, than Slavish, Mercenary Marriage'. The younger generation in *The Man of Mode* is in revolt against the repressions of an older generation, and feels itself to have achieved an important degree of freedom.

Lady Woodvill and Old Bellair represent an extreme response to Dorimant, one which is to be upended by the comedy's conclusion: Lady Townley, whose role is that of a worldly-wise member of the elder generation, tolerant and in sympathy with the young, rightly forecasts that Lady Woodvill will 'find Mr Dorimant as civil a gentleman as you thought Mr Courtage' (V.ii, 287–8). But the reaction to Dorimant among his immediate associates is equally confused. Sir Fopling regards him as an English exemplar of French gallantry, but grievously mistakes the purpose of gallantry in Dorimant's world – 'women', says Sir Fopling, 'are the prettiest things we can fool away our time with' (IV.i, 225–6). For Medley he is a mentor in dissembling, cunning, and malice; for servants and tradespeople he is a generous man of the world who refuses to stand on ceremony; Mrs Loveit's responses range from violent rejection of him as a 'prodigy of ill nature' (V.i. 245) and a barbarian, to an unwilling admiration – 'I know he is a devil, but he has something of the angel yet undefaced in him, which makes him so charming and agreeable that I must love him, be he never so wicked' (II.ii,15–17). If Bellinda is forced to recognize his 'ill nature' (II.ii, 258), Dorimant himself ironically lays claim to good nature (I, 5), while Emilia thinks that the 'town does him a great deal of injury', and that he is 'a very witty man' (III.ii, 22, 27). In Lady Townley's eyes he is 'a very well-bred man' and 'a very pleasant acquaintance' (ibid., 25, 35–6). Young Bellair believes Dorimant to have 'something extreme delightful in his wit and person' and, above

16 'Marriage of Convenience and the Moral Code of Restoration Comedy', *Essays in Criticism*, 12 (1962), 370–87, citing Habakkuk's 'Marriage Settlements in the Eighteenth Century', *Transactions of the Royal Historical Society*, 4th series, 32 (1950), 15–32, and 'English Land Ownership, 1680–1740', *Economic History Review*, 10 (1940), 2–17.

all, to be 'so easy and so natural' an ease and naturalness which Harriet castigates as affectation – 'He's agreeable and pleasant, I must own,
but he does so much affect being so, he displeases me ... It passes on
the easy town, who are favourably pleased in him to call it humour'
(III.iii, 18–27). The protean nature of Dorimant is a natural consequence of his role as trickster, though it equally reflects on many of
the play's characters' inability to distinguish between appearance and
reality in the world of manners, and to grasp the questioning relationship in which he stands to 'true love'.

Young Bellair and Emilia are true love's representatives in *The Man of
Mode*, and what passes in this play for the *ingénu* lovers. They are very
carefully set apart from the young rakes about town. Dorimant describes
Young Bellair as a 'handsome, well-bred, and by much the most tolerable
of all the young men that do not abound in wit' (I, 380–1). Emilia is
similarly described in partly negative terms by Medley –

> Emilia, give her her due, has the best reputation of any young
> woman about the town who has beauty enough to provoke detrac-
> tion. Her carriage is unaffected, her discourse modest – not at all
> censorious nor pretending, like the counterfeits of the age.
>
> (I, 392–6)

The positive and vital quality of 'wit' then, which is allied to 'malice',
belongs to Dorimant and Medley, 'men of sense, who will be talking
reason' (I, 288), men who argue, that is, the irrationality of marriage
when the irregular demands of sexuality are more easily and satisfactorily
answered outside the narrow obligations of a legal tie. 'Is it not', Medley
asks of Young Bellair, who is firmly committed to marrying Emilia, 'great
indiscretion for a man of credit, who may have money enough on his
word, to go and deal with Jews, who for little sums make men enter into
bonds and give judgements [i.e., securities]?' (I, 305–7). As 'wits' Medley
and Dorimant embody what the word had come to mean in colloquial
language. Richard Flecknoe, in a work published in 1675 and probably
alluded to satirically by Medley as belonging to the last age, observes, '*wit*
now [is] but new names for an *Atheist* and *Debauchée*'.[17] The alliance
between the wits and libertine strains of thought was one felt by contemporaries, and given countenance by the circulation of Rochester's
libertine lyrics in the 1670s even had they not been backed up by his
well-known escapades.

17 *A Treatise of the Sports of Wits*, 1675, p. 5: the probable allusion is at II.i, 124.

From this viewpoint, Young Bellair's love for Emilia denies him the 'heaven' of promiscuity in return for the 'hell' of marriage. Although *The Man of Mode* respects the relationship of Emilia and Young Bellair, they are seen as less perceptive, less exciting, and less vital than Harriet or Dorimant. Their idealism as romantic lovers necessarily limits them. Emilia's distaste for fools is regarded by Lady Townley as 'a little too delicate' (III.ii, 120), exhibiting a lack of the robust tolerance of the older woman. ''Tis good to have an universal taste. We should love wit, but for variety be able to divert ourselves with the extravagancies of those who want it' (ibid., 114–16). (An attitude endorsed by the audience to the extent that it finds Sir Fopling's idiocies laughable.) Even so, in this comedy Emilia is as sharply aware of the unsurety of the human heart as the wits – 'Do not vow – our love is frail as is our life, and full as little in our power; and are you sure you shall outlive this day?' (II.i, 26–7). Even the romantic lovers must take account of a realism based on 'reasonable' arguments. Love is again and again described in images which demystify its claims to absoluteness by presenting it in naturalistic and materialistic terms – as a sickness, a legal battle, a pleasurable 'business', a kind of hunting, a card-game, a battle, and so on. Love is essentially irrational and temporary in its nature, a fact recognized both by the characters and by the audience. Men, in a society which countenances it, are only too likely to give rein to their appetites (women too, though they must guard against their reputations being affected). Harriet, speaking of Dorimant, remarks on the 'sordidness of men's natures' (III.iii, 69). It is an unflattering assumption, but is nevertheless one kind of observable truth about human behaviour. These attitudes and the assumption of impermanence leave very little reasonable space for 'true love'.

Yet *The Man of Mode* does finally allow the two different pairs of young lovers to come together. Young Bellair and Emilia arrange a secret marriage, a benign and easily accomplished trick, in order to circumvent the parental generation, but Dorimant and Harriet have to approach one another much more warily through the rites of a witty courtship and other dangers.

'Wildness' and 'Extravagance'

The way in which *The Man of Mode* balances apparent cynicism, comic tolerance, and emotional honesty, depends very importantly on the interplay between key words which embody a complex of tensions in contemporary anxieties about love and manners. From the first act Dorimant and Harriet are linked by their 'wildness', which distinguishes them from all other characters in the play. Dorimant is one of 'the wild young men o' the town' (I, 104): Harriet has more wit 'than is usual in her sex, and as much malice. Then, she's as wild as you would wish her, and has a demureness in her looks that makes it so surprising' (I, 133–5). The combination of wit, wildness, and the ability to dissemble are shared by both future lovers, and it is their wildness and malice which separate them from Young Bellair and Emilia. In Dorimant's eyes Harriet is above all 'wild, witty, lovesome, beautiful, and young' (III.iii, 318–19). The word's frequent occurrences in the play call on a wide range of meanings. It can mean merely 'restive', as when Harriet threatens to shake her hair our of order (III.i, 3), but the word's connotations extend to the ideas of gaiety, of fecklessness, of resisting control, even of ferocity and savagery. Harriet makes its links with her sexual attractiveness apparent when she says, 'My eyes are wild and wandering like my passions, and cannot yet be tied to rules of charming' (IV.i, 106–7). Dorimant, of course, is characterized as 'wild' (I, 104, IV.i, 64–5, 308), and Harriet calls him 'ridiculously wild and apish' (V.ii, 57), mockingly though significantly relating him to the animal world. This clustering of meaning suggests that when Bellinda calls him a 'wild man' (II.ii, 94), we are to remember the 'wild man' of legend.[18] The figure of the wild man, sexually and morally unconstrained by society's restrictions, clearly echoes Libertine aspirations, and Maximillian Novak has pointed out that the word has particular resonance in the comedy of the 1670s.[19] The hero's and heroine's 'wildness' in *The Man of Mode* is dangerous for others and, potentially, for the lovers, in particular Harriet. Both choose to live at risk, Dorimant obviously so, but Harriet's preference for the 'scandalous Mall' (III.iii, 277), with its assignations and dangerous 'conversations', over the more formal and reputable Hyde Park, is telling – '. . . I abominate the dull diversions there [Hyde Park] – the formal bows, the affected smiles, the silly by-words and amorous tweers in passing. Here one meets with a little conversation now and then' (III.iii, 35–8). Style and good conversation go together, and it is to the point that Pall Mall was close to St James's and had been built at Charles II's instructions.

18 Maximillian Novak makes the same connection in 'Margery Pinchwife's "London Disease": Restoration Comedy and the Libertine Offensive of the 1670s', *Studies in the Literary Imagination*, 10 (1977), 1–24 (at p. 16). For a brief account, with helpful references, of the history of the 'wild man' see Frank Kermode, ed., *The Tempest* (Arden Shakespeare), 5th ed., 1954, pp. xxxviii–ix and note.

19 Novak, op. cit., who points out that the heroines of Shadwell's *Epsom-Wells*, 1675, worry that Bevil and Rains are 'so very wild', while 'wildness' is associated with Libertine values throughout Wycherley's *The Country Wife* (acted 1675).

Harriet's 'wildness' is integral to her sexual attractiveness, and Medley's connoisseur's description lingers over her 'lively, large, wanton eyes' (I, 124–5). Although able to remain within the bounds of propriety through her charm and manipulation of those about her, Harriet is essentially untamed, and her sometimes freakish and 'extravagant' behaviour (III.i. 28, III.iii, 6) is an accepted part of her character.[20] 'Extravagance' and wildness are also joined in the character of Dorimant. With sharp dramatic irony Lady Woodvill describes 'a wild, extravagant fellow of the times' as 'a Dorimant' when she believes herself to be talking to Mr Courtage (IV.i, 308).

It has been suggested that the idea of extravagance is a defining quality of several rake-heroes in Restoration comedy:

> Wycherley's Horner (an extravagant trickster), Etherege's Dorimant (an extravagant narcissist) and Congreve's Valentine, who assumes madness for much of *Love for Love*, are all extravagants. In making the extravagant city rake into a comic protagonist, the playwrights gave him something equivalent to the qualities that were supposed to arouse 'admiration' in the rhymed heroic plays of this decade, including a degree of excess in word and character.[21]

In *The Man of Mode*, however, extravagance seems to be regarded as one element of the wild and witty hero and heroine, for extravagance is a dubious quality. Mrs Loveit's 'mighty spirit' prevents her from maintaining a balance between her passionate nature and the need for self-control: Medley says, 'She's the most passionate in her love and the most extravagant in her jealousy of any woman I ever heard of' (I, 166–7). The extravagance of uncontrolled passion creates a fatal vulnerability – Dorimant even throws in her face the 'extravagancies' to which he claims to have been driven by his passion for her (V.i, 186). Love and jealousy rage strangely within her, and her attraction to Dorimant meets the needs of a self-destructive element in her character, as Medley observes – 'She could not have picked out a devil upon earth so proper to torment her' (II.i, 111–12). The psychological accuracy of Etherege's portrait of Mrs Loveit is important: she too is driven by arrogance and a love of power, and is therefore doomed to choose a man like Dorimant. Mrs

---

20 See Robert Jordan, 'The Extravagant Rake in Restoration Comedy', *Restoration Literature*, ed. Harold Love, 1972, pp. 69–88.
21 Novak, art. cit., p. 16, who modifies Jordan's findings.

Loveit is the creature of her own excesses and, consequently, the butt of
the comedy's most savage ridicule. She shows a foolish disregard for the
realities of life when she tells Pert that she 'had rather be made infamous
[by Dorimant's malicious gossip] than owe my reputation to the dull
discretion of those fops you talk of' (II.ii, 46–7). Even when she nearly
has Dorimant in retreat (after raising his jealousy by pretending to be
attracted by Sir Fopling), her feelings cause her to throw away her advantage (V.i, 206–7). Her outcries against Dorimant are marked by their
hysterical rhetoric: 'Plague, war, famine, fire – all that can bring universal
ruin and misery on mankind – with joy I'd perish to have you in my
power but this moment!' (II.ii, 253–5). Her last extravagance, before she
abandons the stage, is to advise Bellinda to give herself up to goodness
(V.ii, 342–3).

If the world of the play punishes Mrs Loveit savagely – Dorimant's
assessment of her future is coldly clinical (V.i, 139–42), and Harriet is
brutally tart ('Mr Dorimant has been your God Almighty long enough.
'Tis time to think of another' (V.ii, 344–5)) – it is because Mrs Loveit,
unlike Sir Fopling, knows the penalties but chooses to ignore them. Passion reduces her to the level of a comic automaton. The sternness of her
rejection stems from her demonstration of the destructiveness of love:
she has believed what Dorimant calls the 'extravagant words' men speak

Royal Shakespeare Company, Swan Theatre, 1988: Mrs Loveit (Marie Mullen) and
Sir Fopling (Simon Russell Beale). Photograph by Joe Cocks. Joe Cocks Studio
Collection © Shakespeare Birthplace Trust.

in love. ''Tis as unreasonable to expect we should perform all we promise then, as do all we threaten when we are angry' (V.ii, 268–70). It is the extravagance of love's hopes in a materialistically reasonable world which makes both Dorimant and Harriet slow to admit their feelings for one another, and which means that they must engage in a carefully indirect courtship. *The Man of Mode* is unforgiving only towards Mrs Loveit. Her exclusion at the end of the play can only be handled openly and schematically because comedy's conventions allow it to encompass what would be profoundly painful and embarrassing in life. More radically, she cannot be forgiven because she represents the fate of Dorimant and Harriet if they lose their balance and control. This is not to deny that Dorimant's character is in some part compromised by his affair with Mrs Loveit, but from the comic standpoint Mrs Loveit gets what she deserves.

The other obvious extravagant in the play is Sir Fopling, who mistakes manner for substance. There is a marked undertow which hints that Dorimant may, in his own way, be as much a man of mode as the Frenchified knight. Harriet's accusations of affectation show her realization that Dorimant plays to his audience. And it is Mrs Loveit and Bellinda who recognize that Dorimant's pursuit of women is self-regarding, more a pursuit of the town's admiration than anything more – 'You take a pride of late in using of me ill, that the town may know the power you have over me . . .' (V.i, 157–9). Vanity, then, may be a motive force behind Dorimant as it is for Sir Fopling, who is at least harmless. Dorimant's other main drive, the love of power, is even less morally attractive. He takes more pleasure in a woman's ruin than her love (V.i, 177–8), and, as Bellinda says, is 'never well but when he triumphs – nay, glories – to a woman's face in his villainies' (V.i, 254–5). The connection with Hobbes's definition of 'glory' is one made by Dale Underwood: '*Joy*, arising from the imagination of a mans own power and ability, is that exultation of the mind which is called GLORYING . . .'[22] The driving forces behind the sophistication of this modish society are those of domination and self-gratification. The vitalism of 'wildness' and 'extravagance' is offset by the dubious materialism which certainly informs the attitudes of Medley, and perhaps even those of Lady Townley.

'Complaisance' and Manners
Within the social world depicted by *The Man of Mode*, the pursuit of these ends is contained and made tolerable by the Town's code of man-

22 *Leviathan, or The Matter, Forme, & Power of a Commonwealth, Ecclesiasticall and Civill,* 1651, pp. 26–7.

ners which places a high valuation upon 'easiness' and 'complaisance'. Etherege's 'easy' style, at once stylish and colloquial, impressed his contemporaries immediately, and fifty years later was still the mark of his achievement for Pope.[23] In *The Man of Mode* the word can be used of manners and behaviour, as when Young Bellair describes Dorimant to Harriet: 'Lord, madam, all he does and says is so easy and so natural' (III.iii, 22). It can also apply to the grace and attractiveness of Harriet's figure, which Medley says is 'a fine, easy, clean shape' (I, 123), a phrase echoed by Dorimant (III.iii, 28). But when Harriet remarks upon the 'easy town', she comments both upon its tolerance and its gullibility.[24] The Town's tolerance is of only doubtful humanity, for it is marked by malice and by its love of gossip. The double nature of society's good nature and ease is embodied in the multi-faceted idea of 'complaisance', a recent word drawn from the French, and one which focuses the aspirations and unease of a society reaching after a new form of *politesse*, in which appearance and true feeling might be widely at variance. One of the many conduct books published at this time is *The Art of Complaisance or the Means to oblige in Conversation* . . .(1673).[25] Its motto, '*Quis nescit dissumulare, nescit vivere*' ('he who does not know how to dissimulate does not know how to live') underscores the moral ambivalence which these works show towards the need to disguise feelings in order to succeed in social intercourse. Although they normally argue that such dissimulation is necessary and for the good of society, they shy away from the more cynical implications of such a division. The extent of the stress caused by this tension appears in the embarrassingly wide definition given by the author of *The Art of Complaisance* to his topic: 'I hope I may without provoking the too Critical, use this word Complaisance in such an extensive signification, as to comprehend reservation, dissimulation, dexterity, patience, humility, civility, and affability . . .' (p. 8). The same width of meaning is evident in *The Man of Mode*. On several occasions it means no more than acting in such a way as to please others, as when Sir Fopling explains that his unwillingness to dance is not 'want of complaisance' (IV.i, 274; see too IV.i, 119, V.i, 37). But when the word comes into Dorimant's orbit, the concept becomes much more slippery,

23 'None of our writers have a freer, easier way for comedy than Etherege and Vanbrugh' (Spence, ed. cit., No. 483 (28 or 29 November 1730)).

24 'Easiness' again means gullibility at V.ii, 169; at IV.i, 149 it may carry the sense of unchastity.

25 For an essay which interestingly relates this book and other French works to the play, see John G. Hayman, 'Dorimant and the Comedy of A Man of Mode', *Studies in English Literature 1500–1900*, 10 (1970), 459–68.

for his wildness is accommodated within an effectively complaisant manner, a deliberate cover for his depredations. When Dorimant complains that women are as 'unreasonable' in their love affairs as at cards because unless they have won the game 'a man can never quietly give over when he's weary', Medley replies, 'If you would play without being obliged to complaisance, Dorimant, you should play in public places'. Taking his pursuit of women into 'private houses' means that Dorimant must obey the social niceties (III.ii, 92–9). Consequently, he is under a necessity to create an image of politeness. His friendship with Young Bellair, 'always complaisant', is, as he explains to Medley, aimed at the town –

> It is our mutual interest to be so. It makes the women think the better of his understanding and judge more favourably of my reputation; it makes him pass upon some for a man of very good sense [i.e., as a witty rake], and I upon others for a very civil person.
>
> (I, 384–7)

Dorimant's appearance of civility is essential to his continued success. Hence the involutions of his rejection of Mrs Loveit: it is in the interest of both Dorimant and Bellinda that he should not appear to do a 'barbarous thing' (I, 203). The problem is that Dorimant's 'complaisance', while dangerous for its victims, is a valuable asset in Lady Townley's society (she, like Emilia, finds him 'civil'). His civility is both feigned and real. Dorimant's case is the sharpest presentation of contemporary unease before the ambiguity inherent in the ideal of complaisance. It falls to Harriet to perceive his 'affectation', and to demand that if they are to marry, he must change.

An Uneasy Balance: Cynicism or Romance?

Structurally, the play distinguishes between Dorimant's activities when he is heart-free and when courting Harriet. On the evidence of his relationships with Mrs Loveit and Bellinda, Dorimant is right to say, half-cynically, half-regretfully, that 'Love gilds us over and makes us show fine things to one another for a time, but soon the gold wears off, and then again the native brass appears' (II.ii, 186–8). In his relations with Mrs Loveit, whoever knows what is in the other's heart can win the victory. As long as Dorimant knows that Loveit is jealous of him, he can manipulate her to his ends. The turning-point comes when he thinks she might really be interested in Sir Fopling. Admittedly, the cause is less passion for Loveit than concern for his reputation, but when he first mentions his fears in an aside, Dorimant significantly blames them on the irrationality of the heart:

MEDLEY
> . . . I have known men fall into dangerous relapses when they
> have found a woman inclining to another.

DORIMANT (*To himself*)
> He guesses the secret of my heart. I am concerned but dare not
> show it, lest Bellinda should mistrust all I have done to gain her.
>
> (III.iii, 269–73)

His anger and jealousy almost lead to the disruption of his carefully
ordered life. When Bellinda finds him at Mrs Loveit's in Act V, Scene i, he
has to bear with the two women berating him, and to admit, 'I am to
blame in some circumstances, I confess . . .' (ll. 267–8). Even then he is
not entirely free of the danger, for when both his mistresses appear in the
final scene he is taken aback – 'Loveit and Bellinda! The devil owes me a
shame today, and I think never will have done paying it' (V.ii, 221–2).
Although Dorimant recovers balance, and these temporary setbacks can
hardly be rated as punishment, it is clear that his ascendancy depends
wholly upon his wit controlling his passions.

Dorimant's real defeat is at Harriet's hands. The play almost goes out
of its way to assure the audience that it is a case of love at first sight for
them both. On Dorimant's first glimpse of Harriet he thinks of marriage
– 'I'll follow the lottery and put in for a prize with my friend Bellair'
(III.iii, 30–1), and left in a 'reverie' after his first conversation with her, he
quotes from Waller's 'Of Loving at First Sight':

> Snatched from myself, how far behind
> Already I behold the shore!
>
> (III.iii, 119–20)

Simultaneously, Dorimant is sharply aware of the danger this represents:
'. . . she has left a pleasing image of herself behind that wanders in my
soul. – It must not settle there' (ibid., 115–17). Dorimant fears the ultim-
ate irrationality of love, and recognizes the danger of the loss of his own
sense of identity (just as Mrs Loveit has) in a world in which, since
everyone pursues 'glory', a coherent identity is extremely hard to main-
tain: 'I love her and dare not let her know it. I fear she has an ascendant
o'er me and may revenge the wrongs I have done her sex' (IV.i, 134–6).
Equally, Harriet is overwhelmed by her attraction to Dorimant. Even
when she has only seen him at a distance, she is inclined towards him
(III.i, 51, 90), and at their first meeting has to hide her feelings – 'I feel as
great a change within, but he shall never know it' (III.iii, 57). Other
observers in the play, such as Busy, Medley, and Young Bellair, are sure of

her feelings towards Dorimant (IV.ii, 157, V.ii, 50, 53). Harriet is at root a romantic heroine, opposed to the mercenary values of her mother's generation: 'Shall I be paid down by a covetous parent for a purchase? I need no land. No, I'll lay myself out all in love. It is decreed' (III.i, 63–4). But she is realistic enough to recognize Dorimant's fear of committing himself to love, and shrewd enough to know that she must not only prove herself his equal but establish a superiority in their courtship. Their mutual ability as actors sets them apart from the other characters. Dorimant, acting the part of Mr Courtage, takes in Lady Woodvill (IV.i) and later mimics Sir Fopling (V.i, 80 ff): Harriet acts out the role of young lover with Young Bellair to fool their parents (III.i), and mimics Dorimant (I, 59–60, III.iii, 92–3, IV.i, 96–9). Both accuse each other of acting for their respective audiences in the Mall (III.iii, 85–93). Their adroitness allows each to approach the other warily, to explore the reality of their own and their prospective partner's feelings. In their exchange in Act IV, Scene i, Harriet establishes her ascendancy by forcing Dorimant to come to the point of professing his love, only for her to mock the foolish appearance of a lover's protestations. At his refusal to continue, Harriet makes it clear that she needs to test his love – 'When your love's grown strong enough to make you bear being laughed at, I'll give you leave to trouble me with it' (160–1). Although very unlike *Love's Labours Lost* in mood or emphasis, the parallel between Harriet's treatment of Dorimant and Rosalind's punishment of Berowne's excessive wit and her imposition of a time limit before she will reward his suit, brings out the conventional and idealistic comic pattern shared by the two plays. Both plays too are concerned with the falsity and inflation of love's rhetoric. When Dorimant, adopting the language of the *précieux* lover 'in prospect of such a heaven', renounces wine and women, Harriet cuts through – 'Hold! Though I wish you devout, I would not have you turn fanatic' (V.ii, 135–6). Where Shakespeare's comedy belongs to a romance world, the Town in Etherege's play is inimical to love, hence the poignancy of those moments in which, against all the odds, and despite aspects of Dorimant's character, the two lovers recognize their feelings for one another. Behind the affectation and verbal games, what Harriet responds to is a vitality and aliveness in Dorimant that matches her own. She also sees the need for Dorimant to change, and for her to allow him time. The comedy sees that mere manners degenerate into emptiness (Sir Fopling) or incapacitate the man from action or involvement (Medley is no more than an observer). The wildness of Harriet and Dorimant lies ultimately in their willingness to risk themselves, while they, like the audience, know the risks involved.

The final scene brings together the various strands of the comedy, but allows the audience no easy resting place. Harriet's recognition of Dorimant's love is expressed in a new rhetoric of love which is knowing and realistic. In the following exchange Harriet's reminders of Dorimant's past would be acerbic if it were not understood by both that behind the parleying lies real feeling, that real 'generosity' is involved on both sides –

EMILIA

... Here are dreadful preparations, Mr Dorimant—writings sealing, and a parson sent for.

DORIMANT

To marry this lady?

BUSY

Condemned she is; and what will become of her I know not, without you generously engage in a rescue.

DORIMANT

In this sad condition, madam, I can do no less than offer you my service.

HARRIET

The obligation is not great; you are the common sanctuary for all young women who run from their relations.

DORIMANT

I have always my arms open to receive the distressed. But I will open my heart and receive you where none yet did ever enter. You have filled it with a secret, might I but let you know it—

HARRIET

Do not speak it if you would have me believe it. Your tongue is so famed for falsehood, 'twill do the truth an injury.

> *Turns away her head*
> (V.ii, 105–18)

The real conversation here is unspoken. In the lovers' hands the cynical patterns of witty town conversation have become the vehicle for expressing the sentiments of Waller, who is quoted by both, but whose language and vocabulary are no longer viable.[26] The comedy moves in its conclusion to re-establishing the norms of generosity, good nature, and

---

26 See Ronald Berman, 'The Comic Passions of *The Man of Mode*', *Studies in English Literature 1500–1900*, 10 (1970), 459–68.

mutual love, so discovering a new stylishness through which to affirm their value.

What distinguishes *The Man of Mode* from Shakespearean comedy is the way in which this moment of affirmation is not allowed to conclude the play's movement. Instead, *The Man of Mode* turns back to the problem of Mrs Loveit and Bellinda, and Dorimant faces both women with Harriet. His just-discovered faith in love does not prevent him from telling Mrs Loveit that his forthcoming marriage is purely materialistic in motive – 'Believe me – a wife to repair the ruins of my estate that needs it' (V.ii, 261–2).The placing of this scene after the exchange between Harriet and Dorimant does mean that it hangs threateningly over their future relationship: it is significant that although Harriet (like the town) knows that Mrs Loveit has been Dorimant's mistress, she does not know of his affair with Bellinda. The play, like all good jokes, looks in two directions. The comic pattern imposes the wish for a happy ending, yet the play has shown all too clearly the enemies to that happiness within the characters and within their society. Nevertheless, the ideal remains a possible if difficult one, and it is this balance between the possible and probable that gives the poignancy to Dorimant's and Harriet's final exchange, an exchange which turns on the opposition between Town and Country underlying the whole play. An essential condition placed by Harriet upon Dorimant is that he should prove his love by visiting her in the country:[27]

> To a great, rambling, lone house that looks as it were not inhabited, the family's so small. There you'll find my mother, an old lame aunt, and myself, sir, perched up on chairs at a distance in a large parlour, sitting moping like three or four melancholy birds in a spacious volary. Does not this stagger your resolution?
>
> DORIMANT
> Not at all, madam. The first time I saw you, you left me with the pangs of love upon me, and this day my soul has quite given up her liberty.
>
> (V.ii, 372–80)

---

27 Novak, art. cit., places *The Man of Mode* near the conclusion of a debate in the 1670s between Town and Country values. The significance of Harriet's ignorance of Dorimant's relationship with Bellinda was pointed out to me by Jane Challinor, a postgraduate student at Leeds.

In obeying the Rake-reformed pattern *The Man of Mode* does not simply fall back upon conventional values. Dorimant and Harriet have chosen marriage freely and knowingly, and their witty understanding accommodates a direct and unblinkered knowledge of the dangers facing their love.

Recent stage history

Terry Hands's production of *The Man of Mode* for the Royal Shakespeare Company, which began its run at the Aldwych Theatre on 13 September 1971, was the first performed on the London stage since 1766.[28] Yet the comedies of Wycherley, Congreve and Vanbrugh had been recovered for the repertory early in the twentieth century. This neglect of *The Man of Mode* was undoubtedly because it is so difficult to perform as an 'artificial comedy'. Irving Wardle, reviewing the 1971 production, noted that Etherege's 'unusually cruel' comedy could not be made to conform to the then conventional 'Restoration style' with 'its standard parade of bloodless gallants and simpering misses': 'Dorimant, the principal lover, acts as much from sadism and ruthless vanity as from desire.'[29] Hands's production, at once classical and contemporary, was staged in an abstract but modern setting, and stressed the continuities between Restoration London and the sexual liberation of the Sixties. The dances and songs were scored by the jazz composer, John Dankworth, while the characters' costumes (long dresses, broad brimmed hats) belonged to an earlier period. Alan Howard, with an auburn beard and moustache, played Dorimant to Helen Mirren's Harriet, the 'embodiment of rebellious natural life'. The play opened with Dorimant 'voluptuously' starting his day, 'relishing the prospect of rejecting a mistress and stripping off to drop into his morning bath to await news of the latest virgins in town'. His performance made no appeal to the audience's sympathies, and his humiliations were relished 'as much as his successes'. John Wood's Sir Fopling was 'a cause of entertainment, not irritation, to the other characters', and by the end

---

28 On Saturday, 15 March 1766, at Covent Garden Theatre as a benefit performance for Henry Woodward (1714–77), who played Sir Fopling: the playbill, however, noted, 'Not acted these 20 years' (*The London Stage 1660–1800: Part 4 1747–1776*, ed. George Winchester Stone, Jr., 1962). John Conaghan notes that there was a professional production of *The Man of Mode* by the Prospect Theatre in the Georgian Theatre, Richmond, North Yorkshire, in 1965 (claiming to be the first performance since 1793, though there is no record of a London performance in that year), and another by the English Department of Glasgow University (John Conaghan, ed., 1973, *The Man of Mode* (Fountainwell Drama Series), p. 3).

29 Irving Wardle, *The Times*, 14 September 1971. The account of this production is based on Wardle's review and the original cast list.

Out of Joint Theatre Company in association with the Royal Court, 1994:
Dorimant (left) (David Westhead) and Sir Fopling (Tim Potter).
Photograph by John Haynes.

he had earned the audience's sympathy through 'a lovely, highly vulnerable performance.'

A television programme of selected scenes from *The Man of Mode*, made by the BBC for the Open University ten years later and shown at prime time, was perhaps seen by a wider audience than any version of the play since the seventeenth century. The selection was created in collaboration with the University as illustrative material for its course A203, 'Seventeenth Century England: A Changing Culture' and was filmed between 28 and 30 April 1980. It was first shown on BBC2 at 9.45–10.35 p.m., then on 29 August and 1 October 1981, and repeated in 1982 and 1984.[30] Dorimant was played by John Harding, Harriet by Prue Clarke, and Mrs. Loveit by Cyd Hayman: it was produced by Richard Callanan.

The selection had to fit into a running-time of just under fifty minutes, and is made up of ten scenes taken from Act II, Scene ii, to the end of the

30 On 7 September 1982 and 18 August and 19 September 1984.

play.[31] The production makes very substantial cuts, and concentrates exclusively on Dorimant's casting off of Mrs Loveit, his seduction of Bellinda, and his wooing of Harriet. The parental generations of Lady Woodvill, Old Bellair, and the more worldly Lady Townley, are omitted altogether, as is the love between Young Bellair and Emilia. Sir Fopling is reduced to an off-stage role, entirely depriving the action of the comic counterpoint to the real man of mode. The effect is to foreground Dorimant's highly manipulative triangular relationship with Mrs Loveit and Bellinda, in which Bellinda betrays her 'friend', and is wholly complicit with Dorimant's male sexual code. The selection throws the self-gratifying dexterity of Dorimant's sexual intrigues into high relief, and reduces Etherege's comedy to a one dimensional demonstration of Dorimant's duplicity and amorality.

The next professional performance of Etherege's comedy was a modern dress production (brightly coloured rehearsal jump-suits and leg-warmers for everyone but Sir Fopling) in the tiny acting space of the Orange Tree Theatre, Richmond, directed by Sam Walters in January 1984. It was well reviewed, with 'a clutch of excellent performances ... that lay bare the cruelty behind the smiling artifice'; David Timson's Sir Fopling was notable for its 'outrageous' but not 'excessive camp' (Lyn Gardner). Unusually, Liz Crowther chose to play Bellinda as 'the acme of innocence, all the more pathetic when we realise that she is likely to follow Mrs Loveit on the game' (B. A. Young).[32]

In March 1986, Cheek by Jowl premiered Declan Donellan's touring production at the Donmar Warehouse. There were complaints about poor articulation. The small circular stage meant that the cast, when not performing, sat upstage, applauding the action or mocking the spectators' reactions, and seemed to be offering a critique of Etherege's play. Harriet (Saskia Reeves) was played as a 'hard little Hampshire heiress' in a 'loveless world' with Martin Turner's 'unusually vinegary' Dorimant the 'essence of male vanity'. The production revealed 'a harsh melancholy' behind 'the frills and froth' of Restoration comedy, 'a treadmill of intrigue, ostentation and artifice'.[33]

In June the following year the M.A. students of the Workshop Theatre, University of Leeds, put on a partly modernized performance directed by Dorrian Lambley. David Pope and Julia Haythorn acted Dorimant and

31 The following account is based on the archival copy of the camera script (A203/14), a Xerox of which was kindly supplied by Amanda Worthy of the Open University Library.
32 First acted on 27 January 1984. For the reviews, see *London Theatre Record*, 4 (1–30 January 1984), 41–4.
33 For the reviews, see *London Theatre Record*, 6 (12–15 March 1986), 285–7.

Harriet, and James Frieze took the part of Sir Fopling. The production, like that by Terry Hands, stressed that the issues raised by the play were as pertinent to the 1980s as they were to a Restoration audience. The programme noted how the comedy sets 'the appearance of success and "savoir faire", [against] real, deeply personalised values; the ability of women to challenge their institutionalised role as either playthings or financial assets of men in an attempt to satisfy their own passions and their own intelligence; [and] the seemingly timeless presence of the "generation gap" . . .'[34] Lambley's production of *The Man of Mode* cut out topical allusions to seventeenth-century London, and, like all other modern productions, omitted the prologue and epilogue. With considerable ingenuity, the production totally excised the roles of both Emilia and Bellinda.[35] This, despite the production's other virtues, meant that Dorimant's duplicity and amorality, and the harshness with which Mrs Loveit is treated were foregrounded in the final scene of Act V (as in the Open University selection). However, the omission of Bellinda draws attention to an essential function of her character in the play. Bellinda's seduction is vivid proof of Dorimant's dangerous attractiveness even for a woman who recognizes the risk she runs. She demonstrates the Town's complaisant acceptance of the inevitability of inconstancy in love.

Garry Hynes made her directorial debut with the Royal Shakespeare Company on 6 July 1988 with a production of *The Man of Mode* in the Swan Theatre, Stratford-upon-Avon.[36] This was part of an imaginative season of Restoration comedies, in which Etherege's comedy, William Wycherley's *The Plain Dealer* (published 1677), and George Farquhar's *The Constant Couple* (1699) were performed alongside a revival of Edward Bond's *Restoration* (1981). Taking advantage of the part-round thrust-stage of the Swan, opened only two years earlier, the production established an intimate relation with its audience and maintained a free-flowing staging throughout. Unlike most of it predecessors, Hynes's production set out to show 'Restoration comedy with a heart: beneath the usual preoccupation with sex and money lie characters who have the texture and vitality of real life.'[37] Despite this, most critics stressed the play's heartlessness. For Michael Coveney, Dorimant, played by Miles Anderson, was 'an unsalvable degenerate', and Mrs Loveit (Marie Mul-

---

34 Programme note, Special Collections, University of Leeds.
35 The director's script, an annotated pasted-up Xerox of the text of John Barnard, ed., 1979, *The Man of Mode* (New Mermaids), Special Collections, University of Leeds.
36 For the cast and other details of the production, see the programme-text, Simon Trussler, ed., *The Man of Mode*, 1988 (Methuen Swan Theatre Plays).
37 Programme for RSC's summer season, 2 May-24 September 1988.

len) was 'a one-track minded termagant': he thought, as most critics did, that Simon Russell Beale, then early in his career, stole the show as Sir Fopling.[38] In the *Guardian*, Michael Billington thought it 'an austerely brilliant production that takes the camp out of Restoration comedy' presenting instead 'a world of resonant solitude and sexual cruelty'. But elsewhere he recognized the psychological realism of Mrs Loveit's character: 'Etherege pins down exactly the way decayed passion turns into a form of sexual revenge.'[39] Lois Potter responded to the play's ambiguity, saying that Hynes was 'equally sensitive to the play's cruelty and its melancholy', and to the doubleness with which we regard its intrigues – 'time and time again, we are shown how the trick is done, yet the trick, when it comes, is utterly convincing'. Of the play's conclusion she writes, 'The last scene, which includes two women who Dorimant ruins, makes it clear that Harriet's triumph over her rivals is due to her having her fortune in her own power, but allows us the option of finding the ending romantic.'[40] However, Mel Gussow, in the *New York Times*, thought that Amanda Root's Harriet, played as 'a clear-eyed and determined challenger', made Dorimant 'to a great extent, her victim.'[41]

Very few cuts were made for this 1988 production.[42] The prologue and epilogue were omitted, as were some topical allusions: the occasional French words were translated, there were a few cuts in the dialogue, and the last two verses of Sir Car Scroope's song were not sung. The most significant omission was a relatively short one – the irruption of the four 'ill-fashioned' Bullies into the Mall for their attack on Mrs Loveit and Sir Fopling, singing at them mockingly and making leering comments on Mrs Loveit's sexual availability (III.iii, 204–14, 222–42). Although this brief episode is wholly irrelevant to the plot, what it does is to remind the audience that there exists alongside, and contiguous with, the fashionable world of the wits and the Woodvill, Bellair, and Townley families, an altogether more brutal and openly aggressive level of urban society. The Bullies' brief appearance serves, that is, the same function as the begging letter from the prostitute, Molly, read out to Dorimant at the end of Act I. The other interesting feature of Garry Hynes's script is that the

38 *Financial Times*, 15 July 1988.
39 *Guardian*, 15 July, 1988, *Country Life*, 21 July 1988.
40 *Times Literary Supplement*, 22 July 1988.
41 'Stage View: Englishwomen make an Impact as Directors', *New York Times*, 7 August 1988.
42 Royal Shakespeare Company Archive, RSC/SM/1/1988/MAM1. Although the Methuen Swan Theatre Plays programme-text (Simon Trussler, ed., cit., p. xx), says 'The cuts made in the RSC version are indicated by square brackets in the text', they are not in fact so marked.

production ran for approximately two and three quarters hours including one interval of 20 minutes,[43] which means the text published in 1676 could have been originally performed in its entirety.

Six years later Max Stafford-Clark's Out of Joint theatre company's production of *The Man of Mode* in association with the Royal Court Theatre was cleverly paired with Stephen Jeffreys's new play, *The Libertine*. Jeffreys's play was premiered on 9 December 1994 and *The Man of Mode* on 15 December 1994, and the two plays ran together for seven weeks.[44] Jeffreys's *Libertine* re-interprets the biographical facts and myths generated by Rochester's notorious life-style, frequently using his words and those of his contemporaries, presenting his excesses as wit, rake, pornographic writer and satirist as the enraged reaction of a disappointed idealist faced by the corruption and cynicism of Charles II's England.[45] The essential premisses of Jeffreys's play (most of them not certain facts) are that Dorimant is a direct portrayal of Rochester, that Rochester fell seriously in love with Elizabeth Barry, and that he trained her to act. Hence, in the penultimate scene, Rochester watches from backstage a performance of *The Man of Mode* with Barry playing Harriet, thus emphatically pointing up the distance between Etherege's fashionable society comedy and the unpleasant actualities of Rochester's self-destructive life-style. Not only did the modern play invite comparison with its predecessor, but, because the same company acted the characters in both plays, the audience and the critics unavoidably read the one against the other. This certainly increased the interest in both plays. Since Jeffreys's play can be seen as digging 'for dirt, [and] depicting the despair and disgust underlying the poet's reckless hedonism' (Charles Spencer), at least one reviewer thought that in comparison with *The Libertine* 'the sprightly opportunism' and 'romantic deceptions' of Etherege's Dorimant (played by David Westhead) 'endeared' the audience to him (Neil Smith). Most critics, however, thought that Stafford-Clark's dour and harsh production stripped *The Man of Mode* 'of all the beguiling artifice we normally associate with Restoration comedies' and brought out instead 'all the cruelty that lies beneath the surface' of Etherege's play (Charles Spencer). The 'two-way mirror between these productions is the

---

43 Trussler, ed. cit., p. iii: Stephen Jeffreys's *The Libertine* takes up the same amount of time.
44 *Theatre Record* [previously *London Theatre Record*], 14 (3–31 December 1994), 1551–8.
45 For the text, cast list, production, and introductory material, see Stephen Jeffreys, *The Libertine*, 1994, published by Nick Hern Books. Jeffrey's play had been read as a first draft at Los Angeles Central Library on 18 May 1994, and performed for the first time at the Warwick Arts Centre, University of Warwick, 20 October 1994, ibid., pp. i, xv.

National Theatre, 2007: Photographer (Mark Tintner), Sir Fopling (Rory Kinnear) and Mrs Loveit (Nancy Carroll). Photograph by Tristram Kenton.

sour reflection both plays cast on an age praised for its cynical wit and damned for its licentiousness' (James Christopher).[46]

(Although not strictly part of the *The Man of Mode*'s reception history, the film version of Stephen Jeffreys's *The Libertine* (2004) depicts Etherege as a subsidiary character, whose great stage success is wholly parasitic upon Rochester's life. Johnny Depp gave a remarkable performance as Rochester, John Malkovich took the part of Charles II and Rosamund Pike played the role of Elizabeth Malet, Rochester's wife; Etherege was acted by Tom Hollander.)

Nicholas Hytner's production of *The Man of Mode* for the National Theatre began its successful run on 29 January 2007. It was 'set in a London obsessed with having it all', taking 'a steely look at young people driven by the need to have the latest clothes, the latest gossip and each others bodies.'[47] The play's translation to twenty-first century London was consistently thought through. Act I opened with a magazine photoshoot of a bare-chested, tattooed Dorimant (Tom Hardy) in his designer

46 Quotations taken from reviews reprinted in *Theatre Record*, op. cit., 1994, 1551–8.
47 Pre-performance publicity, National Theatre website, 2006.

flat, Lady Townley's townhouse was transformed into an Indian restaurant or upmarket members' club ('Townleys'), Mrs Loveit's lodgings were a luxury boutique ('Loveits'), and the Mall a fashionable art gallery. Old Bellair and Lady Woodvill became wealthy Indian parents from Yorkshire attempting to set up arranged marriages for their children. All this, together with mobile phones, laptops, references to Diptyque candles and Égoïste perfume, and the between-scenes choreography necessitated by the revolve, gave a satiric 'kaleidoscopic vision of modern London's hectic consumerist fever' and its 'metrosexual bustle'.[48] The eruption into this world of Rory Kinnear's brilliantly conceived Sir Fopling, desperately mimicking French manners and fashions, provided much of the production's fun (though most of the time the laughter was directed at Sir Fopling).

However, translating the Restoration into present-day London came at a cost. The importance of the by-play between Dorimant and his inferiors was diminished (the Shoemaker disappeared entirely from the truncated Act I) as was that of the class distinctions within the play (Mrs Loveit does not run a shop but belongs to a *demi-monde*, the parents' generation all belong to a landowning gentry class, and the play includes, though off-stage, Dorimant's former whore, Molly). More importantly, the emotional range of the production was narrowed. Dorimant not only kept open the possibility of further relations with both Mrs Loveit and Bellinda after marriage to Harriet, but this production had him, watched by Harriet, sidle up to a blonde at the bar in 'Townleys' at the play's conclusion. Dorimant's self-seeking pursuit of power over women was entirely unqualified.

Perhaps in consequence, there was only limited affect between Harriet (Amber Agar) and Tom Hardy's Dorimant, who was played as all of a cynical piece. The few crucial moments at which he and Harriet admit their love in a world seemingly inimical to its possibility never really convinced. Further, by cutting out all the quotations from Waller and Suckling, which provide Dorimant and Harriet with a private (and nostalgic) language of love, the production denied them the change of linguistic register which sets them apart from everyone else in the play. In contrast, Bertie Carvel's brilliant interpretation of Medley as a gay man about town, a gossip much in demand among the ladies, and an observer of the antics of the heterosexual world, seemed to offer the only settled viewpoint in the play, one of cynical amusement (like Scandal in

48 Michael Billington, *Guardian*, 7 February 2007. For other reviews, see for instance, Susannah Clapp, *Observer*, 11 February 2007, Rosie Millard, *New Statesman*, 19 February 2007, and the roundup in *The Week*, 17 February 2007.

Congreve's *Love for Love*). In the gap left by Harriet and Dorimant, Nancy Carroll's powerful performance as Mrs Loveit, out of control emotionally and as much the victim of her own passion as of Dorimant's manipulation, threatened at times to pull the production towards more dangerous, and disturbing, areas.[49]

In different ways all these productions demonstrate the play's complicated and ambiguous balance between comic affirmation and hard, near cynical, realism. All of them highlight the importance of Sir Fopling's role in moderating the audience's view of Dorimant's behaviour, and demonstrate the difficulties posed to both directors and actors at the end of Act V by the possibility that Dorimant may well continue his relations with either or both Mrs Loveit and Bellinda. More unexpectedly, the cuts in the 1987 Leeds production demonstrated the importance of Bellinda's role in determining how Dorimant is to be interpreted, just as Garry Hynes's omission of the Bullies in Act III, Scene iii, shows how a relatively unimportant change in this closely worked play can diminish its resonances. These modern productions, if they show the attractions of highlighting the continuities between a crisis in sexual mores in the Restoration and the Sixties or early twenty-first century London, also demonstrate the difficulties of doing so. *The Man of Mode* reflected with extraordinary intimacy the verbal and social distinctions among its mixed audience. Its original prologue and epilogue subtly inducted its early auditors into and out of the play's fiction. Presenting *The Man of Mode* on the contemporary stage will continue to be a challenge to its directors, actors and audience. Susannah Clapp's review of Nicholas Hytner's 2007 production describes 'Etherege's sceptical, scabrous and gorgeously worded play' as one which hides its own 'steeliness'. She rightly concludes that he is 'the most theatrical of writers' whose 'dialogue can be savoured on the page but comes to life in action.'[50]

Note on the text

The Man of Mode presents no complicated textual difficulties. It was licensed for publication on 3 June 1676, and entered in the Stationers' Register on 15 June. The first edition, printed by John Macock for Henry Herringman, is a quarto, spaciously and well printed in comparison with many Restoration editions of play-texts. It collates A–N^4, and is the only

---

49 In addition to the productions discussed here, *The Man of Mode* has been performed on at least the following occasions: Department of Theatre, Vanderbilt University, 1994–5 season; Rochester University (paired with Stephen Jeffrey's *The Libertine*), autumn 1999; Northcott Theatre Company, University of Exeter, 18 October-10 November 2001; Colby College, Maine, 14–15, 21–22 March 2003; and Simpson College, Iowa, 4–6 March 2005.
50 *Observer*, 11 February 2007.

text with any authority. Judging by internal evidence, it derives from Etherege's manuscript rather than a playhouse copy (for example, 'Young' Bellair is not distinguished from 'Old' Bellair until Act II, and in some places stage directions are lacking).

A second quarto of 1684 (Q2) is based on Q1, but introduces minor errors, followed by the quarto of 1693 (Q3), which was published two years after Etherege's death. The text given in *The Collected Plays* of 1704 (W) was set up from Q1, again making unimportant changes, mostly for the worse. There are no signs of authorial intervention in any of these editions, and Q1 must provide the basis for a modern text.

The copy in the Brotherton Collection, the University of Leeds, is the copy-text for this edition. Collation with five other copies[51] revealed an uncorrected state in the outer forme of G, not present in any of the twelve copies examined by John Conaghan.[52] As he first discovered, two substantive alterations in the outer forme of I, which occur in a Bodleian copy (Ashmole 1041 (1)) and one of the Worcester copies (Plays 5.38), are of particular interest. The phrase 'to an English Dancer' is inserted in corrected copies at IV.i, 294 as if it were part of Sir Fopling's speech. Conaghan shrewdly suggests that this is in fact meant as a stage direction, and I have adopted this emendation (see Textual Note). This attempted correction, along with the removal of 'had' (l. 297), resembles the kind of correction an author might make, but is probably to be accounted for by foul copy or a failure in communication between proof-reader and compositor. Even if Etherege were involved, the text as a whole indicates that he read proofs with some carelessness.

A peculiarity of Q1 is that it printed Etherege's prose in the form of rough verse. Although his sentences are antithetically patterned, they do not fall into a loose blank verse (as, for instance, Vanbrugh's do in parts of *The Relapse* (1697)). In all probability, Q1 follows the lineation of Etherege's manuscript, but gives each line an initial capital. As Conaghan notes, Thomas Southerne's *The Wive's Excuse* (1692) supplies convincing proof that this layout originated in the printing-shop – half the play is in 'verse', half in prose, and each half was printed in a different shop. This edition therefore treats the play as one written in prose.

---

51 Bodleian Library (Malone 107 (7), which lacks pp. 95ff., and Ashmole 1041 (1), Worcester College Library (Plays 5.38 and 7.20), and the Victoria and Albert Museum (Dyce copy).

52 For a full record and discussion of the other press variants, see Conaghan, ed. cit., pp. 12–13 and Textual Notes. None of the press variants in the Brotherton copy are significant, but they are worth recording for the sake of completeness – 'beliès' for 'belles' (III.ii, 133; G1ʳ), and 'Hey.' for 'Hey,' (III.iii, 141; G4ᵛ).

The major decision in modernizing the comedy concerns the spelling and accentuation of French words and phrases. In the early editions the spelling of French words is as eccentric as the placing of accents, and might be thought to be an indication of Sir Fopling's ignorance and mispronunciation. There are several arguments against this. No clear pattern emerges, the wits, as well as Sir Fopling, would be guilty of a similar degree of ignorance, and Restoration play-quartos regularly treat French in this way ('deux' for 'doux'). Further, as Carnochan observes, 'If Sir Fopling's French is lame, he becomes a character of farce' instead of a fool whom, as Dryden's Epilogue says, the ladies might mistake for a wit.[53]

A delicate problem is posed by the large number of words recently imported from the French. Some of these were in the process of being naturalized, and it is not always possible to distinguish between those which would have been accepted as English in 1676, and those felt to be French. The matter is the more complicated since the acceptance of such words would have varied among different generations and different classes. Although it is hardly a satisfactory answer, the *OED* has normally been followed in modernizing. On occasion it seems necessary to distinguish between a newly accepted importation and its French root: see 'dishabille' (II.ii, 76) and '*déshabillé*' (IV.ii, 105) and notes.

Variant texts of Dryden's Epilogue exist, two in the British Library (MSS. Sloane 203, f. 95, and 1485, f. 23), one in the Bodleian (MS. Don. 8, pp. 558–9), and a fourth in Nottingham University Library (MS. Portland PwV 203). The text of Q1 is independent of these version. Brett-Smith and Carnochan adopt unnecessarily one reading from the Bodleian text ('it' for 'they', l. 6), but the antecedent of 'they' is 'fools' (see Paul Hammond, ed., *The Poems of John Dryden*, 1995–2005, I, p. 301).

All substantive departures from the copy-text are given in the Textual Notes, along with some of the more interesting variants from Q1–3 and W. The decisions of four important modern editors, Verity, Brett-Smith, Carnochan, and Conaghan, are also recorded where significant (when a variant is given, all later editions follow Q1 unless otherwise noted). The handling of punctuation is indebted to Carnochan's, though his changes, generally tactful, are not followed where Q1, Verity, or some alternative arrangement seems preferable. In modernizing some silent alterations have been made. Names and abbreviations of names have been

53 W. B. Carnochan, ed., 1966, *The Man of Mode* (Regents Restoration Drama Series), p. ix n.

normalized, expanded, and capitalized in speech prefixes and stage directions; some stage directions have been shifted slightly in the interests of clarity; typographical slips have been corrected; spellings have been modernized according to the *OED* (e.g., 'ungrateful' for 'ingrateful'); and contractions in the dialogue ('H'as', 'th' next', 'wo'not', etc.) have been either expanded ('He has') if the cadence or emphasis demands it, or given in modernized form ('He's', 'won't'). Etherege regularly spells Hyde Park and the Mall as 'High Park' and the 'Mail', but these forms have been modernized throughout: no modern production would employ either on the stage, even though they reflect Etherege's probable pronunciation (see notes to III.iii, 34 and II.ii, 158). All editorial insertions are marked by square brackets.

Sir Car Scoope's song ('Amoret with Phillis sat') in Act V, Scene ii, has sometimes been attributed to Etherege or Sedley in error. Two other songs, 'Caelia with mournful pleasure hears' and 'That you alone my heart possess', have been falsely identified as songs from *The Man of Mode* (James Thorpe, ed., *The Poems of Sir George Etherege*, 1963, pp. 144–5).

Early stage history and reception

The first recorded performance of *The Man of Mode*, which may also have been its premiere, was given before the King at the Duke's Theatre, Dorset Gardens, on 11 March 1676.[54] Although the Company's move to their new theatre, designed by Wren, had brought them closer to the City (near the Thames just south of Fleet Street), the King's presence at this early performance, Sir Car Scroope's prologue and song, Dryden's epilogue, and the eventual dedication to the Duchess of York, all proclaim the comedy's allegiance to the ethos and social assumptions surrounding the Court.

The Duke's Men, who had presented Etherege's two earlier plays, provided a strong cast. Thomas Betterton, famous for both his tragic roles and his portrayal of rake-heroes, took the part of Dorimant, while Mrs Barry, the tragic actress and current mistress of Rochester, probably played Mrs Loveit: the remainder of the cast offered more than effective support, and in John Downes's professional judgement 'this Comedy

---

54 'His Ma¹ˢ Bill from His Royall Highness Theatre', dated 29 June 1676, P. R. O., L. C. 5/142, p. 1 (cited by Allardyce Nicoll, *A History of English Drama*, vol. I, *Restoration Drama 1660–1700*, 4th ed., 1952, p. 51). The King also attended a performance in April and took a 'Box for the Mayds of Hono".

being well Cloath'd and well *Acted*, got a great deal of Money'.[55] The 'extraordinary Success' of the production was long remembered.[56] Three days after the first recorded performance, a contemporary witness reported, 'This Sr Fopling makes at present all the discourse, to discover the persons meant by it',[57] an account supported many years later by John Dennis. Identifications varied wildly. At least one member of the audience identified Dorimant with the Duke of Monmouth '& his intrigue with Moll Kirke, Mrs Needham, & Lady Harriott Wentworth'.[58] The most common identification, however, was with Rochester:

> I remember very well that upon the first acting this Comedy, it was ... unanimously agreed, that [Dorimant] had in him several of the qualities of *Wilmot* Earl of *Rochester*, as, his Wit, his amorous Temper, the Charms that he had for the fair Sex, and his Inconstancy; the agreeable Manner of his chiding his Servants, which the late Bishop of *Salisbury* takes notice of in his Life; and lastly, his repeating, on every Occasion, the Verses of *Waller*, for whom that noble Lord had a very particular Esteem.[59]

Dryden, though, is surely right to deny that any individual was hunted

---

55 John Downes, *Roscius Anglicanus*, 1708, p. 36. Downes gives the cast as: Dorimant – Betterton; Medley – Harris; Sir Fopling – Smith; Old Bellair – Leigh; Young Bellair – Jevon; Loveit – Mrs Barry; Bellinda – Mrs Betterton; Lady Woodvill – Mrs Leigh; Emilia – Mrs Twiford. J. H. Wilson thought that the role of Mrs Loveit was created by Mary Leigh, and only given to Elizabeth Barry after Mrs Lee's retirement in 1685 (*All the King's Ladies*, 1958, p. 111), but see Robert D. Hume, 'Elizabeth Barry's First Roles and the Cast of *The Man of Mode*', *Theatre History Studies*, 5 (1985), 16–19.

56 Charles Gildon, *Lives and Characters of the English Dramatick Poets*, [1699], p. 53.

57 Peter Killigrew to his sister, 14 March; quoted in Spence, ed. cit., Vol. 2, p. 638.

58 Ibid.

59 John Dennis, *A Defense of Sir Fopling Flutter* (1722) in *The Critical Works of John Dennis*, ed. E. N. Hooker, 2 vols., 1939–43, Vol. 2, p. 248. Dean Lockier also identified Dorimant with Rochester in 1730: see Spence, *Anecdotes*, ed. cit., No. 678 (1–6 September 1730). The other main sources for contemporary identifications are Peter Killigrew (cited above); John Bowman (1651–1739) who was William Oldys's informant for his article in *Biographica Britannica*, 1750, Vol. 3, p. 1841; the information given by Charles Sackville's descendants to Thomas Davies (*Dramatic Miscellanies*, 1784, Vol. 3, pp. 169–70); and the testimony falsely ascribed to St Évremond in the 1707 edition of Rochester. In addition, the anonymous writer of *Poeta De Tristibus* (1681) thought Sir Fopling a self-portrait (Harold Love, 'The Satirised Characters in *Poeta De Tristibus*', *Philological Quarterly*, 47 (1968), 553). Excluding St Évremond, the identifications are as follows: Dorimant = Rochester (Dennis, Lockier, Bowman), Monmouth (Killigrew), Dorset and Rochester (Sackville family); Harriet = Harriet Wentworth (Killigrew); Mrs Loveit = Moll Kirke (Killigrew); Bellinda = Mrs Needham (Killigrew); Sir Fopling = Villiers (Killigrew), 'Beau' Hewitt (Bowman), Etherege (*Poeta De Tristibus*); Medley = Etherege (Bowman: Sir Charles Sedley has also been suggested as a possible model by later writers).

from the herd, and it is mistaken to search for any *à clef* pattern.[60] What is important is that the comic truthfulness of the play's representation of contemporary life was at once recognized. Sir Fopling quickly became a byword, and, more surprisingly, both Dorimant and Sir Fopling appear in a theological dispute in the same year.[61]

Unfortunately, records of performances in the seventeenth century are fragmentary.[62] *The Man of Mode* still enjoyed the Court's favour when it was performed at Whitehall in 1685 'with the usuall applause', and it was put on in Edinburgh, possibly in 1679 or 1680, by a group of actors who had broken away from the King's Men, led by Clarke and Goodman, and then by Haines.[63] There is some evidence to suggest that Etherege's comedy, along with Wycherley's *The Plain-Dealer*, temporarily lost favour and lay 'untouch'd and unsought-for' in the public theatre in the late 1680s while lesser plays succeeded.[64] In 1693 the play was reprinted, and a revival was probably staged, a supposition supported by a cast list in a Harvard copy of the play.[65] *The Man of Mode*, along with Etherege's two other comedies, was performed at the Smock Alley Theatre, Dublin, in 1698–9, and may also have been acted in an earlier season.[66] There was sufficient interest to justify a *Collected Works* in 1704.

Looking back in 1722, John Dennis claimed that the comedy had been 'well receiv'd, and believ'd by the people of *England* to be the most agreeable Comedy for about Half a Century.'[67] Dennis's *A Defense of Sir Fopling Flutter* is a deliberate reply to the covert Whig attack, mounted by

---

60 But see J. M. Auffret, art. cit., who attempts to prove that Moll Kirke is 'the common origin of both comedies.' He further makes the interesting suggestion that the model for Sir Fopling was Charles Mordaunt, who was connected with the Duchess of York.

61 Andrew Marvell, *Mr Smirke: or, the Divine in Mode . . .* (1676), cited in *Dramatic Works of Sir George Etherege*, ed. H. F. B. Brett-Smith, 2 vols., 1927, Vol. 1, p. xxvi n.

62 Further see *The London Stage 1660–1800*, ed. E. L. Avery, A. H. Scouten, G. W. Stone, and C. B. Hogan, 11 vols., 1960–68.

63 Charles, Earl of Middleton, writing to Etherege on 7 December 1685 (*Letters of Sir George Etherege*, ed. Frederick Bracher, 1974, p. 269) reported on the success at Court. For the Edinburgh performance, see John Conaghan, 'A Prompt Copy of Etherege's *Man of Mode*', *Library Review*, 21 (1968), pp. 387–8.

64 *The Lacedemonian Mercury*, 7 March 1692, cited in *The London Stage*.

65 See Edward A. Langhans, 'New Restoration Manuscript Casts', *Theatre Notebook*, 27 (1972–3), 156–7. The cast included Betterton as Dorimant, Mrs Barry as Loveit, and Elinor Leigh as Lady Woodvill.

66 The cast was as follows: Medley = Booth; Shoemaker = Bowen; Old Bellair = Estcourt; Young Bellair = Elliott; Handy = Norris; Parson = Trefusis; Dorimant = Wilks; Harriet = Mrs Ashbury; Orange-woman = Mrs Cross; Emilia = Mrs Elliott; Busy = Mrs Harrison; Pert = Mrs Hook; Mrs Loveit = Mrs Knightley; Lady Woodvill = Mrs Martin; Bellinda = Mrs Schoolding; Lady Townley = Mrs Smith (W. S. Clark, *The Irish Stage: The Beginnings to 1720*, 1959, pp. 113–14). If it is true that Farquhar played Young Bellair at Smock Alley, the comedy was probably performed in an earlier season (ibid., pp. 105, 205).

67 *A Defense of Sir Fopling Flutter*, ed. cit., Vol. 2, p. 243.

Addison and Steele in the *Spectator*, which sought to discredit the Stuarts by criticizing the immorality of the period's drama. The immediate cause of Dennis's pamphlet was the rehearsal of Steele's *The Conscious Lovers*, which was bourgeois and Whig in its sympathies. At root, the argument, though coloured by political considerations, was an aesthetic confrontation over the nature of comedy. Steele believed in exemplary comedy while Dennis's classical theory of ridicule, finding its origins in Aristotle, was doomed to failure with the later eighteenth-century audience. Although Horace Walpole in 1775 or 1776 thought *The Man of Mode* 'our first genteel comedy',[68] by that time the play had disappeared from the London stage, driven out by a changed public taste which insisted that its stage be 'moral'.

The author

According to William Oldys, Sir George Etherege's birth took place in 1636: if so, he cannot have been born until after the summer of that year. He was the eldest son, but not the eldest child, of the seven children of Captain George Etherege (b. 1607) and Maria Powney.[69] The family was prosperously middle-class. The dramatist's grandfather, also named George (1576–1658), called himself a gentleman, and was a successful vintner and a shareholder in the Virginia and Bermuda Companies, sufficiently well-to-do to move from London to Bray, near Maidenhead, some time after 1628. In the same year as the future playwright's probable birth, Etherege's father purchased the post of purveyor to Queen Henrietta Maria, a court office 'worth about two hundred pounds per annum before the troubles.'[70] The Civil War, however, disrupted any career within the Court. Captain George Etherege followed the Queen to France after her escape in 1644. He died there in 1650, leaving his children to be supported by their grandfather.

Etherege's letters show that he had a reasonable education. Although there is no firm evidence to support the tradition that he attended Lord William's Grammar School at Thame with Antony à Wood, he was well-read in English poetry, had at least a working knowledge of Horace (despite Dennis's assertion that he knew 'neither Latin nor Greek'), and was fluent in French. He may have travelled in France and Flanders

---

68 'Thoughts on Comedy: Written in 1775 and 1776', *Works*, 5 vols., 1798, Vol. 2, p. 315.
69 William Oldys, *Biographica Britannica*, 1750, Vol. 3, p. 1841. See the entry in *The Oxford Dictionary of National Biography* for an account of Etherege's life and its sources.
70 Eleanore Boswell, 'Sir George Etherege', *Review of English Studies*, 7 (1931), 207, and Dorothy Foster, ibid., 8 (1932), 459.

during his youth, but by 1654 was apprenticed to an attorney at Beacons-
field, George Gosnold, to whom he was still articled in August 1658.

The transformation of articled clerk into a wit and associate of young
aristocrats had taken place by the winter of 1663–4 when he carried on a
bawdy verse correspondence with Lord Buckhurst, to whom his first play,
The Comical Revenge (1664), is dedicated. Etherege was by then
approaching thirty, and, like many a man whose family had suffered for
its Royalist sympathies (though the Ethereges appear to have suffered a
good deal less than some), the obvious course for advancement was
through noble, preferably royal, patronage. By the time his second play,
She Wou'd if She Cou'd, was acted four years later, he was a member of the
group of courtiers, wits, and rakes which included Sir Charles Sedley,
the Earl of Rochester, and the Duke of Buckingham.

Etherege's easy wit and literary success brought court favour. In 1668
he was made Gentleman of the Privy Chamber in Ordinary, and then
appointed to an important and delicate diplomatic mission to Turkey as
Sir Daniel Hervey's secretary. Returning to London in 1671, he once
more took up the rakish life of a man about town. Not until 1676 was
The Man of Mode produced, and by then, according to the play's Dedication, Etherege was in some way in the service of Mary of Modena, wife of
the future James II, brother of the King. That summer, after the success
of his comedy, Etherege was involved in the notorious episode of Rochester's 'scouring' of the watch at Epsom. Although the playwright tried to
act as peacemaker, one of the party was seriously injured. On 29 June
Charles Hatton reported:

> Mr Downs is dead. Y^e Ld Rochester doth abscond, and soe doth
> Etheridge, and Capt Bridges who occasioned ye riot Sunday sen-
> night. They were tossing some fiddlers in a blanket for refusing to
> play, and a barber, upon ye noise, going to see what ye matter, they
> seized upon him, and, to free himself from them, he offered to
> carry them to ye handsomest woman in Epsom, and directed them
> to the constables house, who demanding what they came for, they
> told him a wh . . ., and he refusing to let them in, they broke open
> his doores and broke his head, and beate him very severely. At last,
> he made his escape, called his watch, and Etheridge made a sub-
> missive oration to them and soe far appeased them that ye con-
> stable dismissed his watch. But presently after, ye Ld Rochester drew
> upon ye constable. Mr Downs, to prevent his pass, seized upon him,
> ye constable cryed out murther, and, the watch returning, one
> came behind Mr Downs and with a sprittle staff cleft his scull. Y^e L^d

Rochester and ye rest run away, and Downs, having noe sword, snatched up a sticke and striking at them, they run him into ye side wth a half pike, and soe bruised his arm y^t he wase never able to stir it after.[71]

This episode does little credit to anyone involved except the watch, but it is worth quoting at length since it contrasts sharply with the claims for Dorimant's and his immediate circle's gentility within *The Man of Mode*. It is important to note that Etherege was about forty at the time, while Rochester was in his late twenties. None of this, however, affected Etherege's way of life: in 1677 he was involved in a tavern squabble in which Fleetwood Shepherd was 'runn with a sword under the eye.'[72]

By 1679 the dramatist had gained both a knighthood and a wife. Gildon's assertion that 'for Marrying a Fortune he was Knighted'[73] was seen very differently by contemporary satirists who claim that he had married an ugly, old, rich woman for her money: in 1683 he was said to be gaming away her money at Locket's.[74] It is difficult to distinguish between truth and rumour, but Etherege's extant letters to his wife are notably brief and usually concerned with money: he also refers to playing and losing at the Duchess of Mazarin's basset-table, probably during these years.

When James II became King in 1685, Etherege was again appointed to a diplomatic post, and left London with an eagerness which suggests he was escaping from something. His letters written while Resident at Ratisbon give the most graphic account available of Etherege.[75] They reveal a lonely man, ill adapted to the provincial formality of the envoys to the Diet. They also reveal a wry wit, coupled with a striking *insouciance*, which, in a diplomat, amounted to indiscretion. By 1685 the Diet of the Holy Roman Empire had lost most of its importance, and Etherege's essential duties were those of an observer of the uneasy truce preceding the War of the League of Augsburg. Etherege, bored and missing the delights of London, failed to establish proper relations with the other envoys, while his card-playing and an affair with an itinerant actress

---

71 *Correspondence of the Family of Hatton . . .*, ed. E. M. Thomas, Camden Society, 1 (1878), 133–4.
72 *Historical Manuscripts Commission, Calendar of the Manuscripts of the Marquis of Bath*, Vol. 2 (1907), pp. 160.
73 Gildon, op. cit., p. 53.
74 Thomas Wood, *Juvenalis Redivivum* (1683), p. 17.
75 See *The Letterbook of Sir George Etherege*, ed. Sybil Rosenfeld, 1928, and *Letters of Sir George Etherege*, ed. cit.

caused considerable scandal. At the end of his first year Etherege 'was virtually a social outcast. He reacted by becoming all the more arrogant in his official capacity and apparently more dissolute in his private life.'[76] Yet his letters show another side of Etherege, one not incompatible with his impatience of formality – and with his failure to realise for some time that his secretary was sending adverse and maliciously detailed reports of his behaviour back to London. undercutting Etherege's position at Ratisbon. To a friend he wrote:

> I need not tell you I am good-natur'd. I who have forgiven so many Mistresses who have been false to me can well forgive a friend who has onely been negligent. My heart was never touch'd for any whom there remains not still some impression of kindness.[77]

This is more than the 'open-handedness' of the reprobate, for it is based on a knowledge of the ways of the world and the heart. And his temper is sceptical rather than cynical or atheistic:

> I have ever enjoy'd a liberty of opinion in matters of Religion. 'Tis indifferent to me whether there be an other in the world who thinks as I do. This makes me have no temptation to talk of the business, but quietly following the light within me, I leave that to them who were born with the ambition of becoming Prophets or Legislators.[78]

'Good nature' of this complexion was hardly likely to be appreciated by any but a few in Ratisbon. Not until the spring of 1687 did Etherege realize the seriousness of his position. He then turned his mind to business with an effectiveness which grew into relish. But James's reign was already tottering. From midsummer until November 1688 Etherege was rightly obsessed with the threat of an invasion of England which aimed to replace James II with William of Orange, though the evidence he sent to London seems to have been taken less seriously than it ought. Etherege's loyalty to James was a mixture of gratitude for past favours and an emotional commitment to a concept of royalty sadly out of touch with political reality. When in January 1689 Etherege heard that James had reached Paris safely, he left Ratisbon to throw in his lot with the Jacobites.

---

76 *Letters of Sir George Etherege*, ed. cit., p. xx.
77 To Charles Boyle, 22 May 1687, ibid., p. 118.
78 Unaddressed, 29 December 1687, ibid., p. 168.

The tragi-comedy of these last years concludes in a mystery. Etherege is not mentioned in the list of the Court in exile, so that he may have arrived too late at St Germain to join the cause. Nor is it certain when he died. Although his death probably took place in May 1692, it was earlier reported in February 1691.[79] As a final irony, the Benedictine monks at Ratisbon claimed he died a convert to Catholicism. Such a conversion would fit well with his Jacobite sympathies, and would place Etherege, with Rochester, as a rake whose libertine mores finally concealed a conservative faith in hierarchy and a superstitious belief in religion. Or it may be that he is another victim of the seventeenth-century church's need to enforce the myth of 'surprising conversions'.

79 Ibid., pp. xxiii–iv.

FURTHER READING

Editions

The Dramatic Works of Sir George Etherege, ed. H. F. B. Brett-Smith, 2 vols., 1927.
The Letterbook of Sir George Etherege, ed. Sybil Rosenfeld, 1928.
Letters of Sir George Etherege, ed. Frederick Bracher, 1974.
The Poems of Sir George Etherege, ed. James Thorpe, 1963.
The Plays of Sir George Etherege, ed. Michael Cordner, 1982.

Critical Works

Barnard, John. 'Point of View in *The Man of Mode*', *Essays in Criticism*, 34 (1984), 285–308.

Berman, Ronald. 'The Comic Passions of *The Man of Mode*', *Studies in English Literature, 1500–1900*, 10 (1970), 459–68.

Canfield, J. Douglas. *Tricksters & Estates: On the Ideology of Restoration Comedy*, 1997.

Chernaik, Warren. *Sexual Freedom in Restoration Literature*, 1995.

Corman, Brian. *Genre and Generic Changes in Restoration Comedy*, 1993.

Davies, Paul C. 'The State of Nature and the State of War: A Reconsideration of *The Man of Mode*', *University of Toronto Quarterly*, 39 (1969), 53–62.

Dennis, John. *A Defense of Sir Fopling Flutter* (1722), in *The Critical Woks of John Dennis*, ed. E. N. Hooker, 2 vols., 1939–43.

Fisher, Judith W. 'The Power of Performance: Sir George Etherege's *The Man of Mode*', *Restoration and Eighteenth Century Theater Research*, 10 (1995), 15–28.

Gill, Pat. *Interpreting Ladies: Women, Wit, and Morality in the Restoration Comedy of Manners*, 1994.

Hawkins, Harriet. Chapter on *The Man of Mode* in *Likenesses of Truth in Elizabethan and Restoration Comedy* (Oxford, 1972).

Hayman, John G. 'Dorimant and the Comedy of A Man of Mode', *Modern Language Quarterly*, 30 (1969), 183–97.

Holland, Norman N. *The First Modern Comedies: The Significance of Etherege, Wycherley and Congreve*, 1959.

Holland, Peter. *The Ornament of Action: Text and Performance in Restoration Comedy*, 1979.

Hughes, Derek. *English Drama 1660–1700*, 1996.

Hume, Robert D. *The Development of English Drama in the late Seventeenth Century*, 1976.

—— 'The Myth of the Rake in "Restoration" Comedy', *Studies in the Literary Imagination*, 10 (1977), 25–55.

—— 'Elizabeth Barry's First Roles and the Cast of *The Man of Mode*', *Theatre History Studies*, 5 (1985), 16–19.

Huseboe, Arthur. *Sir George Etherege*, 1987.

Knights, L. C. 'Restoration Comedy: The Reality and the Myth', *Explorations*, 1946.

Krause, David. 'The Defaced Angel: A Concept of Satanic Grace in Etherege's *The Man of Mode*', *Drama Survey*, 7 (1969), 87–103.

Leech, Clifford. 'Restoration Comedy: The Earlier Phase', *Essays in Criticism*, 1 (1951), 165–84.

Markley, Robert. *Two Edg'd Weapons: Style and Ideology in the Comedies of Etherege, Wycherley and Congreve*, 1988.

Milhous, Judith, and Hume, Robert D. *Producible Interpretation: Eight English Plays 1675–1707* (Carbondale, Ill., 1988).

Novak, Maximilian. 'Margery Pinchwife's "London Disease": Restoration Comedy and the Libertine Offensive of the 1670s', *Studies in the Literary Imagination*, 10 (1977), 1–25.

Owen, Susan J. (ed). *Blackwell's Companion to Restoration Drama*, 2001.

Payne Fisk, Deborah. *Cambridge Companion to Restoration Drama*, 2000.

Powell, Jocelyn. 'George Etherege and the Form of a Comedy', *Stratford-upon-Avon Studies 6, Restoration Theatre* (London, 1965), pp. 43–69.

Sauer, David K. 'Apart from Etherege: Stage Directions in *The Man of Mode*', *Restoration and Eighteenth Century Theater Research*, 8 (1993), 29–48.

Steele, Sir Richard. *The Spectator*, No. 65 (15 May 1711).

Traugott, John. 'The Rake's Progress from Court to Comedy: A Study in Comic Form', *Studies in English Literature, 1500–1900*, 6 (1966), 381–407.

Turner, James Grantham. *Libertines and Radicals in Early Modern London: Sexuality, Politics and Literary Culture*, 2002.

Underwood, Dale. *Etherege and the Seventeenth-Century Comedy of Manners*, 1957.

Walpole, Horace. 'Thoughts on Comedy; written in 1775 and 1776', in *The Works*, 1798, Vol. 2, pp. 315–22.

Walsh, Paul. 'Performance, Space, and Seduction in *The Man of Mode* (Dorset Gardens Theatre)', *Essays in Theatre/Études Théâtrales*, 11 (1993), 121–31.

Wess, Robert. 'Utopian Rhetoric in *The Man of Mode*', *Eighteenth Century: Theory and Interpretation*, 27 (1986), 141–61.

Young, Douglas M. *The Feminist Voices in Restoration Comedy: The Virtuous Women in the Play-Worlds of Etherege, Wycherley and Congreve*, 1997.

ABBREVIATIONS

B   *The Dramatic Works of Sir George Etherege*, ed. H. F. B. Brett-Smith, 2 vols., 1927.

CA   *The Man of Mode*, ed. W. B. Carnochan, 1966, 1967 (Regents Restoration Drama Series).

CO   *The Man of Mode*, ed. John Conaghan, 1973 (Fountainwell Drama Series).

Q1   *The Man of Mode* (1676). Quarto.

Q2   *The Man of Mode* (1684). Quarto.

Q3   *The Man of Mode* (1693). Quarto.

Thorpe   *The Poems of Sir George Etherege*, ed. James Thorpe, 1963.

V   *The Works of Sir George Etherege*, ed. A. W. Verity, 1888.

W   *The Works of Sir George Etherege* (1704). Octavo.

Dryden,   *The Works of John Dryden*, ed. H. T. Swedenberg et al, 20 vols.,
Works   1956–2000

M.E.   Middle English

N & Q   *Notes and Queries*

OED   *Oxford English Dictionary*

obs.   obsolescent usage

s.d.   stage direction

var.   variant

Waller,   *The Poems of Edmund Waller*, ed. G. Thorn Drury, new ed.,
Poems   2 vols., 1901

KEY

Opposite: Original Title Page reproduced from the copy in the Brotherton Library, University of Leeds, with permission.

THE

Man of Mode,

OR,

Sʳ Fopling Flutter

A

COMEDY

Acted at the *Duke's Theatre*.

By *George Etherege* Esq;.

LICENSED,

June 3.
1676.

Roger L'Estrange.

LONDON,

Printed by *J. Macock*, for *Henry Herringman*, at the Sign of
the *Blew Anchor* in the Lower Walk of the
New Exchange, 1 6 7 6.

TO HER ROYAL HIGHNESS
THE DUCHESS

MADAM,

Poets, however they may be modest otherwise, have always too
good an opinion of what they write. The world, when it sees
this play dedicated to your Royal Highness, will conclude I have
more than my share of that vanity. But I hope the honour I have   5
of belonging to you will excuse my presumption. 'Tis the first
thing I have produced in your service, and my duty obliges me
to what my choice durst not else have aspired.

I am very sensible, Madam, how much it is beholding to
your indulgence for the success it had in the acting, and your   10
protection will be no less fortunate to it in the printing; for all
are so ambitious of making their court to you, that none can be
severe to what you are pleased to favour.

This universal submission and respect is due to the greatness
of your rank and birth; but you have other illustrious qualities   15
which are much more engaging. Those would but dazzle, did
not these really charm the eyes and understandings of all who
have the happiness to approach you.

Authors on these occasions are never wanting to publish a
particular of their patron's virtues and perfections; but your   20
Royal Highness's are so eminently known that, did I follow
their examples, I should but paint those wonders here of which
everyone already has the idea in his mind. Besides, I do not
think it proper to aim at that in prose which is so glorious a
subject for verse, in which hereafter if I show more zeal than   25

Her ... Duchess Mary Beatrice of Modena (1658–1718), became Duchess of York in
1673. On her husband's accession as James II she became Queen.
7 *service ... duty* this is the only evidence that Etherege served the Duchess in some
capacity at this date. Gildon reported that she held the dramatist 'in particular esteem'.
In 1682 her husband gave Etherege a pension of £100 and, as King, appointed him envoy
to the Diet at Ratisbon in 1685. That appointment was due to the good offices of Lord
Sunderland rather than the Queen as Gildon claimed (*The Letterbook of Sir George
Etherege*, ed. Sybil Rosenfeld (1928), pp. 15–16). What form the Duchess's 'indulgence'
(l. 10) took in helping the comedy's success on the stage is not known.
9 *sensible* aware
beholding Q1 (beholden W)

skill, it will not grieve me much, since I less passionately desire
to be esteemed a poet than to be thought,
   Madam,
      Your Royal Highness's
         most humble, most obedient,   30
            and most faithful servant,

                      GEORGE ETHEREGE

PROLOGUE

By Sir Car Scroope, Baronet

Like dancers on the ropes poor poets fare:
Most perish young, the rest in danger are.
This, one would think, should make our authors wary,
But, gamester-like, the giddy fools miscarry;
A lucky hand or two so tempts 'em on,   5
They cannot leave off play till they're undone.
With modest fears a Muse does first begin,
Like a young wench newly enticed to sin;
But tickled once with praise, by her good will,
The wanton fool would never more lie still.   10
'Tis an old mistress you'll meet here tonight,
Whose charms you once looked on with delight.
But now, of late, such dirty drabs have known ye,
A Muse o'the better sort's ashamed to own ye.
Nature well-drawn and wit must now give place   15
To gaudy nonsense and to dull grimace;
Nor is it strange that you should like so much
That kind of wit, for most of yours is such.
But I'm afraid that while to France we go,   ⎫
To bring you home fine dresses, dance, and show, ⎬   20
The stage, like you, will but more foppish grow. ⎭
Of foreign wares why should we fetch the scum,
When we can be so richly served at home?
For, heav'n be thanked, 'tis not so wise an age
But your own follies may supply the stage.   25
Though often ploughed, there's no great fear the soil
Should barren grow by the too-frequent toil,
While at your doors are to be daily found
Such loads of dunghill to manure the ground.
'Tis by your follies that we players thrive,   30

Sir Car Scroope wit, courtier, and poet (1649–80). He also wrote Dorimant's song in V.ii.
9 *will* puns on the name, Will
13 *drab* slatternly woman or prostitute
14 *ye* Q2–3, V, CA (you Q1)

As the physicians by diseases live;
And as each year some new distemper reigns,
Whose friendly poison helps t'increase their gains,
So, among you, there starts up every day
Some new, unheard-of fool for us to play.   35
Then, for your own sakes, be not too severe,
Nor what you all admire at home, damn here.
Since each is fond of his own ugly face,
Why should you, when we hold it, break the glass?

33 *t'increase* Q2–3, W, V, CA (to increase Q1)

DRAMATIS PERSONAE

MR DORIMANT
MR MEDLEY [*his friend*]
OLD BELLAIR
YOUNG BELLAIR [*his son, in love with Emilia*]
SIR FOPLING FLUTTER } *Gentlemen* 5

LADY TOWNLEY [*sister of Old Bellair*]
EMILIA
MRS LOVEIT [*in love with Dorimant*]
BELLINDA [*in love with Dorimant*] } *Gentlewomen*
LADY WOODVILL, *and* 10
HARRIET, *her daughter*

PERT
and } *Waiting women*
BUSY

A SHOEMAKER 15
AN ORANGE-WOMAN
FOUR SLOVENLY BULLIES
TWO CHAIRMEN
MR SMIRK, *a parson*
HANDY, *a valet de chambre* 20
PAGES, FOOTMEN, *etc.*

17 *four* ed. (Three Q1)   *four . . . bullies* See note to III.iii, 204 s.d.
20 *valet de chambre* See note to IV.ii, 98.

ACT I

A dressing room. A table covered with a toilet; clothes laid ready.

Enter DORIMANT *in his gown and slippers, with a note in his hand made up, repeating verses*

DORIMANT

   'Now, for some ages, had the pride of Spain
   Made the sun shine on half the world in vain'.

           Then looking on the note

'For Mrs Loveit'. What a dull, insipid thing is a billet doux
written in cold blood after the heat of the business is over! It is a
tax upon good nature which I have here been labouring to pay,   5
and have done it, but with as much regret as ever fanatic paid
the Royal Aid or church duties. 'Twill have the same fate, I
know, that all my notes to her have had of late—'twill not be
thought kind enough. Faith, women are i' the right when they
jealously examine our letters, for in them we always first   10
discover our decay of passion.—Hey! Who waits?

Enter HANDY

---

0 s.d. *toilet* cloth cover for a dressing-table, of rich material and workmanship. *OED* cites
  London Gazette (1683), No. 1811/4: 'Stolen the 20th Instant, a Toilet of blew Velvet, with a
  Gold and Silver Fringe'.

  s.d. 3 *made up* normally means sealed up, but here Dorimant's note is unsealed: he has
  Medley read it out at ll. 171–5, and only instructs Handy to seal and send it off at I, 226.

1–2 *Now . . . vain* opening couplet of Waller's 'Of a War with Spain, and a Fight at Sea', ll. 1–2
  (*Poems*, II, p. 23). John Dennis reported that contemporaries, in identifying Rochester
  with Dorimant, instanced his 'repeating, on every Occasion, the Verses of *Waller*, for
  whom that noble Lord had a very particular Esteem' (*Defence of Sir Fopling Flutter*, 1722,
  in *Critical Works*, ed. E. N. Hooker, 2 vols., 1939–43, II, p. 248).

3 *'For Mrs Loveit'* CA (Q1, etc., centre above Dorimant's speech without quotation marks)

6 *fanatic* in the latter part of the seventeenth century a hostile epithet applied to Nonconformists. *OED* cites John Gaule (1657), 'Enthusiasts, Anabaptists, Fanaticks, and
  Familists'. Nonconformists opposed both the Crown and the established Church.

7 *Royal Aid . . . church duties* 'Royal Aid' was an extraordinary subsidy or tax made by
  Parliament for the King. Church duties were levied locally for the services of the parish
  church.

HANDY
Sir—
DORIMANT
Call a footman.
HANDY
None of 'em are come yet.
DORIMANT
Dogs! Will they ever lie snoring abed till noon?   15
HANDY
'Tis all one, sir: if they're up, you indulge 'em so, they're ever poaching after whores all the morning.
DORIMANT
Take notice henceforward who's wanting in his duty—the next clap he gets, he shall rot for an example. What vermin are those chattering without?   20
HANDY
Foggy Nan, the orange-woman, and swearing Tom, the shoemaker.
DORIMANT
Go, call in that overgrown jade with the flasket of guts before her. Fruit is refreshing in a morning.

        Exit HANDY

      'It is not that I love you less,   25
      Than when before your feet I lay—'

     Enter ORANGE-WOMAN [*and* HANDY]

How now, double-tripe, what news do you bring?
ORANGE-WOMAN
News! Here's the best fruit has come to town t' year. Gad, I was up before four o'clock this morning and bought all the choice i' the market.   30
DORIMANT
The nasty refuse of your shop.

---

17 *poaching after* taking game illegally (which carries on the hunting imagery), but possibly containing a sexual pun on the meaning 'poke' (from OF *pocher*, to thrust or dig out with the fingers).
21 *Foggy* unwholesomely bloated, puffy
23 *flasket* 'a long shallow basket' (Johnson), or, possibly, a small flask
25–6 *It . . . lay* Waller, 'The Self-Banished', ll. 1–2 (*Poems*, I, p. 101).

ORANGE-WOMAN

You need not make mouths at it. I assure you, 'tis all culled
ware.

DORIMANT

The citizens buy better on a holiday in their walk to Tot'nam.

ORANGE-WOMAN

Good or bad, 'tis all one; I never knew you commend anything.   35
Lord, would the ladies had heard you talk of 'em as I have done.
Here—   *Sets down the fruit*
Bid your man give me an angel.

DORIMANT [*To* HANDY]

Give the bawd her fruit again.

ORANGE-WOMAN

Well, on my conscience, there never was the like of you—God's   40
my life, I had almost forgot to tell you, there is a young
gentlewoman, lately come to town with her mother, that is so
taken with you.

DORIMANT

Is she handsome?

ORANGE-WOMAN

Nay, gad, there are few finer women, I tell you but so, and a   45
hugeous fortune, they say. Here, eat this peach, it comes from
the stone. 'Tis better than any Newington you've tasted.

DORIMANT

This fine woman, I'll lay my life (*Taking the peach*), is some
awkward, ill-fashioned country toad, who, not having above
four dozen of black hairs on her head, has adorned her baldness   50

---

34 *citizens . . . Tot'nam* Tottenham then lay 4 miles north of the suburbs beginning to grow
outside the City, and so was convenient for tradespeople's outings. Shadwell distinguishes the different classes of Londoner in *The Virtuoso*, 1676, V.i—'your Glass-
Coach will take you to *Hide-Park* for Air. The Suburb-fools trudge to *Lamb's-Conduit* or
Totnam; your sprucer sort of Citizens gallop to *Epsom*; your Mechanick gross Fellows,
shewing much conjugal affection, strut before their Wives, each with a Child in his Arms,
to *Islington*, or *Hogsdon*' (*Complete Works*, ed. M. Summers, 5 vols., 1931–2, III, p. 164).

38 *angel* gold coin, originally called angel-noble, with the archangel Michael and the dragon
as its device. Its value varied from 6s. 8d. to 10s.

39 *bawd* fruit-women were well-known go-betweens. Conaghan cites Dryden's *The Assignation*, 1673, 'Why, if you will have it, you are little better than a procuress: you carry
messages betwixt party and party, and, in one word Sir, she's as arrant a Fruit-woman as
any is about *Rome*' (III.i, 274–6, *Works*, XI, p. 355).

46–7 *peach . . . Newington* presumably a variety of peach from Newington, Kent. The flesh of a
freestone (as opposed to clingstone) separates from the stone.

with a large white fruz, that she may look sparkishly in the
forefront of the King's box at an old play.

ORANGE-WOMAN

Gad, you'd change your note quickly if you did but see her!

DORIMANT

How came she to know me?

ORANGE-WOMAN

She saw you yesterday at the Change. She told me you came   55
and fooled with the woman at the next shop.

DORIMANT

I remember, there was a mask observed me, indeed. Fooled, did
she say?

ORANGE-WOMAN

Ay; I vow she told me twenty things you said too, and acted with
her head and with her body so like you—   60

Enter MEDLEY

MEDLEY

Dorimant, my life, my joy, my darling sin! How dost
thou?   [*Embraces him*]

ORANGE-WOMAN

Lord, what a filthy trick these men have got of kissing one
another!   *She spits*

---

51 *fruz* clearly means a wig with short curled hair. Not recorded in *OED* which gives 'fruz' as
meaning 'A collection of short and small branches, producing a frizzy appearance'.
However, there are several contemporary examples of the word as a verb meaning 'to
frizz out the hair'. Thackeray uses 'fuzz-wig' (1848).
sparkishly a rare adverb: *OED* cites four examples, of which this is the earliest. When used
of a woman, 'spark' meant one of great beauty, elegance, or wit. Applied to a man it is
usually depreciative, and meant a young man of elegant or foppish character.

55 *Change* the New Exchange, an arcade on the south side of the Strand, with two long
double galleries of shops, one above the other. Etherege had used it as a setting in *She
Wou'd if She Cou'd*, 1668, III.i. Fashionable London bought ribbons, knots, and essences
there; consequently lodgings in the Strand over against the Exchange were popular with
country visitors (see Bellinda's remarks at V.i, 50–3). Henry Herringman, the publisher
of Etherege and Court literature, had his shop there.

59–60 *with her head* W, V, B, CA (with head Q1)

60 *like* Q1 (W, V omit)

63–4 *a filthy trick . . . another* Compare with IV.i, 189. Shadwell's *The Sullen Lovers*, 1668, gives
a further example of this exaggerated custom when Woodcock is described as 'A Familiar
loving Coxcombe, that embraces and kisses all men . . .' (*Complete Works*, ed. cit., I, p.
14).

MEDLEY

Why do you suffer this cartload of scandal to come near you 65
and make your neighbours think you so improvident to need a
bawd?

ORANGE-WOMAN [*To* DORIMANT]

Good, now we shall have it! You did but want him to help
you. Come, pay me for my fruit.

MEDLEY

Make us thankful for it, huswife. Bawds are as much out of 70
fashion as gentlemen-ushers: none but old formal ladies use the
one, and none but foppish old stagers employ the other. Go,
you are an insignificant brandy bottle.

DORIMANT

Nay, there you wrong her. Three quarts of canary is her
business. 75

ORANGE-WOMAN

What you please, gentlemen.

DORIMANT

To him! Give him as good as he brings.

ORANGE-WOMAN

Hang him, there is not such another heathen in the town again,
except it be the shoemaker without.

MEDLEY

I shall see you hold up your hand at the bar next sessions for 80
murder, huswife. That shoemaker can take his oath you are in
fee with the doctors to sell green fruit to the gentry that the
crudities may breed diseases.

ORANGE-WOMAN

Pray give me my money.

DORIMANT

Not a penny! When you bring the gentlewoman hither you 85
spoke of, you shall be paid.

---

68 *Good . . . You* V, CA (Good now, we shall have it, you Q1; Good, now we shall have it; you
Q3; Good, now we shall have it, you W)
want need
72 *stagers* Q1 (strangers W, V) veterans, old hands
74 *canary* a light sweet wine from the Canary Islands. Visitors to the bawdy houses of the
day were usually put to the expense of a few bottles of wine. Possibly there is also a pun
on the abbreviation of thieves' slang, 'canary-bird'—'a Rogue or Whore taken, and
clapp'd into the Cage or Round-house' (*A New Canting Dictionary*, 1725).
83 *crudities* undigested (or indigestible) matter in the stomach

ORANGE-WOMAN

The gentlewoman! The gentlewoman may be as honest as
your sisters, for aught as I know. Pray pay me, Mr Dorimant,
and do not abuse me so. I have an honester way of living—you
know it.   90

MEDLEY

Was there ever such a resty bawd?

DORIMANT

Some jade's tricks she has, but she makes amends when she's
in good humour. Come, tell me the lady's name, and Handy
shall pay you.

ORANGE-WOMAN

I must not, she forbid me.   95

DORIMANT

That's a sure sign she would have you.

MEDLEY

Where does she live?

ORANGE-WOMAN

They lodge at my house.

MEDLEY

Nay, then she's in a hopeful way.

ORANGE-WOMAN

Good Mr Medley, say your pleasure of me, but take heed how   100
you affront my house. God's my life, in a hopeful way!

DORIMANT

Prithee, peace. What kind of woman's the mother?

ORANGE-WOMAN

A goodly, grave gentlewoman. Lord, how she talks against the
wild young men o' the town! As for your part, she thinks you
an arrant devil: should she see you, on my conscience she   105
would look if you had not a cloven foot.

DORIMANT

Does she know me?

---

87 *honest* honourable, chaste
88 *sisters* Q1 (sister W, V)
91 *resty* restive or indolent, sluggish
92 *jade* contemptuous name for an inferior horse, applied pejoratively to women
102 *Prithee* I pray thee
104 *wild* See Introduction, pp. xxvi–viii.
105 *arrant* (a) wandering, as in 'knight errant', hence with the sense of genuine, (b) down-
right or manifest, and hence, unmitigated.

ORANGE-WOMAN

Only by hearsay. A thousand horrid stories have been told her
of you, and she believes 'em all.

MEDLEY

By the character, this should be the famous Lady Woodvill and   110
her daughter Harriet.

ORANGE-WOMAN [*Aside*]

The devil's in him for guessing, I think.

DORIMANT

Do you know 'em?

MEDLEY

Both very well. The mother's a great admirer of the forms and
civility of the last age.   115

DORIMANT

An antiquated beauty may be allowed to be out of humour at
the freedoms of the present. This is a good account of the
mother. Pray, what is the daughter?

MEDLEY

Why, first, she's an heiress, vastly rich.

DORIMANT

And handsome?   120

MEDLEY

What alteration a twelvemonth may have bred in her, I know
not, but a year ago she was the beautifullest creature I ever
saw—a fine, easy, clean shape, light brown hair in abundance,
her features regular, her complexion clear, and lively, large,
wanton eyes; but, above all, a mouth that has made me kiss it a   125

114–15 *forms and civility of the last age* i.e., the manners and social decorum of the previous
generation (those of Charles I's Court). 'Forms' carries the sense of a set method of
outward behaviour according with etiquette. *OED* gives its last example of 'forms'
meaning 'manners' from 1639, but it is common in Restoration comedy, usually in a
pejorative sense and with an old-fashioned flavour. See Lady Wishfort, *The Way of the
World*, 1700, III.i, 'I shall never break Decorums . . . I hope Sir Rowland is better bred,
than to put a Lady to the necessity of breaking her Forms'.

115 *civility* Q1 (civilities Q2–3)

123 *easy* a word carrying several meanings in the play. See Introduction, pp. xxx–xxxi. Here
(as at III.iii, 28) the sense is graceful, attractive (a meaning not recorded in *OED*).

125 *wanton* the meaning goes beyond Carnochan's 'lively, roguish'. Medley's libertine
values set the wide range of the word's senses in tension. At the primary level, Harriet's
eyes are sexually alive and playful. The context inverts the morally condemnatory sense
of lascivious, unchaste, and remembers other meanings – free, unrestrained (poet.);
capricious, giddy; reckless of decorum.

thousand times in imagination—teeth white and even, and
pretty, pouting lips, with a little moisture ever hanging on them,
that look like the Provence rose fresh on the bush, ere the
morning sun has quite drawn up the dew.

DORIMANT

Rapture, mere rapture! 130

ORANGE-WOMAN

Nay, gad, he tells you true. She's a delicate creature.

DORIMANT

Has she wit?

MEDLEY

More than is usual in her sex, and as much malice. Then, she's
as wild as you would wish her, and has a demureness in her
looks that makes it so surprising. 135

DORIMANT

Flesh and blood cannot hear this and not long to know her.

MEDLEY

I wonder what makes her mother bring her up to town? An old,
doting keeper cannot be more jealous of his mistress.

ORANGE-WOMAN

She made me laugh yesterday. There was a judge came to visit
'em, and the old man (she told me) did so stare upon her and, 140
when he saluted her, smacked so heartily—who would think it
of 'em?

MEDLEY

God-a-mercy, Judge!

DORIMANT

Do 'em right, the gentlemen of the long robe have not been
wanting by their good examples to countenance the crying sin 145
o' the nation.

MEDLEY

Come, on with your trappings; 'tis later than you imagine.

---

128 *Provence* V (Province Q1; Provins CA) *Provence rose* the cabbage rose (*rosa centifolia*).
 'The misnamed Provence rose was first introduced into France by the Crusaders at
 Provins (Seine and Marne)' (*Westminster Gazette*, 31 July 1905). Carnochan emends to
 'Provins rose', now used to describe *rosa gallica*.
130 *mere* pure, sheer
134 *wild* See Introduction, pp. xxvi–viii.
143 *God-a-mercy* 'God reward you', hence used as an exclamation of thanks (here ironically).
 Judge Q1 (a judge V)
144 *gentlemen . . . robe* members of the legal profession

DORIMANT

Call in the shoemaker, Handy!

ORANGE-WOMAN

Good Mr Dorimant, pay me. Gad, I had rather give you my
fruit than stay to be abused by that foul-mouthed rogue. What   150
you gentlemen say, it matters not much, but such a dirty fellow
does one more disgrace.

DORIMANT [*To* HANDY]

Give her ten shillings. [*To* ORANGE-WOMAN] And be sure you
tell the young gentlewoman I must be acquainted with her.

ORANGE-WOMAN

Now do you long to be tempting this pretty creature. Well,   155
heavens mend you!

MEDLEY

Farewell, bog!

> *Exeunt* ORANGE-WOMAN *and* HANDY

Dorimant, when did you see your *pis aller*, as you call her, Mrs
Loveit?

DORIMANT

Not these two days.   160

MEDLEY

And how stand affairs between you?

DORIMANT

There has been great patching of late, much ado—we make a
shift to hang together.

MEDLEY

I wonder how her mighty spirit bears it?

DORIMANT

Ill enough, on all conscience. I never knew so violent a creature.   165

MEDLEY

She's the most passionate in her love and the most extravagant
in her jealousy of any woman I ever heard of. What note is that?

DORIMANT

An excuse I am going to send her for the neglect I am guilty of.

---

157 *bog* bugbear (*OED*, sb. 2, cites this example)
158 *pis aller* last resource
162 *late . . . we* V, B, CA, CO (late, much Ado we Q1; late; with much ado we Q3)
166 *extravagant* See Introduction, pp. xxvi–xxx.

MEDLEY
> Prithee, read it.

DORIMANT
> No, but if you will take the pains, you may.   170

MEDLEY (*Reads*)
> 'I never was a lover of business, but now I have a just reason to
> hate it, since it has kept me these two days from seeing you. I
> intend to wait upon you in the afternoon, and in the pleasure of
> your conversation forget all I have suffered during this tedious
> absence'.—This business of yours, Dorimant, has been with a   175
> vizard at the playhouse; I have had an eye on you. If some
> malicious body should betray you, this kind note would hardly
> make your peace with her.

DORIMANT
> I desire no better.

MEDLEY
> Why, would her knowledge of it oblige you?   180

DORIMANT
> Most infinitely; next to the coming to a good understanding
> with a new mistress, I love a quarrel with an old one. But the
> devil's in't, there has been such a calm in my affairs of late, I
> have not had the pleasure of making a woman so much as break
> her fan, to be sullen, or forswear herself, these three days.   185

MEDLEY
> A very great misfortune! Let me see, I love mischief well enough
> to forward this business myself. I'll about it presently, and
> though I know the truth of what you've done, will set her a-
> raving. I'll heighten it a little with invention, leave her in a fit o'
> the mother, and be here again before you're ready.   190

---

174 *conversation* although the word carries the more limited modern meaning, it includes
the idea of social intimacy. Medley may be playing on a further meaning, sexual
intercourse.

176 *vizard* mask, hence a woman wearing a mask; often used of a masked prostitute. Masks
were fashionable in the early Restoration period, but fell into disfavour because of their
use by courtezans. In *She Wou'd if She Cou'd*, 1668, III.iii, Mr Rakehell, 'A Knight of the
Industry', is expected with a 'Coach full or two of Vizard-masks and silk Petticoats'.

190 *mother* hysteria. Compare *King Lear*, II.ii, 246–7, 'O, how this mother swells up toward
my heart!/ *Hysterica passio*, down . . .' R. A. Foakes cites Edward Jorden, *A Briefe Discourse . . .*, 1605, sig. C1ʳ: '. . . the Mother, or the Suffocation of the Mother, because,
most commonly it takes them with choaking in the throat; *and it is an affect of the
Mother or wombe . . .*' (Arden Three).

DORIMANT

Pray, stay; you may spare yourself the labour. The business is undertaken already by one who will manage it with as much address and, I think, with a little more malice than you can.

MEDLEY

Who i' the devil's name can this be?

DORIMANT

Why, the vizard, that very vizard you saw me with.   195

MEDLEY

Does she love mischief so well as to betray herself to spite another?

DORIMANT

Not so neither, Medley; I will make you comprehend the mystery. This mask, for a farther confirmation of what I have been these two days swearing to her, made me yesterday at the   200 playhouse make her a promise, before her face, utterly to break off with Loveit; and because she tenders my reputation and would not have me do a barbarous thing, has contrived a way to give me a handsome occasion.

MEDLEY

Very good.   205

DORIMANT

She intends, about an hour before me this afternoon, to make Loveit a visit; and having the privilege, by reason of a professed friendship between 'em, to talk of her concerns—

MEDLEY

Is she a friend?

DORIMANT

Oh, an intimate friend!   210

MEDLEY

Better and better! Pray proceed.

DORIMANT

She means insensibly to insinuate a discourse of me, and artificially raise her jealousy to such a height that, transported with the first motions of her passion, she shall fly upon me with

202 *tenders* regards, treats with tenderness
208 *'em, to . . . concerns*—Q1 ('em) to . . . concerns. W, V)
213 *artificially* artfully

17

all the fury imaginable as soon as ever I enter. The quarrel being   215
thus happily begun, I am to play my part: confess and justify
all my roguery, swear her impertinence and ill humour makes
her intolerable, tax her with the next fop that comes into my
head, and in a huff march away, slight her, and leave her to be
taken by whosoever thinks it worth his time to lie down before   220
her.

MEDLEY

This vizard is a spark, and has a genius that makes her worthy
of yourself, Dorimant.

Enter HANDY, SHOEMAKER, *and* FOOTMAN

DORIMANT [*To* FOOTMAN]

You rogue there, who sneak like a dog that has flung down a
dish, if you do not mend your waiting, I'll uncase you and   225
turn you loose to the wheel of fortune.—Handy, seal this and
let him run with it presently.

Exeunt HANDY *and* FOOTMAN

[HANDY *re-enters after a few moments*]

MEDLEY

Since you're resolved on a quarrel, why do you send her this
kind note?

DORIMANT

To keep her at home in order to the business. (*To the*   230
SHOEMAKER) How now, you drunken sot?

SHOEMAKER

'Zbud, you have no reason to talk. I have not had a bottle of
sack of yours in my belly this fortnight.

---

222 *genius* prevailing character or spirit
225 *uncase you* strip you (of your livery)
227 *presently* immediately
     s.d. *Exeunt . . . moments* ed. (*Exeunt . . .* FOOTMAN Q1; *Exit Footman* CA) Handy leaves
     with the footman to seal the note, but returns before l. 278. His entry is unmarked, but
     there is no need to emend with Carnochan.
230 *in order to* for the sake of (obs.)
232 *'Zbud* 'Sblood, i.e. 'God's blood'
233 *sack* a class of white wine formerly imported from the Canaries and Spain

MEDLEY

The orange-woman says your neighbours take notice what a
heathen you are, and design to inform the bishop and have you   235
burned for an atheist.

SHOEMAKER

Damn her, dunghill! If her husband does not remove her, she
stinks so, the parish intend to indict him for a nuisance.

MEDLEY

I advise you like a friend, reform your life. You have brought the
envy of the world upon you by living above yourself. Whoring   240
and swearing are vices too genteel for a shoemaker.

SHOEMAKER

'Zbud, I think you men of quality will grow as unreasonable as
the women: you would engross the sins o' the nation. Poor
folks can no sooner be wicked but they're railed at by their
betters.   245

DORIMANT

Sirrah, I'll have you stand i' the pillory for this libel.

SHOEMAKER

Some of you deserve it, I'm sure. There are so many of 'em that
our journeymen nowadays, instead of harmless ballads, sing
nothing but your damned lampoons.

DORIMANT

Our lampoons, you rogue?   250

SHOEMAKER

Nay, good master, why should not you write your own
commentaries as well as Caesar?

MEDLEY

The rascal's read, I perceive.

---

243 *engross* monopolize, wholly absorb
248 *harmless* inoffensive
248–9 *harmless ballads . . . your damned lampoons* the city journeymen's traditional taste for
popular ballads has been corrupted by the flood of scurrilous satires and lampoons
which the Shoemaker identifies with the wits. According to the *OED* 'lampoon' first
occurs in 1649. Lampoons and libels circulated widely through manuscript copies in
Restoration London, but also found their way into print as well as being sometimes
nailed to the victim's door. Etherege himself was regarded as the writer of 'airy songs
and soft lampoons' (Thorpe, p. vi).

SHOEMAKER

You know the old proverb—ale and history.

DORIMANT

Draw on my shoes, sirrah. 255

SHOEMAKER

Here's a shoe—

DORIMANT

Sits with more wrinkles than there are in an angry bully's forehead.

SHOEMAKER

'Zbud, as smooth as your mistress's skin does upon her. So, strike your foot in home. 'Zbud, if e'er a monsieur of 'em all 260 make more fashionable ware, I'll be content to have my ears whipped off with my own paring knife.

MEDLEY

And served up in a ragout, instead of cockscombs, to a company of French shoemakers for a collation.

SHOEMAKER

Hold, hold! Damn 'em caterpillars! Let 'em feed upon 265 cabbage!—Come master, your health this morning!—next my heart now!

---

254 *ale and history* 'Truth is in ale as in history' (M. P. Tilley, *A Dictionary of Proverbs in England in the Sixteenth and Seventeenth Centuries*, 1950, T578). But G. L. Apperson, *English Proverbs and Proverbial Phrases*, 1929, p. 4, regards the evidence as too slight for the sentence to be regarded as a proverb. However, the phrase was current in the seventeenth century, occurring in Bishop Corbett's *Iter Boreale* (*Poems of Richard Corbett*, ed. J. A. W. Bennett and H. R. Trevor-Roper, 1955, p. 43). Fielding quotes the couplet from Pope's *Dunciad* (1728), III, 171–2, in *Tom Jones*, 1749, IV.i—'While [happier] history with her Comrade Ale,/ Sooths the sad Series of her serious Tale'— and also refers to Butler's couplet, 'Thou that with Ale, or viler Liquors,/ Didst inspire *Withers, Pryn* and *Vickars*' (*Hudibras*, Part I, 1663, Canto i, 645–6).

257 *bully* blustering gallant, swashbuckler

263 *ragout* highly flavoured stew

263–4 *ragout . . . collation* cockscombs can be used in French cooking as a garnish or in a sauce. The joke was still current in 1733: James Bramston satirizes a Frenchified taste for '. . . frogs fricasseed, and coxcomb pies' (*The Man of Taste*, p. 14).

264 *collation* light repast

266–7 *Come . . . now!* Carnochan suggests that the Shoemaker asks Dorimant for money to drink his health: but 'next my heart' is used by Sir Frederick Frollick when he embraces Jenny, Wheadle's maid (*The Comical Revenge; or, Love in a Tub*, 1664, I.ii, 57), and Brett-Smith thinks the Shoemaker uses the phrase insolently.

266 *morning!—next* ed. (Morning next Q1, CA; morning! next B)

DORIMANT

Go, get you home, and govern your family better! Do not let your wife follow you to the alehouse, beat your whore, and lead you home in triumph.   270

SHOEMAKER

'Zbud, there's never a man i' the town lives more like a gentleman with his wife than I do. I never mind her motions; she never inquires into mine. We speak to one another civilly, hate one another heartily, and because 'tis vulgar to lie and soak together, we have each of us our several settle-bed.   275

DORIMANT [*To* HANDY]

Give him half a crown.

MEDLEY

Not without he will promise to be bloody drunk.

SHOEMAKER

Tope's the word, i' the eye of the world. [*To* HANDY] For my master's honour, Robin!

272 *motions* either, (1) movements, or (2) emotions, inner promptings (obs.)
275 *several* separate
     settle-bed wooden bench used as a bed
277 *without* unless
     bloody drunk the adverbial use of 'bloody' in colloquial language was recent, and OED cites this as its earliest example. However, the word appears in Dryden's *The Wild Gallant*, 1663, I.i. 68–9, where Bibber, using tavern slang, says, '. . . I was drunk; damnably drunk with Ale; great Hogen Mogen bloody Ale; I was porterly drunk . . .' (*Works*, VIII, p. 10). The modern usage as an intensifier or as an adjective only dates from the nineteenth century.
278–9 *Tope's . . . Robin* CA (Q1, CO have no punctuation; Q2–3, B give a comma after 'honour'; W, V give commas after 'world' and 'honour') Brett-Smith suggests that the Shoemaker rebukes Medley's vulgarism 'bloody drunk': 'tope' is the gentlemanly word. The Shoemaker, with a wink at Handy, then performs the motions of drinking Dorimant's health. 'Tope' was a relatively new word (OED cites its first example from 1654), but was less recent than 'bloody'. But 'tope' may be used as an exclamation, 'I pledge you' (from Fr. *tope*, to accept an offer or proposal, or, in gambling, to cover a bet, accept a challenge): Palmer uses the word in this sense in Etherege's *The Comical Revenge; or, Love in a Tub*, 1664—'Tope—here, pledg me' (II.iii, 48). 'In that case, the Shoemaker accepts Medley's conditions, as (he asserts) would the *world*' (Carnochan). This meaning would make the reading of the early editions possible though difficult. Some support may be given to this by the emendation of Suckling's *The Goblins*, 1646, I.iv, 6 (*The Works of Sir John Suckling*, ed. Thomas S. Clayton and Lester Beaurline, 2 vols., 1971, II, p. 133)—'TAYLOR. Oh no! He seldome wears his Sword. SERGEANT. *Tope* is the word if he do . . .' Suckling's play was written between 1637 and 1641, so that this occurrence precedes the OED's first example.

DORIMANT
Do not debauch my servants, sirrah.   280
SHOEMAKER
I only tip him the wink; he knows an alehouse from a hovel.

Exit SHOEMAKER

DORIMANT [*To* HANDY]
My clothes, quickly!
MEDLEY
Where shall we dine today?

Enter YOUNG BELLAIR

DORIMANT
Where you will. Here comes a good third man.
YOUNG BELLAIR
Your servant, gentlemen.   285
MEDLEY
Gentle sir, how will you answer this visit to your honourable
mistress? 'Tis not her interest you should keep company with
men of sense, who will be talking reason.
YOUNG BELLAIR
I do not fear her pardon, do you but grant me yours for my
neglect of late.   290
MEDLEY
Though you've made us miserable by the want of your good
company, to show you I am free from all resentment, may the
beautiful cause of our misfortune give you all the joys happy
lovers have shared ever since the world began.
YOUNG BELLAIR
You wish me in heaven, but you believe me on my journey to   295
hell.
MEDLEY
You have a good strong faith, and that may contribute much
towards your salvation. I confess I am but of an untoward
constitution, apt to have doubts and scruples; and in love they
are no less distracting than in religion. Were I so near marriage, 300
I should cry out by fits as I ride in my coach, 'Cuckold, cuckold!'

281 *tip . . . wink* give a private signal (orig. rogue's cant)
298 *untoward* awkward, perverse

with no less fury than the mad fanatic does 'Glory!' in
Bethlem.

YOUNG BELLAIR

Because religion makes some run mad, must I live an atheist?

MEDLEY

Is it not great indiscretion for a man of credit, who may have   305
money enough on his word, to go and deal with Jews, who for
little sums make men enter into bonds and give judgments?

YOUNG BELLAIR

Preach no more on this text. I am determined, and there is no
hope of my conversion.

DORIMANT (*To* HANDY, *who is fiddling about him*)

Leave your unnecessary fiddling. A wasp that's buzzing about a   310
man's nose at dinner is not more troublesome than thou art.

HANDY

You love to have your clothes hang just, sir.

DORIMANT

I love to be well-dressed, sir, and think it no scandal to my
understanding.

HANDY

Will you use the essence, or orange-flower water?   315

DORIMANT

I will smell as I do today, no offence to the ladies' noses.

HANDY

Your pleasure, sir.   [*Exit* HANDY]

DORIMANT

That a man's excellency should lie in neatly tying of a ribbon or
a cravat! How careful's nature in furnishing the world with
necessary coxcombs!   320

302–3 *mad fanatic . . . Bethlem* Brett-Smith identifies as Oliver Cromwell's porter, Daniel, a
religious maniac confined in Bethlehem Hospital, the London lunatic asylum usually
known as Bedlam. He cites the dialogue in 'A New Song of the Times, 1683' between
'Olivers Porter, Fidler, *and* Poet I *In* BEDLAM' in which the Porter begins, 'O Glory!
Glory! who are these Appear?' (*A Second Collection of the Newest and most Ingenious
Poems, Satyrs, Songs &c. against Popery*, 1689, p. 12). There are other contemporary
references: the Prologue to Thomas D'Urfey's *Sir Barnaby Whigg*, 1681, has, 'Like
Lunaticks ye roar . . . Like *Oliver*'s Porter, but not so devout'.

307 *judgments* judicial assignment of chattels, hence the certificate of such a judgment used
as security

315 *essence* perfume, scent
orange-flower water see note to III.ii, 209.

23

YOUNG BELLAIR

That's a mighty pretty suit of yours, Dorimant.

DORIMANT

I am glad 't has your approbation.

YOUNG BELLAIR

No man in town has a better fancy in his clothes than you have.

DORIMANT

You will make me have an opinion of my genius. 325

MEDLEY

There is a great critic, I hear, in these matters lately arrived piping hot from Paris.

YOUNG BELLAIR

Sir Fopling Flutter, you mean.

MEDLEY

The same.

YOUNG BELLAIR

He thinks himself the pattern of modern gallantry. 330

DORIMANT

He is indeed the pattern of modern foppery.

MEDLEY

He was yesterday at the play, with a pair of gloves up to his elbows and a periwig more exactly curled than a lady's head newly dressed for a ball.

YOUNG BELLAIR

What a pretty lisp he has! 335

DORIMANT

Ho, that he affects in imitation of the people of quality of France.

MEDLEY

His head stands for the most part on one side, and his looks are more languishing than a lady's when she lolls at stretch in her coach or leans her head carelessly against the side of a box i' the 340 playhouse.

DORIMANT

He is a person indeed of great acquired follies.

---

323 *fancy* taste, critical judgment in matters of art or elegance. *OED* cites Mrs Hutchinson's *Memoirs of Colonel Hutchinson*, 1665, p. 23, 'He was ... genteel in his habit [i.e., dress] and had a very good fancy in it'.

MEDLEY

He is like many others, beholding to his education for making him so eminent a coxcomb. Many a fool had been lost to the world, had their indulgent parents wisely bestowed neither 345 learning nor good breeding on 'em.

YOUNG BELLAIR

He has been, as the sparkish word is, brisk upon the ladies already. He was yesterday at my Aunt Townley's and gave Mrs Loveit a catalogue of his good qualities under the character of a complete gentleman, who (according to Sir Fopling) ought to 350 dress well, dance well, fence well, have a genius for love letters, an agreeable voice for a chamber, be very amorous, something discreet, but not over-constant.

MEDLEY

Pretty ingredients to make an accomplished person!

DORIMANT

I am glad he pitched upon Loveit. 355

YOUNG BELLAIR

How so?

DORIMANT

I wanted a fop to lay to her charge, and this is as pat as may be.

YOUNG BELLAIR

I am confident she loves no man but you.

DORIMANT

The good fortune were enough to make me vain, but that I am in my nature modest. 360

YOUNG BELLAIR

Hark you, Dorimant.—With your leave, Mr Medley—'tis only a secret concerning a fair lady.

MEDLEY

Your good breeding, sir, gives you too much trouble. You might have whispered without all this ceremony.

YOUNG BELLAIR (*To* DORIMANT)

How stand your affairs with Bellinda of late? 365

---

343 *beholding* Q1 (beholden Q3)

343–6 David Vieth (*N & Q*, 203 (Nov. 1958), 473–4) points out the parallel with Dryden's Epilogue (ll. 13–14) and with Rochester's 'Letter from Artemisia … to Chloe', ?Nov. 1673–spring 1675, ll. 150–61. He notes a further parallel between V.i, 94–131 and ll.101–35 of Rochester's poem.

347 *brisk* sharp

DORIMANT

She's a little jilting baggage.

YOUNG BELLAIR

Nay, I believe her false enough, but she's ne'er the worse for your purpose. She was with you yesterday in a disguise at the play.

DORIMANT

There we fell out and resolved never to speak to one another   370
more.

YOUNG BELLAIR

The occasion?

DORIMANT

Want of courage to meet me at the place appointed. These young women apprehend loving as much as the young men do fighting at first; but once entered, like them too, they all turn   375
bullies straight.

Enter HANDY

HANDY (*To* YOUNG BELLAIR)

Sir, your man without desires to speak with you.

YOUNG BELLAIR

Gentlemen, I'll return immediately.   *Exit* YOUNG BELLAIR

MEDLEY

A very pretty fellow, this.

DORIMANT

He's handsome, well-bred, and by much the most tolerable of   380
all the young men that do not abound in wit.

MEDLEY

Ever well-dressed, always complaisant, and seldom impertinent. You and he are grown very intimate, I see.

---

366 *baggage* used familiarly or playfully of any young woman (from 1672), but the earlier meaning, a worthless good-for-nothing woman, a strumpet, remained current. *OED* cites W. Robertson, *Phraseologia Generalis . . .*, 1693 ed., p. 197, 'A baggage, or Souldier's Punk'.

376 *bullies* probably plays on different senses of the word: 1) sweetheart (of either men or women), 2) blustering gallant, swashbuckler, 3) the 'gallant' or protector of prostitutes.

382 *complaisant* obliging, courteous, accommodating. Cf. Hobbes, *Leviathan*, I.xv, 76, 'Compleasance; that is to say, That every man strive to accomodate himselfe to the rest', and Johnson's *Dictionary*, 'Civility, desire of pleasing . . .' A recent word (first example in *OED* dated 1647). See Introduction, pp. xxx–xxxii.

DORIMANT

It is our mutual interest to be so. It makes the women think the
better of his understanding and judge more favourably of my 385
reputation; it makes him pass upon some for a man of very
good sense, and I upon others for a very civil person.

MEDLEY

What was that whisper?

DORIMANT

A thing which he would fain have known, but I did not think it
fit to tell him. It might have frighted him from his honourable 390
intentions of marrying.

MEDLEY

Emilia, give her her due, has the best reputation of any young
woman about the town who has beauty enough to provoke
detraction. Her carriage is unaffected, her discourse modest—
not at all censorious nor pretending, like the counterfeits of the 395
age.

DORIMANT

She's a discreet maid, and I believe nothing can corrupt her but
a husband.

MEDLEY

A husband?

DORIMANT

Yes, a husband. I have known many women make a difficulty of 400
losing a maidenhead, who have afterwards made none of
making a cuckold.

MEDLEY

This prudent consideration, I am apt to think, has made you
confirm poor Bellair in the desperate resolution he has taken.

DORIMANT

Indeed, the little hope I found there was of her, in the state she 405
was in, has made me by my advice contribute something
towards the changing of her condition.

Enter YOUNG BELLAIR

388–91 *that whisper . . . marrying* the 'whisper' is the exchange between Young Bellair and
  Dorimant (ll. 365–76), from which Medley has been excluded. Thus, Dorimant first
  disguises his relationship with Bellinda from Young Bellair (l. 366), so protecting her
  reputation (cf. IV.ii, 74–5), and then uses Emilia as a blind when speaking to Medley.
394 *carriage* either, deportment, or habitual manner of conduct

Dear Bellair, by heavens I thought we had lost thee! Men in love are never to be reckoned on when we would form a company.

YOUNG BELLAIR

Dorimant, I am undone. My man has brought the most 410
surprising news i' the world.

DORIMANT

Some strange misfortune is befallen your love?

YOUNG BELLAIR

My father came to town last night and lodges i' the very house where Emilia lies.

MEDLEY

Does he know it is with her you are in love? 415

YOUNG BELLAIR

He knows I love, but knows not whom, without some officious sot has betrayed me.

DORIMANT

Your Aunt Townley is your confidante and favours the business.

YOUNG BELLAIR

I do not apprehend any ill office from her. I have received a 420
letter, in which I am commanded by my father to meet him at my aunt's this afternoon. He tells me farther he has made a match for me, and bids me resolve to be obedient to his will or expect to be disinherited.

MEDLEY

Now's your time, Bellair. Never had lover such an opportunity 425
of giving a generous proof of his passion.

YOUNG BELLAIR

As how, I pray?

MEDLEY

Why, hang an estate, marry Emilia out of hand, and provoke your father to do what he threatens. 'Tis but despising a coach, humbling yourself to a pair of galoshes, being out of 430
countenance when you meet your friends, pointed at and pitied

---

418 *confidante* this should perhaps be regarded as another instance of a French word. First instance in *OED*, from Lady Mary Wortley Montagu, dates from 1709. The word may have been formed to represent the sound of Fr. *confidente*.

430 *galoshes* CA (goloshoes Q1; goloshes V). 'Galloches, high wooden Pattins or Clogs . . . It also means a Sort of Slipper worn over the Shoes' (Ozell's *Rabelais*, 1737, II, p. 219: cited *OED*)

wherever you go by all the amorous fops that know you, and
your fame will be immortal.

YOUNG BELLAIR

I could find in my heart to resolve not to marry at all.

DORIMANT

Fie, fie! That would spoil a good jest and disappoint the well-   435
natured town of an occasion of laughing at you.

YOUNG BELLAIR

The storm I have so long expected hangs o'er my head and
begins to pour down upon me. I am on the rack and can have
no rest till I'm satisfied in what I fear. Where do you dine?

DORIMANT

At Long's or Locket's.   440

MEDLEY

At Long's let it be.

YOUNG BELLAIR

I'll run and see Emilia and inform myself how matters stand. If
my misfortunes are not so great as to make me unfit for
company, I'll be with you.   *Exit* YOUNG BELLAIR

Enter a FOOTMAN *with a letter*

FOOTMAN (*To* DORIMANT)

Here's a letter, sir.   445

DORIMANT

The superscription's right: 'For Mr Dorimant'.

MEDLEY

Let's see. [*Looks at the letter*] The very scrawl and spelling of a
true-bred whore.

DORIMANT

I know the hand. The style is admirable, I assure you.

MEDLEY

Prithee, read it.   450

· 440 *Long's or Locket's* well-known eating-places. There was a tavern called Long's in the
Haymarket and another in Covent Garden, kept by two brothers. Locket's, named after
its landlord, Adam Locket, is continually referred to in Restoration comedies, and was
frequented by Etherege himself. Lord Foppington speaks of going 'to Dinner at *Lacket's*,
where you are so nicely and delicately serv'd, that, stap my Vitals, they shall compose
you a Dish no bigger than a Saucer, shall come to Fifty shillings' (*The Relapse,* 1697, II.i,
p. 19).

DORIMANT (*Reads*)

'I told a you you dud not love me, if you dud, you would have seen me again ere now. I have no money and am very malicolly. Pray send me a guynie to see the operies. Your servant to command, Molly'.

MEDLEY

Pray let the whore have a favourable answer, that she may spark   455
it in a box and do honour to her profession.

DORIMANT

She shall, and perk up i' the face of quality. [*To* HANDY] Is the coach at door?

HANDY

You did not bid me send for it.

DORIMANT

Eternal blockhead! (HANDY *offers to go out*) Hey, sot!   460

HANDY

Did you call me, sir?

DORIMANT

I hope you have no just exception to the name, sir?

HANDY

I have sense, sir.

DORIMANT

Not so much as a fly in winter.——How did you come, Medley?

MEDLEY

In a chair.   465

FOOTMAN

You may have a hackney coach if you please, sir.

DORIMANT

I may ride the elephant if I please, sir. Call another chair and let my coach follow to Long's.

---

457 *perk up* assume or have a lively or self-conceited attitude or air; lift one's head, or thrust oneself forward briskly, boldly, or impudently. But possibly 'perk' (*OED*, v. 2), to perch, used of birds, though also transferred to people.

467 *I . . . elephant* Harold Brooks cites *City Mercury*, No. 3, 11-18 Nov. 1675, where an advertisement headed 'The Elephant' reads, 'That Wonderful Beast lately sent from *East India* to . . . Lord Berkley, And since sold for Two thousand pounds sterling: Is now to be seen at the *White Horse* Inn over against *Salisbury* Court in Fleet-street . . .', and notes Rochester's reference to an elephant at Smithfield Fair in 'My Lord All-Pride', ?1679, ll. 23–6 (*The Poems of John Oldham*, ed. Harold F. Brooks in collaboration with Raman Selden, 1987, p. 447).

'Be calm, ye great parents, etc.'

Exeunt, [DORIMANT] *singing*

469 *Be . . . parents, etc.* Conaghan identifies as from the song 'My Lord: Great *Neptune,* for my Sake' in the final scene of Shadwell's operatic version of *The Tempest,* first performed at the Dorset Garden Theatre in 1674. Lines 17–18 run: 'Be calm, ye great Parents of the Flouds and the Springs,/ While each *Nereide* and *Triton* Plays, Revels, and Sings' (*Complete Works,* ed. cit., II, p. 266). But Dorimant could be quoting instead the version of these lines from Thomas Duffett's bawdy burlesque, *The Mock-Tempest: or the Enchanted Castle,* 1675, 'Be calme ye great Parents of the Punck, and the Pad,/ While each Bully and Lass sing and revel like mad' (pp. 51–2). Further, see Barnard, art. cit., pp. 295–7.

ACT II, SCENE I

[LADY TOWNLEY's *house*]

Enter my LADY TOWNLEY *and* EMILIA

LADY TOWNLEY
I was afraid, Emilia, all had been discovered.

EMILIA
I tremble with the apprehension still.

LADY TOWNLEY
That my brother should take lodgings i' the very house where
you lie!

EMILIA
'Twas lucky we had timely notice to warn the people to be   5
secret. He seems to be a mighty good-humoured old man.

LADY TOWNLEY
He ever had a notable smirking way with him.

EMILIA
He calls me rogue, tells me he can't abide me, and does so bepat
me.

LADY TOWNLEY
On my word, you are much in his favour then.   10

EMILIA
He has been very inquisitive, I am told, about my family, my
reputation, and my fortune.

LADY TOWNLEY
I am confident he does not i' the least suspect you are the
woman his son's in love with.

EMILIA
What should make him then inform himself so particularly of   15
me?

LADY TOWNLEY
He was always of a very loving temper himself. It may be he has
a doting fit upon him, who knows?

EMILIA
It cannot be.

Enter YOUNG BELLAIR

LADY TOWNLEY

    Here comes my nephew.—Where did you leave your father?   20

YOUNG BELLAIR

    Writing a note within. Emilia, this early visit looks as if some
kind jealousy would not let you rest at home.

EMILIA

    The knowledge I have of my rival gives me a little cause to fear
your constancy.

YOUNG BELLAIR

    My constancy! I vow—   25

EMILIA

    Do not vow—our love is frail as is our life, and full as little in
our power; and are you sure you shall outlive this day?

YOUNG BELLAIR

    I am not, but when we are in perfect health, 'twere an idle thing
to fright ourselves with the thoughts of sudden death.

LADY TOWNLEY

    Pray, what has passed between you and your father i' the garden?   30

YOUNG BELLAIR

    He's firm in his resolution, tells me I must marry Mrs Harriet,
or swears he'll marry himself and disinherit me. When I saw I
could not prevail with him to be more indulgent, I dissembled
an obedience to his will, which has composed his passion and
will give us time—and I hope opportunity—to deceive him.   35

Enter OLD BELLAIR *with a note in his hand*

LADY TOWNLEY

    Peace, here he comes.

OLD BELLAIR

    Harry, take this and let your man carry it for me to Mr
Fourbe's chamber, my lawyer, i' the Temple.

                                     [*Exit* YOUNG BELLAIR]

    (*To* EMILIA) Neighbour, adod, I am glad to see thee here.—

---

38 *Fourbe's* Q1 varies spelling to 'Furb' at V.ii, 29, but 'fourbe' (from the French) meant a
cheat, an impostor, or a trick, imposture. A short-lived word: *OED* gives examples of the
noun and verb from 1654 to 1761, and cites Denham's *Passion of Dido*, 1668, 1. 107,
'Thou art a false Impostor and a Fourbe'.
Temple the Inner and Middle Temple of London's Inns of Court are so-called because
they stand on the site of the buildings of the Knights Templar.

Make much of her, sister. She's one of the best of your   40
acquaintance. I like her countenance and her behaviour well;
she has a modesty that is not common i' this age, adod she has.

LADY TOWNLEY

I know her value, brother, and esteem her accordingly.

OLD BELLAIR

Advise her to wear a little more mirth in her face. Adod, she's
too serious.   45

LADY TOWNLEY

The fault is very excusable in a young woman.

OLD BELLAIR

Nay, adod, I like her ne'er the worse; a melancholy beauty has
her charms. I love a pretty sadness in a face which varies now
and then, like changeable colours, into a smile.

LADY TOWNLEY

Methinks you speak very feelingly, brother.   50

OLD BELLAIR

I am but five-and-fifty, sister, you know—an age not altogether
insensible. (*To* EMILIA) Cheer up sweetheart, I have a secret to
tell thee may chance to make thee merry. We three will make
collation together anon. I' the meantime, mum! [*Aloud*] I
can't abide you; go, I can't abide you—   55

Enter YOUNG BELLAIR

Harry! Come, you must along with me to my Lady
Woodvill's.—I am going to slip the boy at a mistress.

YOUNG BELLAIR

At a wife, sir, you would say.

OLD BELLAIR

You need not look so glum, sir. A wife is no curse when she
brings the blessing of a good estate with her. But an idle town   60
flirt, with a painted face, a rotten reputation, and a crazy

---

42 *adod* equivalent to 'egad', 'By God'
54 *meantime . . . I* CA (meantime mum, I Q1; meantime, mum, I Q3). Conaghan cites two
    further contemporary texts for the emendation
    mum two meanings are possible. 1) Hush, be silent! (the meaning assumed by this text).
    2) A vulgar variant of 'madam'.
57 *slip* release (a greyhound or hawk) from a leash or slip
61 *flirt* woman of loose character (1600–1703, *OED*, which cites this example). The first
    example of the modern sense (one who flirts or plays at courtship) given by the *OED* is
    from Richardson in 1748.

fortune, adod, is the devil and all; and such a one I hear you are
in league with.

YOUNG BELLAIR

I cannot help detraction, sir.

OLD BELLAIR

Out a pize o' their breeches, there are keeping fools enough for   65
such flaunting baggages, and they are e'en too good for 'em.
(*To* EMILIA) Remember 'night. [*Aloud*] Go, you're a rogue,
you're a rogue. Fare you well, fare you well. [*To* YOUNG BELLAIR]
Come, come, come along, sir.

Exeunt OLD *and* YOUNG BELLAIR

LADY TOWNLEY

On my word, the old man comes on apace. I'll lay my life he's   70
smitten.

EMILIA

This is nothing but the pleasantness of his humour.

LADY TOWNLEY

I know him better than you. Let it work; it may prove lucky.

Enter a PAGE

PAGE

Madam, Mr Medley has sent to know whether a visit will not be
troublesome this afternoon?   75

LADY TOWNLEY

Send him word his visits never are so.

[*Exit* PAGE]

EMILIA

He's a very pleasant man.

LADY TOWNLEY

He's a very necessary man among us women. He's not
scandalous i' the least, perpetually contriving to bring good
company together, and always ready to stop up a gap at ombre.   80
Then, he knows all the little news o' the town.

EMILIA

I love to hear him talk o' the intrigues. Let 'em be never so dull
in themselves, he'll make 'em pleasant i' the relation.

---

65 *pize* imprecation of uncertain meaning. It may be an arbitrary substitute for 'Pest!' or
'Pox!', the latter being used in the same way as 'pize' from 1600 onwards.
  keeping fools fools who keep mistresses (cf. Dryden's title, *The Kind Keeper; or, Mr
  Limberham*, 1680).
66 *baggages* See note to I, 366.

LADY TOWNLEY

But he improves things so much one can take no measure of the truth from him. Mr Dorimant swears a flea or a maggot is not 85 made more monstrous by a magnifying glass than a story is by his telling it.

Enter MEDLEY

EMILIA

Hold, here he comes.

LADY TOWNLEY

Mr Medley.

MEDLEY

Your servant, madam. 90

LADY TOWNLEY

You have made yourself a stranger of late.

EMILIA

I believe you took a surfeit of ombre last time you were here.

MEDLEY

Indeed I had my bellyful of that termagant, Lady Dealer. There never was so insatiable a carder; an old gleeker never loved to sit to 't like her. I have played with her now at least a dozen 95 times, till she's worn out all her fine complexion and her tour would keep in curl no longer.

LADY TOWNLEY

Blame her not, poor woman. She loves nothing so well as a black ace.

85–6 *flea ... magnifying glass* Robert Hooke's *Micrographia* (1665), pp. 210–13, had described and illustrated a flea and a louse seen through a microscope: Butler's *Hudibras*, II.iii, 305–12, had made us of this as had Marvell's 'Last Instructions to a Painter' (written 1667), ll. 16–18.

92 *ombre* a card-game, fashionable in the seventeenth and early eighteenth centuries. Played by three people, with forty cards, the eights, nines, and tens of the ordinary pack being thrown out. A Spanish game according to Cotgrave, so-called because 'he who under-takes to play [for the stake] saith *Jo soy L'Ombre*, i.e., I am the man ...' Matadore (1. 101) was the name given to the principal cards (the black aces and variable card).

94 *carder* card-player (obs.: *OED* gives examples *c.* 1530–1712)
gleeker player of gleek, a card-game (rare). The game was played by three people; forty-four cards were used, twelve being dealt to each player, the remaining eight forming a common 'stock'.

96 *tour* a crescent of false hair. Another word of French extraction (cf. *tour de cheveux*) newly brought into English (*OED* gives first e.g. from 1674). Chambers's *Cyclopaedia*, 1724–41 describes as 'a tress or border of hair, going round the head, which mingled dextrously with the natural hair, lengthens and thickens it'.

MEDLEY

The pleasure I have seen her in when she has had hope in   100
drawing for a matadore!

EMILIA

'Tis as pretty sport to her as persuading masks off is to you, to
make discoveries.

LADY TOWNLEY

Pray, where's your friend Mr Dorimant?

MEDLEY

Soliciting his affairs. He's a man of great employment—has   105
more mistresses now depending than the most eminent lawyer
in England has causes.

EMILIA

Here has been Mrs Loveit so uneasy and out of humour these
two days.

LADY TOWNLEY

How strangely love and jealousy rage in that poor woman!   110

MEDLEY

She could not have picked out a devil upon earth so proper to
torment her. He's made her break a dozen or two of fans
already, tear half a score points in pieces, and destroy hoods
and knots without number.

LADY TOWNLEY

We heard of a pleasant serenade he gave her t'other night.   115

MEDLEY

A Danish serenade, with kettledrums and trumpets.

EMILIA

Oh, barbarous!

MEDLEY

What, you are of the number of the ladies whose ears are grown

---

106 *depending* pending, like a lawyer's cases (causes)
112 *He's* ed. (Has Q1; h'as Q3, B, CO; H'as CA; he has W, V)
113 *points* pieces of tagged lace or cord for fastening clothes
114 *knots* bows made of ribbon
115–16 *serenade . . . Danish serenade* 'serenade' was a recent word from the French (first e.g. in *OED* is from 1649). Medley indicates that French wind instruments were an expected part of the ensemble (11. 119–20), as they are of Sir Fopling's *equipage* (see IV.i, 259). Dorimant's 'Danish serenade' is a drunken practical joke. Carnochan aptly cites *Hamlet*, I.iv, 8–12, 'The King doth wake tonight and takes his rouse, /Keeps wassail, and the swaggering upspring reels; /And as he drains his draughts of Rhenish down, /The kettledrum and trumpet thus bray out /The triumph of his pledge'.

so delicate since our operas, you can be charmed with nothing
but flutes douces and French hautboys?   120

EMILIA

Leave your raillery and tell us, is there any new wit come
forth—songs, or novels?

MEDLEY

A very pretty piece of gallantry, by an eminent author, called
The Diversions of Brussels—very necessary to be read by all old
ladies who are desirous to improve themselves at questions and   125
commands, blindman's buff, and the like fashionable
recreations.

EMILIA

Oh, ridiculous!

MEDLEY

Then there is *The Art of Affectation*, written by a late beauty of
quality, teaching you how to draw up your breasts, stretch up   130
your neck, to thrust out your breech, to play with your head, to

---

119 *operas* the production of the altered versions of *Macbeth* and *The Tempest* (1674) along
     with Shadwell's *Psyche* (1675), all of them elaborate spectacles which had musical
     elements, marked a new stage in the development of Restoration 'opera'. Brett-Smith
     cites Evelyn's *Diary*, 5 Jan. 1673/74, 'I saw an Italian opera in musiq, the first that had
     been seen of this kind'.

120 *flutes douces* ed. (Flute doux Q1; *flûtes douces* V, CA) Q1's 'doux' is an erroneous
     formation from the French. The flute douce (i.e., the recorder) with its eight holes and
     two octaves succeeded the flageolet (see note to III.iii, 231) in popularity, but was a
     recent introduction to England. Evelyn's *Diary*, 20 Nov. 1679, records, 'There was also a
     flute douce, now much in request for accompanying the voice'.

121 *raillery* imported from the French. First recorded instance in *OED* dates from 1653:
     'The word Raillery you return'd me for interpretation . . . is now grown here so com-
     mon with the better sort, as there are few of the meaner that are not able to construe it'
     (R. Loveday, *Letters*, 1663 ed., p. 245).

124 *The Diversions of Brussels* identified by R. S. Cox as Richard Flecknoe's *A Treatise of the
     Sports of Wits*, 1675. See 'Richard Flecknoe and *The Man of Mode*', *Modern Language
     Quarterly*, 29 (1968), 183–9.

125–6 *questions and commands* a game in which one person addressed ludicrous questions
     and commands to each member of the company. The game is seen as similarly
     unfashionable in Wycherley's *The Gentleman Dancing-Master*, 1673, 'He is as dull as a
     country-squire at questions and commands' (*The Plays of William Wycherley*, ed.
     Arthur Friedman, 1979, II. i, 189).

129 *The Art of Affectation* Medley is mocking Hannah Woolley's *The Gentlewoman's
     Companion*, 1675. Conaghan notes that the book advises the raising of the eyes heaven-
     wards ('Of the Government of the Eye', pp. 39–42) and refers to washing and painting
     as 'innocently helpful to the beauties of modest women' (p. 240). Medley's attribution
     to 'a late beauty of quality' may be based on the portrait at the front of the book.

toss up your nose, to bite your lips, to turn up your eyes, to speak in a silly soft tone of a voice, and use all the foolish French words that will infallibly make your person and conversation charming; with a short apology at the latter end, in the behalf of   135
young ladies who notoriously wash and paint, though they have naturally good complexions.

EMILIA

What a deal of stuff you tell us!

MEDLEY

Such as the town affords, madam. The Russians, hearing the great respect we have for foreign dancing, have lately sent over   140
some of their best baladines, who are now practising a famous ballet which will be suddenly danced at the Bear Garden.

LADY TOWNLEY

Pray forbear your idle stories, and give us an account of the state of love as it now stands.

MEDLEY

Truly, there has been some revolutions in those affairs—great   145
chopping and changing among the old and some new lovers, whom malice, indiscretion, and misfortune have luckily brought into play.

LADY TOWNLEY

What think you of walking into the next room and sitting down, before you engage in this business?   150

MEDLEY

I wait upon you; and I hope (though women are commonly unreasonable), by the plenty of scandal I shall discover, to give you very good content, ladies.

Exeunt

136 *wash* use cosmetic washes
141 *baladine* a theatrical dancer; a mountebank, buffoon (from the French). This occurrence is the *OED*'s first clear example of the word being restricted to dancers, though it occurs as early as 1599.
142 *ballet* originally employed to illustrate dramatically the costumes and manners of other nations. A new word from the French: the only earlier occurrence in the *OED* is from Dryden's *Essay of Dramatick Poesie*, 1667.
   suddenly soon
   Bear Garden a hit both at the contemporary craze for music and dancing by foreign troupes, and at the proverbial barbarity of the Russians. The Bear Garden, on Bankside, was a venue for bear-baiting and prizefighting with swords. (Perhaps the bears there danced?)
146 *chopping and changing* the phrase originally meant buying and selling, bartering. As Carnochan observes, the words keep something of that force here.

ACT II, SCENE II

[MRS LOVEIT's]

Enter MRS LOVEIT *and* PERT. MRS LOVEIT *putting up a letter, then pulling out her pocket-glass and looking in it*

MRS LOVEIT
Pert.

PERT
Madam?

MRS LOVEIT
I hate myself, I look so ill today.

PERT
Hate the wicked cause on't, that base man, Mr Dorimant, who makes you torment and vex yourself continually. 5

MRS LOVEIT
He is to blame, indeed.

PERT
To blame to be two days without sending, writing, or coming near you, contrary to his oath and covenant! 'Twas to much purpose to make him swear! I'll lay my life there's not an article but he has broken—talked to the vizards i' the pit, waited upon 10 the ladies from the boxes to their coaches, gone behind the scenes and fawned upon those little insignificant creatures, the players. 'Tis impossible for a man of his inconstant temper to forbear, I'm sure.

MRS LOVEIT
I know he is a devil, but he has something of the angel yet 15 undefaced in him, which makes him so charming and agreeable that I must love him, be he never so wicked.

PERT
I little thought, madam, to see your spirit tamed to this degree,

---

0   s.d. *putting up* putting away
    s.d. 2 *pocket-glass* Under 're-adjust' *OED* cites a much later example from Fielding's *Joseph Andrews*, 1742, IV.xi, 'The beau . . . taking out a pocket-glass . . . re-adjusted his hair'.

who banished poor Mr Lackwit but for taking up another lady's
fan in your presence.   20

MRS LOVEIT

My knowing of such odious fools contributes to the making of
me love Dorimant the better.

PERT

Your knowing of Mr Dorimant, in my mind, should rather
make you hate all mankind.

MRS LOVEIT

So it does, besides himself.   25

PERT

Pray, what excuse does he make in his letter?

MRS LOVEIT

He has had business.

PERT

Business in general terms would not have been a current
excuse for another. A modish man is always very busy when he
is in pursuit of a new mistress.   30

MRS LOVEIT

Some fop has bribed you to rail at him. He had business; I will
believe it, and will forgive him.

PERT

You may forgive him anything, but I shall never forgive him his
turning me into ridicule, as I hear he does.

MRS LOVEIT

I perceive you are of the number of those fools his wit has   35
made his enemies.

PERT

I am of the number of those he's pleased to rally, madam; and if
we may believe Mr Wagfan and Mr Caperwell, he sometimes
makes merry with yourself, too, among his laughing
companions.   40

MRS LOVEIT

Blockheads are as malicious to witty men as ugly women are to
the handsome; 'tis their interest, and they make it their business
to defame 'em.

---

28 *current* genuine
29 *modish* from the French, *mode*, a recent importation. First example in *OED* dates from
    1660.
35 *has* W, V, B, CA (had Q1)

PERT

    I wish Mr Dorimant would not make it his business to defame
you.   45

MRS LOVEIT

    Should he, I had rather be made infamous by him than owe my
reputation to the dull discretion of those fops you talk of.

Enter BELLINDA

    Bellinda!   *Running to her*

BELLINDA

    My dear!

MRS LOVEIT

    You have been unkind of late.   50

BELLINDA

    Do not say unkind, say unhappy.

MRS LOVEIT

    I could chide you. Where have you been these two days?

BELLINDA

    Pity me rather, my dear, where I have been so tired with two or
three country gentlewomen, whose conversation has been more
insufferable than a country fiddle.   55

MRS LOVEIT

    Are they relations?

BELLINDA

    No, Welsh acquaintance I made when I was last year at St
Winifred's. They have asked me a thousand questions of the
modes and intrigues of the town, and I have told 'em almost as
many things for news that hardly were so when their gowns   60
were in fashion.

MRS LOVEIT

    Provoking creatures, how could you endure 'em?

BELLINDA (*Aside*)

    Now to carry on my plot; nothing but love could make me

---

47 *of* Q3, V, B, CA (off Q1)

57–8 *St Winifred's* St Winifred's Well at Holywell, Flintshire, a place of pilgrimage, particu-
    larly for Roman Catholics.

59 *intrigues* liaisons, recently imported from the French. OED cites Charleton, *Ephesian and
    Cimmerian Matrons*, 1668, 'She in like manner falls into an Intrigue (as they nowadays
    call it)'. Also Dryden, *Marriage à-la-Mode*, 1673, 'Intrigue, Philotis! that's an old phrase; I
    have laid that word by; *Amour* sounds better' (II.i, 14–15, *Works*, XI, p. 243).

capable of so much falsehood. 'Tis time to begin, lest Dorimant
should come before her jealousy has stung her.   65

                            (*Laughs, and then speaks on*)
I was yesterday at a play with 'em, where I was fain to show 'em
the living, as the man at Westminster does the dead. That is
Mrs Such-a-one, admired for her beauty; this is Mr Such-a-one,
cried up for a wit; that is sparkish Mr Such-a-one, who keeps
reverend Mrs Such-a-one; and there sits fine Mrs Such-a-one,   70
who was lately cast off by my Lord Such-a-one.

MRS LOVEIT

Did you see Dorimant there?

BELLINDA

I did, and imagine you were there with him and have no mind
to own it.

MRS LOVEIT

What should make you think so?   75

BELLINDA

A lady masked, in a pretty dishabille, whom Dorimant
entertained with more respect than the gallants do a common
vizard.

MRS LOVEIT (*Aside*)

Dorimant at the play entertaining a mask! Oh, heavens!

BELLINDA (*Aside*)

Good!   80

MRS LOVEIT

Did he stay all the while?

BELLINDA

Till the play was done, and then led her out, which confirms me
it was you.

---

67 *man at Westminster* a guide at Westminster Abbey. Conaghan cites Walter Pope, 'It is a
Custom for the Servants of the Church upon all Holidays, *Sundays* excepted, betwixt the
Sermon and Evening Prayers, to shew the Tombs, and Effigies of the Kings and Queens in
Wax, to the meaner sort of People, who then flock thither from all the corners of the
Town, and pay their Twopence to see *The Play of the Dead Volks*, as I have heard a
Devonshire Clown not improperly call if' (*The Life of . . . Seth, Lord Bishop of Salisbury*,
1697, p. 147–8).

76 *dishabille* ed. (dishabillié Q1; *déshabillé* V, CA) a negligent style of dress. Wycherley's *The
Gentleman Dancing-Master*, 1673, has 'her Dishabiliee, or Flame-colour Gown call'd
Indian' (*Plays*, ed. cit., V.i, 632–3). Another word newly taken over from the French: the
spellings in Wycherley and Q1 indicate that the word was in process of being naturalized,
so there is no need to give it as French (as do Verity and Carnochan).

MRS LOVEIT

Traitor!

PERT

Now you may believe he had business, and you may forgive him   85
too.

MRS LOVEIT

Ungrateful, perjured man!

BELLINDA

You seem so much concerned, my dear, I fear I have told you
unawares what I had better have concealed for your quiet.

MRS LOVEIT

What manner of shape had she?   90

BELLINDA

Tall and slender. Her motions were very genteel. Certainly she
must be some person of condition.

MRS LOVEIT

Shame and confusion be ever in her face when she shows it!

BELLINDA

I should blame your discretion for loving that wild man, my
dear—but they say he has a way so bewitching that few can   95
defend their hearts who know him.

MRS LOVEIT

I will tear him from mine, or die i' the attempt!

BELLINDA

Be more moderate.

MRS LOVEIT

Would I had daggers, darts, or poisoned arrows in my breast, so
I could but remove the thoughts of him from thence!   100

BELLINDA

Fie, fie, your transports are too violent, my dear. This may be
but an accidental gallantry, and 'tis likely ended at her coach.

PERT

Should it proceed farther, let your comfort be, the conduct Mr
Dorimant affects will quickly make you know your rival—ten
to one let you see her ruined, her reputation exposed to the   105
town—a happiness none will envy her but yourself, madam.

---

91 *genteel* graceful, elegant
94 *wild man* possibly a reference to the traditional figure of the wild or 'salvage' man (Q1
   capitalizes 'wild': both words are capitalized in W). On the range of meanings of 'wild' in
   the play see Introduction, pp. xxvi–viii.

MRS LOVEIT

Whoe'er she be, all the harm I wish her is, may she love him as
well as I do, and may he give her as much cause to hate him!

PERT

Never doubt the latter end of your curse, madam!

MRS LOVEIT

May all the passions that are raised by neglected love—jealousy, 110
indignation, spite, and thirst of revenge—eternally rage in her
soul, as they do now in mine!

Walks up and down with a distracted air

Enter a PAGE

PAGE

Madam, Mr Dorimant—

MRS LOVEIT

I will not see him.

PAGE

I told him you were within, madam. 115

MRS LOVEIT

Say you lied, say I'm busy, shut the door—say anything!

PAGE

He's here, madam. [*Exit* PAGE]

Enter DORIMANT

DORIMANT

'They taste of death who do at heaven arrive,
But we this paradise approach alive'.

(*To* MRS LOVEIT) What, dancing the galloping nag without a 120
fiddle? (*Offers to catch her by the hand; she flings away and walks
on*) I fear this restlessness of the body, madam, (*Pursuing her*)
proceeds from an unquietness of the mind. What unlucky
accident puts you out of humour—a point ill-washed, knots

118–19 *They . . . alive* from Waller's 'Of her Chamber', ll. 1–2 (*Poems*, I, p. 26). Dorimant
has 'who' for Waller's 'that'.
120 *galloping nag* country dance

spoiled i' the making up, hair shaded awry, or some other little   125
mistake in setting you in order?

PERT

A trifle, in my opinion, sir, more inconsiderable than any you
mention.

DORIMANT

Oh, Mrs Pert! I never knew you sullen enough to be silent.
Come, let me know the business.   130

PERT

The business, sir, is the business that has taken you up these two
days. How have I seen you laugh at men of business, and now to
become a man of business yourself!

DORIMANT

We are not masters of our own affections; our inclinations daily
alter. Now we love pleasure, and anon we shall dote on business.   135
Human frailty will have it so, and who can help it?

MRS LOVEIT

Faithless, inhuman, barbarous man—

DORIMANT [*Aside*]

Good. Now the alarm strikes—

MRS LOVEIT

—Without sense of love, of honour, or of gratitude! Tell me, for
I will know, what devil masked she was, you were with at the   140
play yesterday.

DORIMANT

Faith, I resolved as much as you, but the devil was obstinate and
would not tell me.

MRS LOVEIT

False in this as in your vows to me! You do know!

DORIMANT

The truth is, I did all I could to know.   145

MRS LOVEIT

And dare you own it to my face? Hell and furies!

Tears her fan in pieces

DORIMANT

Spare your fan, madam. You are growing hot and will want it to
cool you.

MRS LOVEIT

Horror and distraction seize you, sorrow and remorse gnaw
your soul, and punish all your perjuries to me!   *Weeps*   150

DORIMANT (*Turning to* BELLINDA)

'So thunder breaks the cloud in twain,
And makes a passage for the rain'.

(*To* BELLINDA) Bellinda, you are the devil that have raised this
storm. You were at the play yesterday and have been making
discoveries to your dear.   155

BELLINDA
You're the most mistaken man i' the world.

DORIMANT
It must be so, and here I vow revenge—resolve to pursue and
persecute you more impertinently than ever any loving fop did
his mistress, hunt you i' the Park, trace you i' the Mall, dog
you in every visit you make, haunt you at the plays and i' the   160
drawing room, hang my nose in your neck and talk to you
whether you will or no, and ever look upon you with such dying
eyes till your friends grow jealous of me, send you out of town,
and the world suspect your reputation. (*In a lower voice*)—At
my Lady Townley's when we go from hence—   165
                                        He looks kindly on BELLINDA

BELLINDA
—I'll meet you there.

DORIMANT
Enough.

MRS LOVEIT (*Pushing* DORIMANT *away*)
Stand off! You shan't stare upon her so!

DORIMANT [*Aside*]
Good! There's one made jealous already.

MRS LOVEIT
Is this the constancy you vowed?   170

151–2 *So . . . rain* from Mathew Roydon's 'An Elegie, or Friend's Passion for his Astrophill',
    ll. 59-60: identified by R. G. Howarth, 'Untraced Quotations in Etherege', *N & Q*, 188
    (June 1945), 281. Dorimant has 'breaks' for the original's 'rends'. Roydon's elegy for Sir
    Philip Sidney was published in *The Phoenix Nest* (1593).
159 *Park* either Hyde Park or St James's Park, which were both fashionable meeting-places,
    but probably the latter.
    the Mall a broad avenue with four lines of trees laid out on the border of St James's Park
    by Charles II as a place to play pall mall (hence the name). Q1 regularly spells 'Mail',
    reflecting the French origin of 'mall' (avenue, mallet used in the game). It is likely that
    Etherege intended the French pronunciation: See Blount's *Glossographia*, 1656, '*Pale
    Maille,* This game was heretofore used at the Alley near St Jameses, and vulgarly called
    Pel-Mel'.

DORIMANT

Constancy at my years? 'Tis not a virtue in season; you might as
well expect the fruit the autumn ripens i' the spring.

MRS LOVEIT

Monstrous principle!

DORIMANT

Youth has a long journey to go, madam. Should I have set up
my rest at the first inn I lodged at, I should never have arrived   175
at the happiness I now enjoy.

MRS LOVEIT

Dissembler, damned dissembler!

DORIMANT

I am so, I confess. Good nature and good manners corrupt me. I
am honest in my inclinations and would not, wer't not to avoid
offence, make a lady a little in years believe I think her young,   180
wilfully mistake art for nature, and seem as fond of a thing I am
weary of as when I doted on't in earnest.

MRS LOVEIT

False man!

DORIMANT

True woman.

MRS LOVEIT

Now you begin to show yourself!   185

DORIMANT

Love gilds us over and makes us show fine things to one another
for a time, but soon the gold wears off, and then again the
native brass appears.

MRS LOVEIT

Think on your oaths, your vows, and protestations, perjured
man!   190

DORIMANT

I made 'em when I was in love.

MRS LOVEIT

And therefore ought they not to bind? Oh, impious!

DORIMANT

What we swear at such a time may be a certain proof of a
present passion; but to say truth, in love there is no security to
be given for the future.   195

175 *rest* abode
182 *of as* Q2–3, V, B, CA (off as Q1)

MRS LOVEIT

Horrid and ungrateful, begone! And never see me more!

DORIMANT

I am not one of those troublesome coxcombs who, because they were once well-received, take the privilege to plague a woman with their love ever after. I shall obey you, madam, though I do myself some violence.   200

He offers to go, and MRS LOVEIT *pulls him back*

MRS LOVEIT

Come back, you shan't go! Could you have the ill nature to offer it?

DORIMANT

When love grows diseased, the best thing we can do is to put it to a violent death. I cannot endure the torture of a lingering and consumptive passion.   205

MRS LOVEIT

Can you think mine sickly?

DORIMANT

Oh, 'tis desperately ill! What worse symptoms are there than your being always uneasy when I visit you, your picking quarrels with me on slight occasions, and in my absence kindly listening to the impertinences of every fashionable fool that   210 talks to you?

MRS LOVEIT

What fashionable fool can you lay to my charge?

DORIMANT

Why, the very cock-fool of all those fools, Sir Fopling Flutter.

MRS LOVEIT

I never saw him in my life but once.

DORIMANT

The worse woman you, at first sight to put on all your charms,   215 to entertain him with that softness in your voice and all that wanton kindness in your eyes you so notoriously affect when you design a conquest.

MRS LOVEIT

So damned a lie did never malice yet invent. Who told you this?

DORIMANT

No matter. That ever I should love a woman that can dote on a   220 senseless caper, a tawdry French ribbon, and a formal cravat.

213   *cock-fool* a nonce formation

MRS LOVEIT
You make me mad!

DORIMANT
A guilty conscience may do much! Go on, be the game-mistress
of the town and enter all our young fops, as fast as they come
from travel.   225

MRS LOVEIT
Base and scurrilous!

DORIMANT
A fine mortifying reputation 'twill be for a woman of your
pride, wit, and quality!

MRS LOVEIT
This jealousy's a mere pretence, a cursed trick of your own
devising. I know you.   230

DORIMANT
Believe it and all the ill of me you can. I would not have a
woman have the least good thought of me that can think well of
Fopling. Farewell. Fall to, and much good may do you with
your coxcomb.

MRS LOVEIT
Stay! Oh stay, and I will tell you all.   235

DORIMANT
I have been told too much already.   *Exit* DORIMANT

MRS LOVEIT
Call him again!

PERT
E'en let him go. A fair riddance!

MRS LOVEIT
Run, I say! Call him again, I will have him called!

PERT
The devil should carry him away first, were it my concern.   240

                                                    Exit PERT

BELLINDA
He's frighted me from the very thoughts of loving men. For

---

233   *to* Q2–3, W, V, CA (too Q1)
    much good may do you a conventional ironic formula. Brett-Smith cites Ravenscroft's
    The London Cuckolds, 1682, I.i: '*Wiseacre*. You have a witty wife, much good may doe
    you with her./ *Doodle*. And much good may doe you with your fool'.
    may Q1 (may [it] V) There is no need for Verity's emendation.

heaven's sake, my dear, do not discover what I told you. I dread
his tongue as much as you ought to have done his friendship.

Enter PERT

PERT

He's gone, madam.

MRS LOVEIT

Lightning blast him!   245

PERT

When I told him you desired him to come back, he smiled,
made a mouth at me, flung into his coach, and said—

MRS LOVEIT

What did he say?

PERT

'Drive away'—and then repeated verses.

MRS LOVEIT

Would I had made a contract to be a witch when first I   250
entertained this greater devil. Monster, barbarian! I could tear
myself in pieces. Revenge, nothing but revenge can ease me.
Plague, war, famine, fire—all that can bring universal ruin and
misery on mankind—with joy I'd perish to have you in my
power but this moment!   *Exit* MRS LOVEIT   255

PERT

Follow, madam. Leave her not in this outrageous passion.

                                      PERT *gathers up the things*

BELLINDA

He's given me the proof which I desired of his love, but 'tis a
proof of his ill nature too. I wish I had not seen him use her so:
        I sigh to think that Dorimant may be
        One day as faithless and unkind to me.   260

                                                          Exeunt

257–8 *but . . . so* Q1 (W, V, B print as verse: But . . . too;/I . . . so)

ACT III, SCENE I

LADY WOODVILL's *lodgings*

Enter HARRIET *and* BUSY, *her woman*

BUSY
Dear madam! Let me set that curl in order.

HARRIET
Let me alone. I will shake 'em all out of order!

BUSY
Will you never leave this wildness?

HARRIET
Torment me not.

BUSY
Look! There's a knot falling off.   5

HARRIET
Let it drop.

BUSY
But one pin, dear madam.

HARRIET
How do I daily suffer under thy officious fingers!

BUSY
Ah, the difference that is between you and my Lady Dapper!
How uneasy she is if the least thing be amiss about her!   10

HARRIET
She is indeed most exact. Nothing ever wants to make her
ugliness remarkable.

BUSY
Jeering people say so.

HARRIET
Her powdering, painting, and her patching never fail in public
to draw the tongues and eyes of all the men upon her.   15

---

3 *wildness* restiveness. On 'wild' see Introduction pp. xxvi–viii.
5 *knot* decorative ribbon
14 *patching* it was fashionable for women to wear small patches, normally of black silk, on
the face.

BUSY

She is indeed a little too pretending.

HARRIET

That women should set up for beauty as much in spite of nature
as some men have done for wit!

BUSY

I hope without offence one may endeavour to make one's self
agreeable.   20

HARRIET

Not when 'tis impossible. Women then ought to be no more
fond of dressing than fools should be of talking. Hoods and
modesty, masks and silence, things that shadow and conceal—
they should think of nothing else.

BUSY

Jesu! Madam, what will your mother think is become of you?   25
For heaven's sake, go in again.

HARRIET

I won't.

BUSY

This is the extravagant'st thing that ever you did in your life, to
leave her and a gentleman who is to be your husband.

HARRIET

My husband! Hast thou so little wit to think I spoke what I   30
meant when I overjoyed her in the country with a low curtsy
and 'What you please, madam; I shall ever be obedient'?

BUSY

Nay, I know not, you have so many fetches.

HARRIET

And this was one, to get her up to London. Nothing else, I
assure thee.   35

BUSY

Well, the man, in my mind, is a fine man!

HARRIET

The man indeed wears his clothes fashionably and has a pretty,
negligent way with him, very courtly and much affected. He
bows, and talks, and smiles so agreeably, as he thinks.

BUSY

I never saw anything so genteel.   40

28 *extravagant'st* See Introduction, pp. xxviii–xxx.
33 *fetches* dodges, tricks

HARRIET

Varnished over with good breeding many a blockhead makes a tolerable show.

BUSY

I wonder you do not like him.

HARRIET

I think I might be brought to endure him, and that is all a reasonable woman should expect in a husband; but there is   45
duty i' the case, and like the haughty Merab, I
        'Find much aversion in my stubborn mind',
which
        'Is bred by being promised and designed'.

BUSY

I wish you do not design your own ruin! I partly guess your   50
inclinations, madam. That Mr Dorimant—

HARRIET

Leave your prating and sing some foolish song or other.

BUSY

I will—the song you love so well ever since you saw Mr Dorimant.

SONG

    When first Amintas charmed my heart,   55
    My heedless sheep began to stray;
    The wolves soon stole the greatest part,
    And all will now be made a prey.

    Ah, let not love your thoughts possess,
    'Tis fatal to a shepherdess;   60

46–9 *Merab . . . designed* Merab, elder daughter of Saul, who should have been given to David, but was married to Adriel (I Samuel 18.19). Harriet adapts Abraham Cowley's description in *Davideis*, 1656, Book III: 'And much aversion in her stubborn mind /Was bred by being *promis'd* and *design'd*' (*Poems*, ed. A. R. Waller, 1905, p. 341).

48 *which* B, CA, CO (omitted Q1, V; Q2-3, W include 'which' but place it at the beginning of the couplet, 'Which is . . . designed'; in Q1 'which' is given as a catchword on p. 32, and is clearly meant to link the two quotations)

54 SONG often reprinted; see Thorpe, p. 102, who also points out that Amintas has something of the charm and dangerousness of Dorimant. For Dr Staggins's setting, published in 1684, see Appendix A.

The dang'rous passion you must shun,
Or else like me be quite undone.

HARRIET

Shall I be paid down by a covetous parent for a purchase? I need
no land. No, I'll lay myself out all in love. It is decreed—

Enter YOUNG BELLAIR

YOUNG BELLAIR

What generous resolution are you making, madam? 65

HARRIET

Only to be disobedient, sir.

YOUNG BELLAIR

Let me join hands with you in that.

HARRIET

With all my heart. I never thought I should have given you mine
so willingly. Here, [*They join hands*]—I, Harriet—

YOUNG BELLAIR

And I, Harry— 70

HARRIET

Do solemnly protest—

YOUNG BELLAIR

And vow—

HARRIET

That I with you—

YOUNG BELLAIR

And I with you—

HARRIET, YOUNG BELLAIR

Will never marry. 75

HARRIET

A match!

YOUNG BELLAIR

And no match! How do you like this indifference now?

HARRIET

You expect I should take it ill, I see.

YOUNG BELLAIR

'Tis not unnatural for you women to be a little angry you miss

64 *lay . . . out* spend myself
79 *for you* Q1 (for young Q2–3)

a conquest—though you would slight the poor man were he in   80
your power.

HARRIET

There are some, it may be, have an eye like Bart'lomew, big
enough for the whole fair, but I am not of the number, and
you may keep your gingerbread. 'Twill be more acceptable to
the lady whose dear image it wears, sir.   85

YOUNG BELLAIR

I must confess, madam, you came a day after the fair.

HARRIET

You own then you are in love?

YOUNG BELLAIR

I do.

HARRIET

The confidence is generous, and in return I could almost find in
my heart to let you know my inclinations.   90

YOUNG BELLAIR

Are you in love?

HARRIET

Yes—with this dear town, to that degree I can scarce endure the
country in landscapes and in hangings.

YOUNG BELLAIR

What a dreadful thing 'twould be to be hurried back to
Hampshire!   95

HARRIET

Ah! Name it not!

YOUNG BELLAIR

As for us, I find we shall agree well enough. Would we could do
something to deceive the grave people!

HARRIET

Could we delay their quick proceeding, 'twere well. A reprieve is
a good step towards the getting of a pardon.   100

82–3 *an eye . . . fair* an allusion to Cokes in Jonson's *Bartholmew Fair*, 1614, Act III. The fair
 was held annually on 24 August in Smithfield.
84 *gingerbread* from 'gingimbrat' (M. E.), preserved ginger. The final syllable was early
 confounded with 'bread', and gingerbread, made into various shapes and often gilded,
 was a staple item at fairs. From 1605 the word also carried the figurative meaning,
 'anything showy and unsubstantial'.
86 *you . . . fair* too late (proverbial)
93 *hangings* wall-tapestries

YOUNG BELLAIR

 If we give over the game, we are undone. What think you of
 playing it on booty?

HARRIET

 What do you mean?

YOUNG BELLAIR

 Pretend to be in love with one another. 'Twill make some
 dilatory excuses we may feign pass the better.   105

HARRIET

 Let us do't, if it be but for the dear pleasure of dissembling.

YOUNG BELLAIR

 Can you play your part?

HARRIET

 I know not what it is to love, but I have made pretty remarks
 by being now and then where lovers meet. Where did you leave
 their gravities?   110

YOUNG BELLAIR

 I' the next room. Your mother was censuring our modern
 gallant.

Enter OLD BELLAIR *and* LADY WOODVILL

HARRIET

 Peace! Here they come. I will lean against this wall and look
 bashfully down upon my fan, while you, like an amorous spark,
 modishly entertain me.   115

LADY WOODVILL [*To* OLD BELLAIR]

 Never go about to excuse 'em. Come, come, it was not so when I
 was a young woman.

OLD BELLAIR

 Adod, they're something disrespectful—

LADY WOODVILL

 Quality was then considered, and not rallied by every fleering
 fellow.   120

OLD BELLAIR

 Youth will have its jest, adod it will.

102 *playing . . . on booty* joining with confederates to 'spoil' or victimize another player; to
  play into the hands of confederates in order to share the 'plunder' with them.
108 *remarks* observations
116–24 Compare Rochester's 'Satyr [Timon]', ?March–July 1674, 11.101-6.
119 *fleering* mocking, jeering

LADY WOODVILL

'Tis good breeding now to be civil to none but players and
Exchange women. They are treated by 'em as much above
their condition as others are below theirs.

OLD BELLAIR

Out a pize on 'em! Talk no more: the rogues ha' got an ill habit   125
of preferring beauty, no matter where they find it.

LADY WOODVILL

See, your son and my daughter. They have improved their
acquaintance since they were within!

OLD BELLAIR

Adod, methinks they have! Let's keep back and observe.

YOUNG BELLAIR [*To* HARRIET]

Now for a look and gestures that may persuade 'em I am saying   130
all the passionate things imaginable.

HARRIET

Your head a little more on one side. Ease yourself on your left
leg and play with your right hand.

YOUNG BELLAIR

Thus, is it not?

HARRIET

Now set your right leg firm on the ground, adjust your belt,   135
then look about you.

YOUNG BELLAIR

A little exercising will make me perfect.

HARRIET

Smile, and turn to me again very sparkish.

YOUNG BELLAIR

Will you take your turn and be instructed?

HARRIET

With all my heart.   140

YOUNG BELLAIR

At one motion play your fan, roll your eyes, and then settle a
kind look upon me.

HARRIET

So.

123 *Exchange women* women serving in the shops of the New Exchange

YOUNG BELLAIR

Now spread your fan, look down upon it, and tell the sticks with
a finger.   145

HARRIET

Very modish.

YOUNG BELLAIR

Clap your hand up to your bosom, hold down your gown.
Shrug a little, draw up your breasts and let 'em fall again, gently,
with a sigh or two, *etc.*

HARRIET

By the good instructions you give, I suspect you for one of those   150
malicious observers who watch people's eyes and from
innocent looks make scandalous conclusions.

YOUNG BELLAIR

I know some, indeed, who out of mere love to mischief are as
vigilant as jealousy itself, and will give you an account of every
glance that passes at a play and i' the Circle.   155

HARRIET

'Twill not be amiss now to seem a little pleasant.

YOUNG BELLAIR

Clap your fan then in both your hands, snatch it to your mouth,
smile, and with a lively motion fling your body a little forward.
So,—now spread it, fall back on the sudden, cover your face
with it, and break out into a loud laughter.—Take up! Look   160
grave, and fall a-fanning of yourself. Admirably well acted!

HARRIET

I think I am pretty apt at these matters.

OLD BELLAIR [*To* LADY WOODVILL]

Adod, I like this well.

LADY WOODVILL

This promises something.

OLD BELLAIR [*Coming forward*]

Come, there is love i' the case, adod there is, or will be.—What   165
say you, young lady?

---

149 *etc.* Carnochan regards this as a stage direction, and comments, 'the actors were, evi-
dently, to improvise'.

155 *the Circle* probably the 'Tour' or Ring in Hyde Park, used by the fashionable for riding
and walking. Carnochan points out that the reference may possibly be to the assembly
at Court (cf. IV.i, 122).

HARRIET

All in good time, sir. You expect we should fall to and love as gamecocks fight, as soon as we are set together. Adod, you're unreasonable!

OLD BELLAIR

Adod, sirrah, I like thy wit well.   170

Enter a SERVANT

SERVANT

The coach is at the door, madam.

OLD BELLAIR

Go, get you and take the air together.

LADY WOODVILL

Will not you go with us?

OLD BELLAIR

Out a pize! Adod, I ha' business and cannot. We shall meet at night at my sister Townley's.   175

YOUNG BELLAIR (*Aside*)

He's going to Emilia. I overheard him talk of a collation.

Exeunt

---

170 *sirrah* applied to a woman seriously or in jest up to 1711, but almost certainly used here to indicate Old Bellair's old-fashioned vulgarity.

ACT III, SCENE II

[LADY TOWNLEY's *house*]

Enter LADY TOWNLEY, EMILIA, *and* MEDLEY

LADY TOWNLEY
I pity the young lovers we last talked of, though to say truth, their conduct has been so indiscreet they deserve to be unfortunate.

MEDLEY
You have an exact account, from the great lady i' the box down to the little orange-wench.   5

EMILIA
You're a living libel, a breathing lampoon. I wonder you are not torn in pieces.

MEDLEY
What think you of setting up an office of intelligence for these matters? The project may get money.

LADY TOWNLEY
You would have great dealings with country ladies.   10

MEDLEY
More than Muddiman has with their husbands.

Enter BELLINDA

LADY TOWNLEY
Bellinda, what has been become of you? We have not seen you here of late with your friend Mrs Loveit.

---

6   *libel ... lampoon* libel in the sense of a broadsheet or manuscript poem attacking a person's character, thus making it almost synonymous with lampoon, and supporting the pun on Medley being torn to pieces. Libels, which were often pinned to their victim's door, circulated in manuscript. Sir Roger L'Estrange complained in 1677 that 'it is notorious that not one in forty libels ever comes to the press, though by the help of manuscripts they are well-nigh as public' (cited in *Poems of Affairs of State, I (1660–78)*, ed. G. de F. Lord, 1963, p. xxxvii). See also I, 248–9 and note.

11 *Muddiman* Henry Muddiman (1629–92), first editor of the *London Gazette*, but referred to here for his newsletters, popular among country gentlemen.

BELLINDA

Dear creature, I left her but now so sadly afflicted.

LADY TOWNLEY

With her old distemper, jealousy? 15

MEDLEY

Dorimant has played her some new prank.

BELLINDA

Well, that Dorimant is certainly the worst man breathing.

EMILIA

I once thought so.

BELLINDA

And do you not think so still?

EMILIA

No, indeed. 20

BELLINDA

Oh, Jesu!

EMILIA

The town does him a great deal of injury, and I will never believe what it says of a man I do not know again, for his sake.

BELLINDA

You make me wonder.

LADY TOWNLEY

He's a very well-bred man. 25

BELLINDA

But strangely ill-natured.

EMILIA

Then he's a very witty man.

BELLINDA

But a man of no principles.

MEDLEY

Your man of principles is a very fine thing, indeed!

BELLINDA

To be preferred to men of parts by women who have regard to 30
their reputation and quiet. Well, were I minded to play the fool,
he should be the last man I'd think of.

MEDLEY

He has been the first in many ladies' favours, though you are so
severe, madam.

LADY TOWNLEY

What he may be for a lover, I know not, but he's a very pleasant 35
acquaintance, I am sure.

BELLINDA

Had you seen him use Mrs Loveit as I have done, you would
never endure him more.

EMILIA

What, he has quarrelled with her again?

BELLINDA

Upon the slightest occasion. He's jealous of Sir Fopling.   40

LADY TOWNLEY

She never saw him in her life but yesterday, and that was here.

EMILIA

On my conscience, he's the only man in town that's her
aversion. How horribly out of humour she was all the while he
talked to her!

BELLINDA

And somebody has wickedly told him—   45

EMILIA

Here he comes.

Enter DORIMANT

MEDLEY

Dorimant, you are luckily come to justify yourself. Here's a
lady—

BELLINDA

—Has a word or two to say to you from a disconsolate
person.   50

DORIMANT

You tender your reputation too much, I know, madam, to
whisper with me before this good company.

BELLINDA

To serve Mrs Loveit, I'll make a bold venture.

DORIMANT

Here's Medley, the very spirit of scandal.

BELLINDA

No matter!   55

EMILIA

'Tis something you are unwilling to hear, Mr Dorimant.

LADY TOWNLEY

Tell him, Bellinda, whether he will or no.

BELLINDA (*Aloud*)

Mrs Loveit—

DORIMANT

Softly, these are laughers. You do not know 'em.

BELLINDA (*To* DORIMANT, *apart*)

In a word, you've made me hate you, which I thought you never   60
could have done.

DORIMANT

In obeying your commands.

BELLINDA

'Twas a cruel part you played. How could you act it?

DORIMANT

Nothing is cruel to a man who could kill himself to please you.
Remember, five o'clock tomorrow morning.   65

BELLINDA

I tremble when you name it.

DORIMANT

Be sure you come.

BELLINDA

I shan't.

DORIMANT

Swear you will.

BELLINDA

I dare not.   70

DORIMANT

Swear, I say!

BELLINDA

By my life, by all the happiness I hope for—

DORIMANT

You will.

BELLINDA

I will.

DORIMANT

Kind.   75

BELLINDA

I am glad I've sworn. I vow I think I should ha' failed you else.

DORIMANT

Surprisingly kind! In what temper did you leave Loveit?

BELLINDA

Her raving was prettily over, and she began to be in a brave way

---

78 *prettily* cleverly, aptly

of defying you and all your works. Where have you been since
you went from thence?   80

DORIMANT

I looked in at the play.

BELLINDA

I have promised and must return to her again.

DORIMANT

Persuade her to walk in the Mall this evening.

BELLINDA

She hates the place and will not come.

DORIMANT

Do all you can to prevail with her.   85

BELLINDA

For what purpose?

DORIMANT

Sir Fopling will be here anon. I'll prepare him to set upon her
there before me.

BELLINDA

You persecute her too much. But I'll do all you'll ha' me.

DORIMANT (*Aloud*)

Tell her plainly, 'tis grown so dull a business I can drudge on no   90
longer.

EMILIA

There are afflictions in love, Mr Dorimant.

DORIMANT

You women make 'em, who are commonly as unreasonable in
that as you are at play: without the advantage be on your side, a
man can never quietly give over when he's weary.   95

MEDLEY

If you would play without being obliged to complaisance,
Dorimant, you should play in public places.

DORIMANT

Ordinaries were a very good thing for that, but gentlemen do
not of late frequent 'em. The deep play is now in private houses.

                              BELLINDA *offering to steal away*

LADY TOWNLEY

Bellinda, are you leaving us so soon?   100

---

96 *complaisance* See note to I, 382.
98 *Ordinaries* eating houses, taverns

BELLINDA

I am to go to the Park with Mrs Loveit, madam. [*Exit* BELLINDA]

LADY TOWNLEY

This confidence will go nigh to spoil this young creature.

MEDLEY

'Twill do her good, madam. Young men who are brought up under practising lawyers prove the abler counsel when they come to be called to the bar themselves. 105

DORIMANT

The town has been very favourable to you this afternoon, my Lady Townley. You use to have an *embarras* of chairs and coaches at your door, an uproar of footmen in your hall, and a noise of fools above here.

LADY TOWNLEY

Indeed, my house is the general rendezvous and, next to the 110 playhouse, is the common refuge of all the young idle people.

EMILIA

Company is a very good thing, madam, but I wonder you do not love it a little more chosen.

LADY TOWNLEY

'Tis good to have an universal taste. We should love wit, but for variety be able to divert ourselves with the extravagancies of 115 those who want it.

MEDLEY

Fools will make you laugh.

EMILIA

For once or twice—but the repetition of their folly after a visit or two grows tedious and insufferable.

LADY TOWNLEY

You are a little too delicate, Emilia. 120

Enter a PAGE

PAGE

Sir Fopling Flutter, madam, desires to know if you are to be seen.

---

102 *confidence* excess of assurance, impudence (or, possibly, intimate relationship)

107–8 *embarras . . . coaches* cf. *embarras de voitures* (Fr.), a congestion of carriages. Although 'embarras' (i.e. embarrassment) occurs as an uncommon English word from 1664 into the eighteenth century, Q1's spelling 'ambara's' suggests that Etherege probably intended the French word. It is used again by Sir Fopling (l. 166).

LADY TOWNLEY

    Here's the freshest fool in town, and one who has not cloyed
you yet.—Page!

PAGE

    Madam? 125

LADY TOWNLEY

    Desire him to walk up.

                                              [*Exit* PAGE]

DORIMANT

    Do not you fall on him, Medley, and snub him. Soothe him up
in his extravagance. He will show the better.

MEDLEY

    You know I have a natural indulgence for fools and need not
this caution, sir. 130

           Enter SIR FOPLING, *with his* PAGE *after him*

SIR FOPLING

    Page, wait without.

                                            [*Exit* PAGE]

    ([*To*] LADY TOWNLEY) Madam, I kiss your hands. I see yesterday
was nothing of chance; the *belles assemblées* form themselves
here every day. (*To* EMILIA) Lady, your servant.—Dorimant, let
me embrace thee. Without lying, I have not met with any of my 135
acquaintance who retain so much of Paris as thou dost—the
very air thou hadst when the marquise mistook thee i'the
Tuileries and cried, '*Hé, chevalier!*' and then begged thy
pardon.

DORIMANT

    I would fain wear in fashion as long as I can, sir. 'Tis a thing to 140
be valued in men as well as baubles.

SIR FOPLING

    Thou art a man of wit and understands the town. Prithee, let

---

127 *Soothe . . . up* encourage or humour a person by expressing assent or approval (1573–
    1705). *OED* cites this as an example.

133 *belles assemblées* fashionable gatherings

137–8 *the Tuileries* the gardens of the Palace of the Tuileries, laid out by Le Nôtre for Louis
    XIV, and so called because the palace occupied the site of an old brick-yard.

142 *understands* Q1 (understand'st W, V)

thee and I be intimate. There is no living without making some
good man the *confident* of our pleasures.

DORIMANT

'Tis true—but there is no man so improper for such a business   145
as I am.

SIR FOPLING

Prithee, why hast thou so modest an opinion of thyself?

DORIMANT

Why, first, I could never keep a secret in my life; and then, there
is no charm so infallibly makes me fall in love with a woman as
my knowing a friend loves her. I deal honestly with you.   150

SIR FOPLING

Thy humour's very gallant, or let me perish. I knew a French
count so like thee.

LADY TOWNLEY

Wit, I perceive, has more power over you than beauty, Sir
Fopling, else you would not have let this lady stand so long
neglected.   155

SIR FOPLING (*To* EMILIA)

A thousand pardons, madam—some civilities due of course
upon the meeting a long absent friend. The *éclat* of so much
beauty, I confess, ought to have charmed me sooner.

EMILIA

The *brillant* of so much good language, sir, has much more
power than the little beauty I can boast.   160

SIR FOPLING

I never saw anything prettier than this high work on your
point d'Espagne.

EMILIA

'Tis not so rich as *point de Venise.*

---

156 *madam . . . civilities* Q1 (madam. Some civility's Q2–3, CA)
   madam . . . of course 'of course' means customary, natural, and Sir Fopling's ellipsis can
   be paraphrased, 'My rudeness to you was occasioned by the need to pay the customary
   civilities . . .' Carnochan's emendation gives the sense, 'some civility is naturally
   due . . .', and is a possible reading.
157 *éclat* brilliance
159 *brillant* glitter
161 *high work* raised needlework
162 *point d'Espagne* Spanish lace
163 *point de Venise* Venetian lace

SIR FOPLING

Not altogether, but looks cooler, and is more proper for the
season.—Dorimant, is not that Medley?   165

DORIMANT

The same, sir.

SIR FOPLING [*To* MEDLEY]

Forgive me, sir; in this *embarras* of civilities I could not come
to have you in my arms sooner. You understand an equipage
the best of any man in town, I hear.

MEDLEY

By my own you would not guess it.   170

SIR FOPLING

There are critics who do not write, sir.

MEDLEY

Our peevish poets will scarce allow it.

SIR FOPLING

Damn 'em, they'll allow no man wit who does not play the fool
like themselves and show it! Have you taken notice of the
gallesh I brought over?   175

MEDLEY

Oh, yes! 'T has quite another air than the English makes.

SIR FOPLING

'Tis as easily known from an English tumbril as an Inns of
Court man is from one of us.

DORIMANT

Truly there is a *bel air* in galleshes as well as men.

167 *embarras* V, CA (Ambara's Q1ᵘ; Ambaras Q1ᶜ) See note to l. 107–8 above.
168 *equipage* presumably in the sense of retinue, train of attendants (*OED*, 1590–1736),
     rather than apparel, costume. (Sir Fopling's comment at ll. 174–5 suggests that he could
     be thinking of 'equipage' as meaning his carriage and attendants, but that appears to be
     an eighteenth-century usage).
175 *gallesh* Q1 (*caléche* V) 'gallesh' (here and at l. 179) is a var. spelling of 'calash' from Fr.
     calèche, a light carriage with low wheels and a removable folding hood or top. Newly
     introduced from France. *OED* records the first occurrence in 1666, and Dryden's *Mar-
     riage-à-la-Mode*, 1673, has, 'I have been at your Lodgings, in my new *Galeche*' (II.i, 214–
     15, *Works*, XI, p. 249).
177 *tumbril* two-wheeled cart which tips to empty its load, especially a dung-cart
177–8 *Inns of Court man* lawyer
179 *bel air* elegant style
     galleshes Q1 (*calèches* V)

MEDLEY

But there are few so delicate to observe it. 180

SIR FOPLING

The world is generally very *grossier* here, indeed.

LADY TOWNLEY [*To* EMILIA]

He's very fine.

EMILIA

Extreme proper!

SIR FOPLING

A slight suit I made to appear in at my first arrival—not worthy
your consideration, ladies. 185

DORIMANT

The pantaloon is very well mounted.

SIR FOPLING

The tassels are new and pretty.

MEDLEY

I never saw a coat better cut.

SIR FOPLING

It makes me show long-waisted, and, I think, slender.

DORIMANT

That's the shape our ladies dote on. 190

MEDLEY

Your breech, though, is a handful too high, in my eye, Sir
Fopling.

SIR FOPLING

Peace, Medley, I have wished it lower a thousand times, but a
pox on 't, 'twill not be!

LADY TOWNLEY

His gloves are well fringed, large, and graceful. 195

---

180 *delicate* Dorimant plays on two meanings: 1) fastidious, discerning, 2) dainty, effemin-
ate (obs.)
181 *grossier* vulgar, coarse
186 *pantaloon* usually in plural, 'pantaloons': a kind of breeches in fashion after the Restoration, hanging wide down to the knees. Evelyn is cited by *OED* as saying in 1661, '. . .
Pantaloons, which are a kind of Hermaphrodite and of neither sex'. Since Dorimant
uses the singular, he may be playing on Pantaloon, the foolish old man in Italian
harlequinade.
mounted Dorimant appears to be punning: 1) the breeches are well-mounted, that is,
raised up away from the legs, 2) metaphorically, the ridiculous pantaloons are ridden
(mounted) by an appropriate fool.

SIR FOPLING

I was always eminent for being *bien ganté.*

EMILIA

He wears nothing but what are originals of the most famous
hands in Paris.

SIR FOPLING

You are in the right, madam.

LADY TOWNLEY

The suit?   200

SIR FOPLING

Barroy.

EMILIA

The garniture?

SIR FOPLING

Le Gras.

MEDLEY

The shoes?

SIR FOPLING

Piccar.   205

DORIMANT

The periwig?

SIR FOPLING

Chedreux.

LADY TOWNLEY, EMILIA

The gloves?

SIR FOPLING

Orangerie—you know the smell, ladies. —Dorimant, I could

---

196 *bien ganté* well-gloved
201–7 *Barroy . . . Chedreux* of this list of fashionable Parisian merchants I can identify only
Chedreux, who gave his name to a kind of wig.
202 *garniture* ornament, trimming of ribbons and jewellery, added to clothing. Strongly
connected to its French origins at this date. First example in *OED* is from 1667. J.
Lacey's *Sir Hercules Buffoon*, 1684, has, 'My French garniture, a pox on 'em, is not yet
arrived from Paris' (II.ii).
209 *Orangerie* scent or perfume extracted from the orange-flower. *OED* records this
instance as its first occurrence. Essence of orange was a popular scent, and in Dryden's
The Kind Keeper; or, Mr Limberham, 1680, Mrs Tricksy tells Limberham, 'I have been
looking over the last Present of orange Gloves you made me; and methinks I do not like
the scent' (III.i, 376–7, *Works*, XIV, p. 50). A quart of orange-flower water is included in
the effects of a fop in *Tatler*, No. 113 (29 December 1709). See also note to V.i., 36.

find in my heart for an amusement to have a gallantry with   210
some of our English ladies.

DORIMANT

'Tis a thing no less necessary to confirm the reputation of your
wit than a duel will be to satisfy the town of your courage.

SIR FOPLING

Here was a woman yesterday—

DORIMANT

Mrs Loveit.   215

SIR FOPLING

You have named her!

DORIMANT

You cannot pitch on a better for your purpose.

SIR FOPLING

Prithee, what is she?

DORIMANT

A person of quality, and one who has a rest of reputation
enough to make the conquest considerable. Besides I hear she   220
likes you too.

SIR FOPLING

Methoughts she seemed, though, very reserved and uneasy all
the time I entertained her.

DORIMANT

Grimace and affectation! You will see her i' the Mall tonight.

SIR FOPLING

Prithee, let thee and I take the air together.   225

DORIMANT

I am engaged to Medley, but I'll meet you at St James's and give
you some information upon the which you may regulate your
proceedings.

SIR FOPLING

All the world will be in the Park tonight.—Ladies, 'twere pity to
keep so much beauty longer within doors and rob the Ring of   230
all those charms that should adorn it.—Hey, Page!

Enter PAGE

219 *rest* remainder
230 *the Ring* See note to III.i, 155.

See that all my people be ready.

[PAGE] *goes out again*

Dorimant, *à revoir*.   [*Exit* SIR FOPLING]

MEDLEY

A fine-mettled coxcomb.

DORIMANT

Brisk and insipid—   235

MEDLEY

Pert and dull.

EMILIA

However you despise him, gentlemen, I'll lay my life he passes
for a wit with many.

DORIMANT

That may very well be. Nature has her cheats, stums a brain,
and puts sophisticate dullness often on the tasteless multitude   240
for true wit and good humour.—Medley, come.

MEDLEY

I must go a little way. I will meet you i' the Mall.

DORIMANT

I'll walk through the garden thither. (*To the women*) We shall
meet anon and bow.

LADY TOWNLEY

Not tonight. We are engaged about a business, the knowledge of   245
which may make you laugh hereafter.

MEDLEY

Your servant, ladies.

231–2 s.d. *Enter . . . again* CA (Q1 and all other texts give as a single sentence after l. 231)
233 *à revoir* ed. (a Revoir Q1; *au revoir* V, CA). In following Q1 here the text adopts Brian
    Gibbons's shrewd observation that since Dorimant mocks Sir Fopling's usage (l. 248),
    the knight is probably pretending that his is the fashionable pronunciation of the
    phrase in Paris. Or it may be an example of his 'pretty lisp' (I, 335).
239 *stum* to renew (wine) by mixing with stum or must and raising a new fermentation
    (from the Dutch). *OED* gives its first occurrence as 1656, and the first figurative use in
    1661. Oldham's *A Letter from the Country*, 1678, has, 'As the poor Drunkard, when
    Wine stums his brains,/ Anointed with that liquor thinks he reigns' (ll. 204–5).
240 *sophisticate* probably in the obsolescent sense, 'adulterated, impure, mixed with some
    foreign substance'. The last example given by *OED* is from Everarde Maynwaringe's
    Praxis Medicorum . . . Ancient and Modern Practice of Physick, 1671, p. 66, 'Yet this *cheap
    sophisticate* Medicine . . . will cost you six times as much'. This sense would continue
    Dorimant's metaphor of adulterated wine passed off upon the 'tasteless multitude'.

DORIMANT

À revoir, as Sir Fopling says.

[*Exeunt* MEDLEY *and* DORIMANT]

LADY TOWNLEY

The old man will be here immediately.

EMILIA

Let's expect him i' the garden.   250

LADY TOWNLEY

Go, you are a rogue!

EMILIA

I can't abide you!

Exeunt

248 *À revoir* ed. (a Revoir Q1; *au revoir* V, CA)
250 *expect* wait for

ACT III, SCENE III

The Mall

Enter HARRIET *and* YOUNG BELLAIR, *she pulling him*

HARRIET
Come along!
YOUNG BELLAIR
And leave your mother?
HARRIET
Busy will be sent with a hue and cry after us; but that's no matter.
YOUNG BELLAIR
'Twill look strangely in me.   5
HARRIET
She'll believe it a freak of mine and never blame your manners.
YOUNG BELLAIR [*Pointing*]
What reverend acquaintance is that she has met?
HARRIET
A fellow beauty of the last king's time, though by the ruins you would hardly guess it.

Exeunt

Enter DORIMANT *and crosses the stage*
Enter YOUNG BELLAIR *and* HARRIET

YOUNG BELLAIR
By this time your mother is in a fine taking.   10
HARRIET
If your friend Mr Dorimant were but here now, that she might find me talking with him!
YOUNG BELLAIR
She does not know him but dreads him, I hear, of all mankind.
HARRIET
She concludes if he does but speak to a woman, she's undone—
is on her knees every day to pray heaven defend me from him.   15

 6 *freak* whim, capricious humour
10 *taking* excited or impassioned state

YOUNG BELLAIR

You do not apprehend him so much as she does?

HARRIET

I never saw anything in him that was frightful.

YOUNG BELLAIR

On the contrary, have you not observed something extreme delightful in his wit and person?

HARRIET

He's agreeable and pleasant, I must own, but he does so much   20
affect being so, he displeases me.

YOUNG BELLAIR

Lord, madam, all he does and says is so easy and so natural.

HARRIET

Some men's verses seem so to the unskilful; but labour i' the one and affectation in the other to the judicious plainly appear.

YOUNG BELLAIR

I never heard him accused of affectation before.   25

Enter DORIMANT *and stares upon her*

HARRIET

It passes on the easy town, who are favourably pleased in him to call it humour.

[*Exeunt* YOUNG BELLAIR *and* HARRIET]

DORIMANT

'Tis she! It must be she—that lovely hair, that easy shape, those wanton eyes, and all those melting charms about her mouth which Medley spoke of. I'll follow the lottery and put in for a   30
prize with my friend Bellair.

[*Exit* DORIMANT, *repeating*]—

'In love the victors from the vanquished fly;
They fly that wound, and they pursue that die'.

---

26 *passes on* goes uncensured by
  easy See note to I, 123, and Introduction, pp. xxx–xxxi.
28–30 *'Tis . . . of* See I, 121–9 and notes.
30 *the lottery* common way of raising money for the government or for individuals.
32–3 *In . . . die* final couplet of Waller's 'To a Friend, of the Different Successes of their Loves'
  (*Poems*, I, 103).

Enter YOUNG BELLAIR *and* HARRIET, *and after them* DORIMANT,
standing at a distance

YOUNG BELLAIR

Most people prefer Hyde Park to this place.

HARRIET

It has the better reputation, I confess; but I abominate the dull   35
diversions there—the formal bows, the affected smiles, the silly
by-words and amorous tweers in passing. Here one meets with
a little conversation now and then.

YOUNG BELLAIR

These conversations have been fatal to some of your sex,
madam.   40

HARRIET

It may be so. Because some who want temper have been
undone by gaming, must others who have it wholly deny
themselves the pleasure of play?

DORIMANT (*Coming up gently and bowing to her*)

Trust me, it were unreasonable, madam.

HARRIET

Lord! Who's this?   *She starts and looks grave*   45

YOUNG BELLAIR

Dorimant.

DORIMANT

Is this the woman your father would have you marry?

YOUNG BELLAIR

It is.

DORIMANT

Her name?

YOUNG BELLAIR

Harriet.   50

---

34 *Hyde Park* Etherege's form in Q1, 'High Park', here and at V.ii, 140, is unusual and
probably went out of use by the early eighteenth century. Brett-Smith knew of no occurrences outside of Etherege, but Conaghan cites Margaret Cavendish, Duchess of Newcas-
tle, *A Piece of a Play*, 'Madam, are you for a Play? or Court? or *High-Park* to day?' (*Plays*,
1668, p. 14).

37 *tweer* var. spelling of 'twire', a glance, leer (obs. slang). *OED* gives this as its first occurrence (the last is from 1719); the verb occurs from 1600, and remained in dialect until the
nineteenth century.

41 *temper* character, self-control

DORIMANT [*Aside*]

I am not mistaken.—She's handsome.

YOUNG BELLAIR

Talk to her; her wit is better than her face. We were wishing for you but now.

DORIMANT (*To* HARRIET)

Overcast with seriousness o' the sudden! A thousand smiles were shining in that face but now—I never saw so quick a   55
change of weather.

HARRIET (*Aside*)

I feel as great a change within, but he shall never know it.

DORIMANT

You were talking of play, madam. Pray, what may be your stint?

HARRIET

A little harmless discourse in public walks, or at most an   60
appointment in a box, barefaced, at the playhouse. You are for masks and private meetings, where women engage for all they are worth, I hear.

DORIMANT

I have been used to deep play, but I can make one at small game when I like my gamester well.   65

HARRIET

And be so unconcerned you'll ha' no pleasure in't.

DORIMANT

Where there is a considerable sum to be won, the hope of drawing people in makes every trifle considerable.

HARRIET

The sordidness of men's natures, I know, makes 'em willing to flatter and comply with the rich, though they are sure never to   70
be the better for 'em.

DORIMANT

'Tis in their power to do us good, and we despair not but at some time or other they may be willing.

HARRIET

To men who have fared in this town like you, 'twould be a great mortification to live on hope. Could you keep a Lent for a   75
mistress?

59 *stint* upper limit
69 *sordidness* low, mean, or mercenary character or motives

DORIMANT

    In expectation of a happy Easter, and though time be very precious, think forty days well lost to gain your favour.

HARRIET

    Mr Bellair! Let us walk. 'Tis time to leave him. Men grow dull when they begin to be particular.   80

DORIMANT

    You're mistaken. Flattery will not ensue, though I know you're greedy of the praises of the whole Mall.

HARRIET

    You do me wrong.

DORIMANT

    I do not. As I followed you, I observed how you were pleased when the fops cried 'She's handsome, very handsome, by God   85 she is!' and whispered aloud your name—the thousand several forms you put your face into; then, to make yourself more agreeable, how wantonly you played with your head, flung back your locks, and looked smilingly over your shoulder at 'em.

HARRIET

    I do not go begging the men's, as you do the ladies' good liking,   90 with a sly softness in your looks and a gentle slowness in your bows as you pass by 'em. As thus, sir—(*Acts him*) Is not this like you?

Enter LADY WOODVILL *and* BUSY

YOUNG BELLAIR

    Your mother, madam!   *Pulls* HARRIET. *She composes herself*

LADY WOODVILL

    Ah, my dear child Harriet!   95

BUSY [*Aside*]

    Now is she so pleased with finding her again, she cannot chide her.

LADY WOODVILL

    Come away!

DORIMANT

    'Tis now but high Mall, madam—the most entertaining time of all the evening.   100

86–7 *name*—. . . *into*; CA (name, . . . into; Q1; name; . . . into; B)
99 *high Mall* the busiest and most fashionable hour for visiting the Mall.

79

HARRIET

I would fain see that Dorimant, mother, you so cry out of for a
monster. He's in the Mall, I hear.

LADY WOODVILL

Come away, then! The plague is here, and you should dread the
infection.

YOUNG BELLAIR

You may be misinformed of the gentleman.   105

LADY WOODVILL

Oh, no! I hope you do not know him. He is the prince of all the
devils in the town—delights in nothing but in rapes and riots.

DORIMANT

If you did but hear him speak, madam—

LADY WOODVILL

Oh, he has a tongue, they say, would tempt the angels to a
second fall.   110

Enter SIR FOPLING *with his equipage, six footmen and a* PAGE

SIR FOPLING

Hey, Champagne, Norman, La Rose, La Fleur, La Tour, La
Verdure!—Dorimant!—

LADY WOODVILL

Here, here he is among this rout! He names him!—Come away,
Harriet, come away!

Exeunt LADY WOODVILL, HARRIET, BUSY, *and* YOUNG BELLAIR

DORIMANT [*Aside*]

This fool's coming has spoiled all. She's gone, but she has left a   115
pleasing image of herself behind that wanders in my soul.—It
must not settle there.

SIR FOPLING

What reverie is this? Speak, man.

101 *of* Q1 (V omits)

110 s.d. *equipage* here 'retinue', but see note to III.ii, 168.

111–12 *Champagne . . . Verdure* see note to III.iii, 256, which accounts for some of these
names. On 'champagne' see note to IV.i, 379.

118 *reverie* bears the modern meaning, but in Middle English it had meant 'revelling,
rejoicing', and was readopted from French *rêverie* in the seventeenth century. OED
records its first instance from 1657, but it retained a strong sense of its French origin
into the eighteenth century.

DORIMANT

      'Snatched from myself, how far behind
      Already I behold the shore!'   120

Enter MEDLEY

MEDLEY

  Dorimant, a discovery! I met with Bellair—

DORIMANT

  You can tell me no news, sir. I know all.

MEDLEY

  How do you like the daughter?

DORIMANT

  You never came so near truth in your life as you did in her
  description.   125

MEDLEY

  What think you of the mother?

DORIMANT

  Whatever I think of her, she thinks very well of me, I find.

MEDLEY

  Did she know you?

DORIMANT

  She did not. Whether she does now or no, I know not. Here was
  a pleasant scene towards, when in came Sir Fopling, mustering   130
  up his equipage, and at the latter end named me and frighted
  her away.

MEDLEY

  Loveit and Bellinda are not far off. I saw 'em alight at St
  James's.

DORIMANT

  Sir Fopling, hark you, a word or two. (*Whispers*)—Look you do   135
  not want assurance.

SIR FOPLING

  I never do on these occasions.

DORIMANT

  Walk on, we must not be seen together. Make your advantage

119–20 *Snatched . . . shore* Waller, 'Of Loving at First Sight', ll. 3–4 (*Poems*, I, p. 100).
130 *towards* imminent
133–4 *St James's* Carnochan thinks the reference is to St James's Palace, opposite the Park.

of what I have told you. The next turn you will meet the
lady. 140

SIR FOPLING

Hey! Follow me all.

Exeunt SIR FOPLING *and his equipage*

DORIMANT

Medley, you shall see good sport anon between Loveit and this
Fopling.

MEDLEY

I thought there was something toward, by that whisper.

DORIMANT

You know a worthy principle of hers? 145

MEDLEY

Not to be so much as civil to a man who speaks to her in the
presence of him she professes to love.

DORIMANT

I have encouraged Fopling to talk to her tonight.

MEDLEY

Now you are here, she will go nigh to beat him.

DORIMANT

In the humour she's in, her love will make her do some very 150
extravagant thing, doubtless.

MEDLEY

What was Bellinda's business with you at my Lady Townley's?

DORIMANT

To get me to meet Loveit here in order to an *éclaircissement*. I
made some difficulty of it and have prepared this rencounter
to make good my jealousy. 155

MEDLEY

Here they come.

Enter MRS LOVEIT, BELLINDA, *and* PERT

DORIMANT

I'll meet her and provoke her with a deal of dumb civility in

---

139 *next turn* next circuit of the Mall
153 *éclaircissement* clearing up (of a mystery, misunderstanding)
154 *rencounter* chance meeting is the primary meaning, but the word could also mean a
military skirmish, a duel, or a contest in wit or argument (*OED*). Verity emends to
rencontre (unnecessarily since Q1's 'rancounter' is a variant spelling of 'rencounter').

passing by, then turn short and be behind her when Sir Fopling
sets upon her—[*Bows to* MRS LOVEIT]

<blockquote>

'See how unregarded now   160
That piece of beauty passes'.
</blockquote>

                   Exeunt DORIMANT *and* MEDLEY

BELLINDA

How wonderful respectfully he bowed!

PERT

He's always over-mannerly when he has done a mischief.

BELLINDA

Methoughts, indeed, at the same time he had a strange,
despising countenance.   165

PERT

The unlucky look he thinks becomes him.

BELLINDA

I was afraid you would have spoke to him, my dear.

MRS LOVEIT

I would have died first. He shall no more find me the loving fool
he has done.

BELLINDA

You love him still!   170

MRS LOVEIT

No.

PERT

I wish you did not.

MRS LOVEIT

I do not, and I will have you think so!—What made you hale
me to this odious place, Bellinda?

BELLINDA

I hate to be hulched up in a coach. Walking is much better.   175

MRS LOVEIT

Would we could meet Sir Fopling now!

BELLINDA

Lord, would you not avoid him?

160–1 *See . . . passes* Suckling, 'Sonnet I', ll. 1–2, which actually begins 'Do'st . . .' (*The Works
of Sir John Suckling*, ed. Thomas S. Clayton and Lester Beaurline, 2 vols., 1971, I, p. 47).
166 *unlucky* mischievous, malicious
175 *hulched up* doubled up (obs.). *OED* gives this as the only example of the verb formed
from 'hulch', hunch-backed (1611–1708).

MRS LOVEIT

I would make him all the advances that may be.

BELLINDA

That would confirm Dorimant's suspicion, my dear.

MRS LOVEIT

He is not jealous, but I will make him so, and be revenged a way   180
he little thinks on.

BELLINDA (*Aside*)

If she should make him jealous, that may make him fond of her
again. I must dissuade her from it.—Lord, my dear, this will
certainly make him hate you.

MRS LOVEIT

'Twill make him uneasy, though he does not care for me. I know   185
the effects of jealousy on men of his proud temper.

BELLINDA

'Tis a fantastic remedy: its operations are dangerous and
uncertain.

MRS LOVEIT

'Tis the strongest cordial we can give to dying love. It often
brings it back when there's no sign of life remaining. But I   190
design not so much the reviving his, as my revenge.

Enter SIR FOPLING *and his equipage*

SIR FOPLING

Hey! Bid the coachman send home four of his horses and bring
the coach to Whitehall. I'll walk over the Park. [*To* MRS
LOVEIT] Madam, the honour of kissing your fair hands is a
happiness I missed this afternoon at my Lady Townley's.   195

MRS LOVEIT

You were very obliging, Sir Fopling, the last time I saw you
there.

SIR FOPLING

The preference was due to your wit and beauty. [*To* BELLINDA]
Madam, your servant. There never was so sweet an evening.

189–90 *'Tis . . . remaining* cf. Etherege's 'Song' (Tell me no more you love; in vain), ll. 13–16,
   'Each smile and kiss which you bestow,/Are like those cordials which we give/To dying
   men, to make them live,/And languish out an hour in pain' (Thorpe, p. 24). First
   published 1669.
189 *cordial* medicine or beverage to stimulate the heart
193 *Whitehall* royal palace, burned down in 1698. It was across St James's Park from the Mall.

BELLINDA

'T has drawn all the rabble of the town hither.   200

SIR FOPLING

'Tis pity there's not an order made that none but the *beau monde* should walk here.

MRS LOVEIT

'Twould add much to the beauty of the place. See what a sort of nasty fellows are coming!

Enter four ill-fashioned fellows singing:

' 'Tis not for kisses alone, etc.'   205

MRS LOVEIT

Foh! Their periwigs are scented with tobacco so strong—

SIR FOPLING

—It overcomes our pulvilio. Methinks I smell the coffee-house they come from.

FIRST MAN

Dorimant's convenient, Madam Loveit.

SECOND MAN

I like the oily buttock with her.   210

---

203 *sort* either 1) variety, kind, or 2) body (of people), company (obs.). The latter meaning persisted into the nineteenth century (*OED* 17c), though Conaghan cites E. Fenton (1730), who felt the usage old-fashioned. See next note.

204 s.d. *four* (three V); the number is given as 'three' in the Dramatis Personae, and Verity emends here to match. Conaghan, noting that 'sort' (l. 203) could mean 'crowd', argues for the present reading—'The author may have considered the theatrical effectiveness of having the "nasty fellows" outnumber the people of fashion on stage'. Since the text of Q1 descends from an authorial manuscript (see Note on the Text), the cast list, which unlike the earlier part of Q1 distinguishes between Young and Old Bellair, must have been prepared after the text. Cutting the 'ill-fashioned fellows' from four to three probably reflects an economy made for production.

205 *'Tis . . . etc.*, Lines from the second stanza of an anonymous song, 'Tell me no more you love'. For the words and source see Appendix B.

207 *pulvilio* scented powder (from It. 'polviglio'). A new word: *OED* gives its first example from Wycherley's *The Country Wife* (1675).

209 *convenient* mistress (obs.). Earliest of *OED*'s three examples. Cf. P. Motteux, *Rabelais* (1708; 1737 ed.), V, p. 217, 'Concubines, Convenients, Cracks'.

210 *oily buttock* 'buttock' was slang for a whore. James Dalton in *A Narrative of all the Street Robberies . . .*, 1728, defines a 'Buttock' as 'One that dispences her Favours without Advantage', i.e., free of charge. 'Oily' could mean greasy or smooth in manner, or slippery. Most obviously the bully refers to Bellinda, but Mrs Loveit apparently knows one of them by sight (ll. 233–4), and the reference is conceivably to her.

THIRD MAN [*Pointing to* SIR FOPLING]
>   What spruce prig is that?

FIRST MAN
>   A caravan, lately come from Paris.

SECOND MAN
>   Peace, they smoke!   *All of them coughing*

>   'There's something else to be done, etc.'

>   *Exeunt singing*

>   *Enter* DORIMANT *and* MEDLEY

DORIMANT
>   They're engaged—   215

MEDLEY
>   She entertains him as if she liked him.

DORIMANT
>   Let us go forward, seem earnest in discourse, and show
>   ourselves. Then you shall see how she'll use him.

BELLINDA
>   Yonder's Dorimant, my dear.

MRS LOVEIT
>   I see him. (*Aside*) He comes insulting, but I will disappoint him   220
>   in his expectation. (*To* SIR FOPLING)—I like this pretty, nice
>   humour of yours, Sir Fopling. [*To* BELLINDA] With what a
>   loathing eye he looked upon those fellows!

SIR FOPLING
>   I sat near one of 'em at a play today and was almost poisoned
>   with a pair of cordovan gloves he wears.   225

MRS LOVEIT
>   Oh, filthy cordovan! How I hate the smell!
>   *Laughs in a loud, affected way*

---

211 *spruce prig* fop, coxcomb (slang)
212 *caravan* object of plunder (thieves' cant). *OED* gives first example, however, from
     Shadwell, *The Squire of Alsatia*, 1689 (*Complete Works*, ed. cit., IV, p. 215), and also cites
     B. E., *Dictionary of the Canting Crew*, 1699, '*Caravan*, a good round Sum of Money
     about a Man, and him that is Cheated of it'.
213 *smoke* take note, 'twig'
214 *There's . . . etc.* See note to l. 205 above.
225 *cordovan* a Spanish leather, originally made from tanned and dressed goatskins, but
     later from split horse-hides (see 'cordwain', *OED*). Q1 spells 'cordivant'.

SIR FOPLING

Did you observe, madam, how their cravats hung loose an inch
from their neck, and what a frightful air it gave 'em?

MRS LOVEIT

Oh! I took particular notice of one that is always spruced up
with a deal of dirty, sky-coloured ribbon.   230

BELLINDA

That's one of the walking flageolets who haunt the Mall o'
nights.

MRS LOVEIT

Oh, I remember him! He has a hollow tooth, enough to spoil
the sweetness of an evening.

SIR FOPLING

I have seen the tallest walk the streets with a dainty pair of   235
boxes, neatly buckled on.

MRS LOVEIT

And a little footboy at his heels, pocket-high, with a flat cap, a
dirty face—

SIR FOPLING

—And a snotty nose.

MRS LOVEIT

Oh, odious! There's many of my own sex, with that Holborn   240
equipage, trig to Gray's Inn Walks, and now and then travel
hither on a Sunday.

MEDLEY [To DORIMANT]

She takes no notice of you.

---

231 *flageolet* a relation of the recorder with six fingerholes, invented in France. 'The flageolet
      was popular in England from about 1666 until it was set aside in favour of the recorder
      some fifteen years later' (*Grove's Dictionary*). Pepys played the flageolet.
233 *He has* ed. (H'has Q1; He's V, B). Brett-Smith defends his reading, which makes the
      'hollow tooth' a metaphor for the man, by citing Sparkish's calling in Wycherley's *The
      Country Wife*, 1675, an 'eternal Rotten-tooth' (*Plays*, ed. cit., V.iv, 323).
236 *boxes* Carnochan suggests, 'wooden overshoes (?)'. The *OED* is of no help, but the
      reference is to some unfashionable form of footwear.
237 *flat cap* round cap with a low, flat crown, worn in the sixteenth and seventeenth centur-
      ies by London citizens, especially apprentices.
240–1 *Holborn equipage* unfashionable retinue characteristic of the City. Holborn was a
      centre of commerce and business.
241 *trig* Q1 (trip V) dress smartly
      Gray's Inn Walks gardens of Gray's Inn, an Inn of Court in Holborn, notorious as a
      place for assignations.

DORIMANT

Damn her! I am jealous of a counterplot.

MRS LOVEIT

Your liveries are the finest, Sir Fopling. Oh, that page! That page   245
is the prettily'st dressed. They are all Frenchmen?

SIR FOPLING

There's one damned English blockhead among 'em. You may
know him by his mien.

MRS LOVEIT

Oh, that's he, that's he! What do you call him?

SIR FOPLING [*Calling* FOOTMAN]

Hey!—I know not what to call him.   250

MRS LOVEIT

What's your name?

FOOTMAN

John Trott, madam.

SIR FOPLING

Oh, insufferable! Trott, Trott, Trott! There's nothing so
barbarous as the names of our English servants. What
countryman are you, sirrah?   255

FOOTMAN

Hampshire, sir.

SIR FOPLING

Then Hampshire be your name. Hey, Hampshire!

MRS LOVEIT

Oh, that sound! That sound becomes the mouth of a man of
quality.

---

248   *mien* Sir Fopling may be using the French word *mine* (Q1 spells 'Meine'): in Etherege's
      earlier plays the word is spelt both 'mine' and 'meen'.
255   *countryman* 'country' here means 'county'.
256   *Hampshire* Brett-Smith draws attention to Congreve's reference: 'The Ancients us'd to
      call their Servants by the names of the Countries from whence they came . . . The
      French to this Day do the same, and call their Footmen *Champagne*, [,]*le Picard, le
      Gascon, le Bourguignon*, &c. and *Sir George Etheridge* in his *Sir Fopling Flutter*, the *Hamp-
      shire*, &c. speaking to his Valet imitates this Custom' ('Notes on the Third Book of
      Ovid's Art of Love', *Ovid's Art of Love in Three Books . . . By Several Eminent Hands*, 1709,
      pp. 253–4). But Arthur Sherbo (*MLN*, 64 (1949), 343–5) points out Etherege's
      indebtedness to Molière's *Les Précieuses Ridicules*, Scene 11, in which Mascarille calls to
      his 'laquais', 'Hola, Champagne, Picard, Bourguignon, Casquaret, Basque, la Verdure,
      Lorrain, Provencal, la Violette,' which provides some of the names for Sir Fopling's
      servants at ll.111–12 above. Sherbo points to further parallels between Mascarille and
      Etherege's fop.

MEDLEY

    Dorimant, you look a little bashful on the matter.   260

DORIMANT

    She dissembles better than I thought she could have done.

MEDLEY

    You have tempted her with too luscious a bait. She bites at the coxcomb.

DORIMANT

    She cannot fall from loving me to that?

MEDLEY

    You begin to be jealous in earnest.   265

DORIMANT

    Of one I do not love?

MEDLEY

    You did love her.

DORIMANT

    The fit has long been over.

MEDLEY

    But I have known men fall into dangerous relapses when they have found a woman inclining to another.   270

DORIMANT (*To himself*)

    He guesses the secret of my heart. I am concerned but dare not show it, lest Bellinda should mistrust all I have done to gain her.

BELLINDA (*Aside*)

    I have watched his look and find no alteration there. Did he love her, some signs of jealousy would have appeared.   275

DORIMANT [*To* MRS LOVEIT]

    I hope this happy evening, madam, has reconciled you to the scandalous Mall. We shall have you now hankering here again.

MRS LOVEIT

    Sir Fopling, will you walk?

SIR FOPLING

    I am all obedience, madam.   280

MRS LOVEIT

    Come along then, and let's agree to be malicious on all the ill-fashioned things we meet.

277 *hankering* 'hanging about'

SIR FOPLING

We'll make a critique on the whole Mall, madam.

MRS LOVEIT

Bellinda, you shall engage—

BELLINDA

To the reserve of our friends, my dear.   285

MRS LOVEIT

No! No exceptions.

SIR FOPLING

We'll sacrifice all to our diversion.

MRS LOVEIT

All—all—

SIR FOPLING

All!

BELLINDA

All? Then let it be.   290

Exeunt SIR FOPLING, MRS LOVEIT, BELLINDA, *and* PERT, *laughing*

MEDLEY

Would you had brought some more of your friends, Dorimant,
to have been witnesses of Sir Fopling's disgrace and your
triumph!

DORIMANT

'Twere unreasonable to desire you not to laugh at me, but pray
do not expose me to the town this day or two.   295

MEDLEY

By that time you hope to have regained your credit?

DORIMANT

I know she hates Fopling and only makes use of him in hope to
work me on again. Had it not been for some powerful
considerations which will be removed tomorrow morning, I
had made her pluck off this mask and show the passion that lies   300
panting under.

Enter a FOOTMAN

---

283 *critique* CA (Critick Q1; *critique* V) probably not the French word as Verity thought.
 OED's first example is from Addison (1702–21). The normal English spelling was
 'critick' (and so pronounced); it altered to the French spelling during the eighteenth
 century, and was given the French pronunciation in the nineteenth.
284 *engage* participate
285 *To . . . of* with the exception of

MEDLEY

Here comes a man from Bellair, with news of your last
adventure.

DORIMANT

I am glad he sent him. I long to know the consequence of our
parting.   305

FOOTMAN

Sir, my master desires you to come to my Lady Townley's
presently and bring Mr Medley with you. My Lady Woodvill
and her daughter are there.

MEDLEY

Then all's well, Dorimant.

FOOTMAN

They have sent for the fiddles and mean to dance. He bid me tell   310
you, sir, the old lady does not know you, and would have you
own yourself to be Mr Courtage. They are all prepared to
receive you by that name.

DORIMANT

That foppish admirer of quality, who flatters the very meat at
honourable tables and never offers love to a woman below a   315
lady-grandmother!

MEDLEY

You know the character you are to act, I see.

DORIMANT

This is Harriet's contrivance—wild, witty, lovesome, beautiful,
and young.—Come along, Medley

MEDLEY

This new woman would well supply the loss of Loveit.   320

DORIMANT

That business must not end so. Before tomorrow sun is set, I
will revenge and clear it.

> And you and Loveit, to her cost, shall find
> I fathom all the depths of womankind.

Exeunt

---

307 *presently* immediately
318–19 *wild . . . young* Brett-Smith compares with Waller, 'Of the Danger his Majesty [Being
   Prince] Escaped in the Road at Saint Andrews', ll. 13–14: 'Of the Fourth Edward was his
   noble song,/Fierce, goodly, valiant, beautiful, and young' (*Poems*, I, p. 1).

ACT IV, SCENE I

[LADY TOWNLEY's *house*]

The scene opens with the fiddles playing a country dance

Enter DORIMANT [*and*] LADY WOODVILL, YOUNG BELLAIR *and*
MRS HARRIET, OLD BELLAIR *and* EMILIA, MR MEDLEY *and* LADY
TOWNLEY, *as having just ended the dance*

OLD BELLAIR
　So, so, so! A smart bout, a very smart bout, adod!
LADY TOWNLEY
　How do you like Emilia's dancing, brother?
OLD BELLAIR
　Not at all, not at all!
LADY TOWNLEY
　You speak not what you think, I am sure.
OLD BELLAIR
　No matter for that—go, bid her dance no more. It don't become   5
　her, it don't become her. Tell her I say so. (*Aside*) Adod, I love
　her.
DORIMANT (*To* LADY WOODVILL)
　All people mingle nowadays, madam. And in public places
　women of quality have the least respect showed 'em.
LADY WOODVILL
　I protest you say the truth, Mr Courtage.   10
DORIMANT
　Forms and ceremonies, the only things that uphold quality and
　greatness, are now shamefully laid aside and neglected.
LADY WOODVILL
　Well, this is not the women's age, let 'em think what they will.
　Lewdness is the business now; love was the business in my time.
DORIMANT
　The women, indeed, are little beholding to the young men of   15
　this age. They're generally only dull admirers of themselves and
　make their court to nothing but their periwigs and their

15 *beholding* Q1 (beholden Q3)

cravats—and would be more concerned for the disordering of
'em, though on a good occasion, than a young maid would be
for the tumbling of her head or handkercher.   20

LADY WOODVILL

I protest you hit 'em.

DORIMANT

They are very assiduous to show themselves at court, well-
dressed, to the women of quality; but their business is with the
stale mistresses of the town, who are prepared to receive their
lazy addresses by industrious old lovers who have cast 'em off   25
and made 'em easy.

HARRIET [*To* MEDLEY]

He fits my mother's humour so well, a little more and she'll
dance a kissing dance with him anon.

MEDLEY

Dutifully observed, madam.

DORIMANT

They pretend to be great critics in beauty—by their talk you   30
would think they liked no face—and yet can dote on an ill one
if it belong to a laundress or a tailor's daughter. They cry a
woman's past her prime at twenty, decayed at four-and-twenty,
old and insufferable at thirty.

LADY WOODVILL

Insufferable at thirty! That they are in the wrong, Mr Courtage, 35
at five-and-thirty there are living proofs enough to convince
'em.

DORIMANT

Ay, madam! There's Mrs Setlooks, Mrs Droplip, and my Lady
Loud. Show me among all our opening buds a face that
promises so much beauty as the remains of theirs.   40

LADY WOODVILL

The depraved appetite of this vicious age tastes nothing but
green fruit and loathes it when 'tis kindly ripened.

---

20 *handkercher* Q1 (handkerchief W, V) unusual variant of 'handkerchief' (not in *OED*),
meaning here a kerchief for the neck or head

28 *kissing dance* i.e., cushion-dance, a round dance formerly danced at weddings, in which
the men and women alternately knelt on a cushion to be kissed. Referred to as 'old' in
1698 (*OED*).

42 *kindly* naturally, seasonably

DORIMANT

Else so many deserving women, madam, would not be so untimely neglected.

LADY WOODVILL

I protest, Mr Courtage, a dozen such good men as you would be enough to atone for that wicked Dorimant and all the under-debauchees of the town. (HARRIET, EMILIA, YOUNG BELLAIR, MEDLEY [and] LADY TOWNLEY *break out into a laughter*)— What's the matter there? 45

MEDLEY

A pleasant mistake, madam, that a lady has made, occasions a little laughter. 50

OLD BELLAIR [*To* DORIMANT *and* LADY WOODVILL]

Come, come, you keep 'em idle! They are impatient till the fiddles play again.

DORIMANT

You are not weary, madam?

LADY WOODVILL

One dance more. I cannot refuse you, Mr Courtage.

They dance.
After the dance, OLD BELLAIR *singing and dancing up to* EMILIA

EMILIA

You are very active, sir. 55

OLD BELLAIR

Adod, sirrah, when I was a young fellow, I could ha' capered up to my woman's gorget.

DORIMANT [*To* LADY WOODVILL]

You are willing to rest yourself, madam?

LADY TOWNLEY [*To* DORIMANT *and* LADY WOODVILL]

We'll walk into my chamber and sit down.

MEDLEY

Leave us Mr Courtage; he's a dancer, and the young ladies are not weary yet. 60

LADY WOODVILL

We'll send him out again.

HARRIET

If you do not quickly, I know where to send for Mr Dorimant.

56–7 *capered . . . gorget* kicked as high as the garment covering my partner's neck and shoulders.

LADY WOODVILL

This girl's head, Mr Courtage, is ever running on that wild
fellow.   65

DORIMANT

'Tis well you have got her a good husband, madam. That will
settle it.

Exeunt LADY TOWNLEY, LADY WOODVILL, *and* DORIMANT

OLD BELLAIR (*To* EMILIA)

Adod, sweetheart, be advised and do not throw thyself away on
a young idle fellow.

EMILIA

I have no such intention, sir.   70

OLD BELLAIR

Have a little patience! Thou shalt have the man I spake of.
Adod, he loves thee and will make a good husband. But no
words—

EMILIA

But, sir—

OLD BELLAIR

No answer—out a pize! Peace, and think on't.   75

Enter DORIMANT

DORIMANT

Your company is desired within, sir.

OLD BELLAIR

I go, I go! Good Mr Courtage, fare you well. (*To* EMILIA) Go, I'll
see you no more!

EMILIA

What have I done, sir?

OLD BELLAIR

You are ugly, you are ugly!—Is she not, Mr Courtage?   80

EMILIA

Better words, or I shan't abide you!

OLD BELLAIR

Out a pize! Adod, what does she say?—Hit her a pat for me
there.   *Exit* OLD BELLAIR

MEDLEY [*To* DORIMANT]

You have charms for the whole family.

DORIMANT

You'll spoil all with some unseasonable jest, Medley.   85

95

MEDLEY

You see I confine my tongue and am content to be a bare spectator, much contrary to my nature.

EMILIA

Methinks, Mr Dorimant, my Lady Woodvill is a little fond of you.

DORIMANT

Would her daughter were. 90

MEDLEY

It may be you may find her so. Try her. You have an opportunity.

DORIMANT

And I will not lose it.—Bellair, here's a lady has something to say to you.

YOUNG BELLAIR

I wait upon her.—Mr Medley, we have both business with you. 95

DORIMANT

Get you all together, then. [*He bows to* HARRIET; *she curtsies*] (*To* HARRIET) That demure curtsy is not amiss in jest, but do not think in earnest it becomes you.

HARRIET

Affectation is catching, I find. From your grave bow I got it.

DORIMANT

Where had you all that scorn and coldness in your look? 100

HARRIET

From nature, sir—pardon my want of art. I have not learnt those softnesses and languishings which now in faces are so much in fashion.

DORIMANT

You need 'em not. You have a sweetness of your own, if you would but calm your frowns and let it settle. 105

HARRIET

My eyes are wild and wandering like my passions, and cannot yet be tied to rules of charming.

DORIMANT

Women, indeed, have commonly a method of managing those messengers of love. Now they will look as if they would kill, and anon they will look as if they were dying. They point and 110 rebate their glances, the better to invite us.

110–11 *point and rebate* sharpen and blunt

HARRIET

I like this variety well enough, but hate the set face that always looks as it would say, 'Come love me'—a woman who at plays makes the *doux yeux* to a whole audience and at home cannot forbear 'em to her monkey.   115

DORIMANT

Put on a gentle smile and let me see how well it will become you.

HARRIET

I am sorry my face does not please you as it is, but I shall not be complaisant and change it.

DORIMANT

Though you are obstinate, I know 'tis capable of improvement,   120
and shall do you justice, madam, if I chance to be at court when the critics of the circle pass their judgment—for thither you must come.

HARRIET

And expect to be taken in pieces, have all my features examined, every motion censured, and on the whole be condemned to be   125
but pretty—or a beauty of the lowest rate. What think you?

DORIMANT

The women—nay, the very lovers who belong to the drawing room—will maliciously allow you more than that. They always grant what is apparent, that they may the better be believed when they name concealed faults they cannot easily be   130
disproved in.

HARRIET

Beauty runs as great a risk exposed at court as wit does on the stage, where the ugly and the foolish all are free to censure.

DORIMANT (*Aside*)

I love her and dare not let her know it. I fear she has an

114 *makes . . . to* make eyes at
119 *complaisant* See note to I, 382 and Introduction pp. xxx-xxxii.
122 *circle* probably 'an assembly surrounding the principal person' (Johnson), as at Court, at a drawing-room or levee, though the *OED*'s first example is from 1714. More broadly it means a 'set' or coterie.
127–8 *drawing room* shortened from 'withdrawing-room', it came to mean a room for receptions. From 1673 the word could refer to the people gathered in the drawing-room, and hence, a levee, or the sovereign's formal reception at which ladies were 'presented' at Court.
132 *risk* as Q1's spelling 'risque' suggests, a relatively recent importation from the French. *OED*'s first example dates from 1661.

ascendant o'er me and may revenge the wrongs I have done   135
her sex. (*To her*) Think of making a party, madam; love will
engage.

HARRIET

You make me start! I did not think to have heard of love from
you.

DORIMANT

I never knew what 'twas to have a settled ague yet, but now   140
and then have had irregular fits.

HARRIET

Take heed, sickness after long health is commonly more violent
and dangerous.

DORIMANT (*Aside*)

I have took the infection from her and feel the disease now
spreading in me. (*To her*) Is the name of love so frightful that   145
you dare not stand it?

HARRIET

'Twill do little execution out of your mouth on me, I am sure.

DORIMANT

It has been fatal—

HARRIET

To some easy women, but we are not all born to one destiny.
I was informed you use to laugh at love, and not make   150
it.

DORIMANT

The time has been, but now I must speak—

HARRIET

If it be on that idle subject, I will put on my serious look, turn
my head carelessly from you, drop my lip, let my eyelids fall and
hang half o'er my eyes—thus, while you buzz a speech of an   155
hour long in my ear and I answer never a word. Why do you not
begin?

---

135 *ascendant* dominance (orig. astrological)
136 *making a party* 'to make one's party good' means to make good one's cause or position;
     'to take a party' means making a resolution on one side or the other, i.e., Harriet should
     take the side of beauty against 'the ugly and the foolish' (1. 133), and love will support
     her. 'Engage' suggests the possibility of a military metaphor—'party' meant a small
     body of troops selected for a particular duty (1645–).
140 *settled ague* chronic fever
150 *use* are accustomed to

DORIMANT

That the company may take notice how passionately I make advances of love and how disdainfully you receive 'em.

HARRIET

When your love's grown strong enough to make you bear being   160
laughed at, I'll give you leave to trouble me with it. Till when, pray forbear, sir.

Enter SIR FOPLING *and others in masks*

DORIMANT

What's here—masquerades?

HARRIET

I thought that foppery had been left off, and people might have been in private with a fiddle.   165

DORIMANT

'Tis endeavoured to be kept on foot still by some who find themselves the more acceptable the less they are known.

YOUNG BELLAIR

This must be Sir Fopling.

MEDLEY

That extraordinary habit shows it.

YOUNG BELLAIR

What are the rest?   170

MEDLEY

A company of French rascals whom he picked up in Paris and has brought over to be his dancing equipage on these occasions. Make him own himself; a fool is very troublesome when he presumes he is incognito.

SIR FOPLING (*To* HARRIET)

Do you know me?   175

158–9 *make advances* the word 'advances' begins to be used in this sense from 1668 according to the *OED*. For the phrase, compare with French, *faire les avances*.

163 *masquerades* Conaghan aptly cites Burnet, 'At this time [1669/70] the court fell into much extravagance in masquerading; both king and queen, and all the court, went about masked, and came into houses unknown, and danced. People were so disguised, that without being in on the secret none could distinguish them' (*History of my Own Time*, ed. O. Airy, 2 vols., 1900, I, p. 473).

169 *habit* dress, attire

172 *dancing equipage* see note to III.ii, 168.

HARRIET

Ten to one but I guess at you.

SIR FOPLING

Are you women as fond of a vizard as we men are?

HARRIET

I am very fond of a vizard that covers a face I do not like, sir.

YOUNG BELLAIR

Here are no masks, you see, sir, but those which came with you.
This was intended a private meeting, but because you look like a   180
gentleman, if you will discover yourself and we know you to be
such, you shall be welcome.

SIR FOPLING (*Pulling off his mask*)

Dear Bellair!

MEDLEY

Sir Fopling! How came you hither?

SIR FOPLING

Faith, as I was coming late from Whitehall, after the King's   185
couchée, one of my people told me he had heard fiddles at
my Lady Townley's, and—

DORIMANT

You need not say any more, sir.

SIR FOPLING

Dorimant, let me kiss thee.

DORIMANT

Hark you, Sir Fopling—   *Whispers*   190

SIR FOPLING

Enough, enough, Courtage.—[*Looking at* HARRIET] A pretty
kind of young woman that, Medley. I observed her in the Mall,
more *éveillée* than our English women commonly are. Prithee,
what is she?

MEDLEY

The most noted coquette in town. Beware of her.   195

---

183 s.d. *off* Q3, W, V, B, CA (of Q1)
185–6 *King's couchée* compare Fr., *coucher le roi*, the reception preceding the King's going to
   bed. *OED* cites this as first example in English. Contemporary spelling varies, reflecting
   its origin. The word was probably brought over by Charles II's Court.
   couchée ed. (Coucheé Q1; *couchée* V, CA)
193 *éveillée* wide awake. Verity cites *Spectator*, No. 45 (21 April 1711), where Addison, advis-
   ing women to stop their 'Sprightliness from degenerating into Levity', says, 'the whole
   Discourse and Behaviour of the *French* is to make the Sex more Fantastical, or (as they are
   pleased to term it,) *more awaken'd*, than is consistent either with Virtue or Discretion'.

SIR FOPLING

Let her be what she will, I know how to take my measures. In
Paris the mode is to flatter the *prude*, laugh at the *faux-prude*,
make serious love to the *demi-prude*, and only rally with the
coquette. Medley, what think you?

DORIMANT

That for all this smattering of the mathematics, you may be out   200
in your judgment at tennis.

SIR FOPLING

What a *coq-à-l'âne* is this? I talk of women, and thou
answerest tennis.

MEDLEY

Mistakes will be, for want of apprehension.

SIR FOPLING

I am very glad of the acquaintance I have with this family.   205

MEDLEY

My lady truly is a good woman.

SIR FOPLING

Ah, Dorimant—Courtage, I would say—would thou hadst
spent the last winter in Paris with me. When thou wert there, La
Corneus and Sallyes were the only *habitudes* we had; a

196   *to . . . measures* to make my plans. From the French idiom, *prendre des mesures*, though
        the first example given by the OED is from 1698, indicating that Sir Fopling uses the
        phrase self-consciously.
196–9   *In Paris . . . coquette* Sir Fopling echoes contemporary French gallantry. See Brett-
        Smith for a parallel with a poem by Comte de Bussy.
197   *prude* OED's first instance is from Cibber's *Careless Husband*, 1704. The spellings in Q1
        ('Prudè', 'Faux-proudè', and 'Demi-proudè') indicate Sir Fopling is using French.
        faux-prude false prude
198   *demi-prude* half prude
        with Q1 (at Q2–3)
202   *coq-à-l'âne* cock and bull story
208–9   *La Corneus and Sallyes* Verity suggests the fashionable Parisians, Mesdames Cornuel
        and Sallé. Madame Cornuel appears in Comte Bussy's *Histoire Amoureuse des Gaules*,
        [1665], who was 'célèbre par ses bon mots' (see *Memoires de Roger de Rabutin Comte
        Bussy . . . suivi de l'Histoire Amoureuse des Gaules . . .*, ed. L. Lalanne, 2 vols., 1857, II,
        pp. 334 and n., 350–8). (For Bussy, see note to ll. 220 below.) 'Une certaine madame
        Sallé, femme d'un maître de comptes' is mentioned in *La France Galante*, 1695, often
        attributed to Comte Bussy and printed with his *Histoire Amoureuse des Gaules* (see
        Histoire Amoureuse des Gaules . . . suivie de La France Galante . . ., ed. A. Poitevin, 2 vols.,
        2nd ed., 1857–8, II, p. 315).
209   *habitudes* i.e., acquaintances. OED gives this single instance. It may reveal Sir Fopling's
        ignorance, or, as Carnochan suggests, come from a memory of the French idiom, *avoir
        ses habitudes dans une maison*, to be at home in someone's house.

comedian would have been a *bonne fortune*. No stranger ever   210
passed his time so well as I did some months before I came over.
I was well received in a dozen families, where all the women of
quality used to visit. I have intrigues to tell thee more pleasant
than ever thou read'st in a novel.

HARRIET

Write 'em, sir, and oblige us women. Our language wants such   215
little stories.

SIR FOPLING

Writing, madam, 's a mechanic part of wit. A gentleman should
never go beyond a song or a *billet*.

HARRIET

Bussy was a gentleman.

SIR FOPLING

Who, d'Ambois?   220

MEDLEY [*Aside*]

Was there ever such a brisk blockhead?

HARRIET

Not d'Ambois, sir, but Rabutin—he who writ the *Loves of
France*.

SIR FOPLING

That may be, madam! Many gentlemen do things that are below
'em.—Damn your authors, Courtage, women are the prettiest   225
things we can fool away our time with.

HARRIET

I hope ye have wearied yourself tonight at court, sir, and will
not think of fooling with anybody here.

SIR FOPLING

I cannot complain of my fortune there, madam.—Dorimant—

---

210 *a comedian . . . fortune* 'The implication is that *even* a comic actor would have been a
    "piece of good luck" ' (Carnochan). Probably Sir Fopling shows his ignorance: Madame
    Cornuel was known for her wit.
213 *to visit* Q1 (to come to visit Q2–3)
220 *d'Ambois* Louis de Clermont d'Amboise, Sieur de Bussy (1549–79), adventurer and
    murderer, familiar to theatregoers as Chapman's *Bussy d'Ambois* (1607), which was still
    performed. Sir Fopling's mistake reveals his French culture as a sham. He knows only
    the popular Bussy, and not the fashionable contemporary writer, Comte de Bussy.
222–3 *Rabutin . . . France* Roger de Rabutin, Comte de Bussy (1618–93), author of the
    famous *Histoire Amoureuse des Gaulles* (1665) and cousin of Madame de Sévigné, with
    whom he corresponded. (See also note to IV.ii, 97 below.)

DORIMANT

    Again! 230

SIR FOPLING

    Courtage, a pox on 't! I have something to tell thee. When I had
made my court within, I came out and flung myself upon the
mat under the state i' the outward room, i' the midst of half a
dozen beauties who were withdrawn to jeer among
themselves, as they called it. 235

DORIMANT

    Did you know 'em?

SIR FOPLING

    Not one of 'em, by heavens, not I! But they were all your
friends.

DORIMANT

    How are you sure of that?

SIR FOPLING

    Why, we laughed at all the town—spared nobody but yourself. 240
They found me a man for their purpose.

DORIMANT

    I know you are malicious to your power.

SIR FOPLING

    And, faith, I had occasion to show it, for I never saw more
gaping fools at a ball or on a Birthday.

DORIMANT

    You learned who the women were? 245

SIR FOPLING

    No matter!—they frequent the drawing room.

DORIMANT

    And entertain themselves pleasantly at the expense of all the
fops who come there.

SIR FOPLING

    That's their business. Faith, I sifted 'em and find they have a
sort of wit among them. (*Pinches a tallow candle*)—Ah, filthy! 250

DORIMANT

    Look, he has been pinching the tallow candle.

233 *state* canopy
234 *jeer* V, CA (jeèr Q1; jeér W) The accent may, as Carnochan suggests, indicate an affected
     mispronunciation by Sir Fopling, but the accenting in Q1 is too eccentric for certainty.
242 *to your* within your
244 *Birthday* celebration of the King's birthday.
249 *sifted* questioned closely, made enquiry of

SIR FOPLING

How can you breathe in a room where there's grease frying?
Dorimant, thou art intimate with my lady—advise her, for her
own sake and the good company that comes hither, to burn wax
lights.   255

HARRIET

What are these masquerades who stand so obsequiously at a
distance?

SIR FOPLING

A set of baladines, whom I picked out of the best in France
and brought over with a flute douce or two—my servants.
They shall entertain you.   260

HARRIET

I had rather see you dance yourself, Sir Fopling.

SIR FOPLING

And I had rather do it—all the company knows it. But,
madam—

MEDLEY

Come, come! No excuses, Sir Fopling!

SIR FOPLING

By heavens, Medley—   265

MEDLEY

Like a woman I find you must be struggled with before one
brings you to what you desire.

HARRIET (*Aside*)

Can he dance?

EMILIA

And fence and sing too, if you'll believe him.

DORIMANT

He has no more excellence in his heels than in his head. He   270
went to Paris a plain, bashful English blockhead, and is returned
a fine, undertaking French fop.

MEDLEY [*To* HARRIET]

I cannot prevail.

---

258 *baladines* see note to II.i, 141
259 *flute douce* ed. (Flutes deux Q1; Flûtes doux CO; *flûtes douces* V; *flûte douce* CA Q1's
      'deux' is probably a misreading of 'doux' in the manuscript) see note to II.i, 120.
267 *to* W, V, B, CA, CO (omitted Q1–3)
272 *undertaking* possibly chiding, reproving, a sense recorded by *OED* in 1691, or, willing to
      take in hand (i.e. affirmative and positive where he had once been 'plain and bashful').

SIR FOPLING

Do not think it want of complaisance, madam.

HARRIET

You are too well-bred to want that, Sir Fopling. I believe it want   275
of power.

SIR FOPLING

By heavens, and so it is! I have sat up so damned late and drunk
so cursed hard since I came to this lewd town that I am fit for
nothing but low dancing now—a *courante*, a *bourrée*, or a
menuet. But St André tells me, if I will but be regular, in one   280
month I shall rise again. (*Endeavours at a caper*)—Pox on this
debauchery!

EMILIA

I have heard your dancing much commended.

SIR FOPLING

It had the good fortune to please in Paris. I was judged to rise
within an inch as high as the Basque in an entry I danced   285
there.

HARRIET [*To* EMILIA]

I am mightily taken with this fool. Let us sit.—Here's a seat, Sir
Fopling.

SIR FOPLING

At your feet, madam. I can be nowhere so much at ease.—By
your leave, gown.   [*Sits*]   290

HARRIET, EMILIA

Ah, you'll spoil it!

SIR FOPLING

No matter, my clothes are my creatures. I make 'em to make my
court to you ladies.—Hey! *qu'on commence*!

Dance

279–80 *low dancing . . . menuet* the three dances are 'low' because they call for no capers.

280 *St André* a French dancer brought over to perform in Shadwell's *Psyche* (1675) and
described as 'the most famous Master of *France*' (Preface). He also heads the list of
dancers in Crowne's *Calisto*, produced at Court in the same year.

285 *the Basque* probably a reference to 'le Basque sauteur', a French dancer whose affair with
Madame de Berthillac is recounted in *La France Galante* (*Histoire Amoureuse des Gaules
. . . suivie de La France Galante . . .*, ed. Poitevin, II, pp. 75–6).

entry a dance introduced between the parts of an entertainment. A fairly new word
(from Fr. *entrée* or *entrée de ballet*). *OED*'s earliest example dates from 1651, 'A masque
at Court, where the French King in person danced five entries' (Evelyn, *Memoirs*, 1857,
I, p. 276).

293 *qu'on commence!* begin!

(*To* [JOHN TROTT, *one of the dancers*])—English
motions! I was forced to entertain this fellow, one of my set   295
miscarrying.—Oh, horrid! Leave your damned manner of
dancing and put on the French air. Have you not a pattern
before you? [*Dances*]—Pretty well! Imitation in time may bring
him to something.

After the dance, enter OLD BELLAIR, LADY WOODVILL, *and*
LADY TOWNLEY

OLD BELLAIR
Hey, adod, what have we here? A mumming?   300
LADY WOODVILL
Where's my daughter?—Harriet!
DORIMANT
Here, here, madam. I know not but under these disguises there
may be dangerous sparks. I gave the young lady warning.
LADY WOODVILL
Lord! I am so obliged to you Mr Courtage.
HARRIET
Lord! How you admire this man!   305
LADY WOODVILL
What have you to except against him?
HARRIET
He's a fop.
LADY WOODVILL
He's not a Dorimant, a wild, extravagant fellow of the times.

293–5 *commence! . . . motions!* ed. (Commencé, English motions. Q1ᵘ; Commencé to an
English Dancer English motions Q1ᶜ; *commence*—to an English dancer English
motions. V, B, CA (who further adds and s.d. after 'fellow' in l. 288, '*pointing to John
Trott*'); in CO, Conaghan, who first discovered the corrected and uncorrected states,
first made 'to an English Dancer' into an s.d., commenting, 'Lack of punctuation in Q1ᶜ
suggests that the compositor made the insertion without attending to its purpose: *to . . .
Dancer* is almost certainly a stage direction') Q1's corrected reading makes possible
sense as Sir Fopling' interjection, but Conaghan's emendation is preferable.

294–7 *English . . . French air* Arthur Sherbo sees a source in Molière's *Les Précieuses ridicules*,
1659, Scene 12, in which Mascarille finds fault with the 'violons' time-keeping (*Modern
Language Notes*, 64 (1949), 344).

295 *entertain* retain, hire

296 *miscarrying* coming to harm, or behaving badly, or going astray

297 *not a* Q1ᶜ (not had a Q1ᵘ). As Conaghan says, the change in Q1ᶜ 'allows for a demonstration of dancing by Sir Fopling'.

308 *wild, extravagant* see Introduction, pp. xxvi–xxx.

HARRIET

    He's a man made up of forms and commonplaces, sucked out
    of the remaining lees of the last age.   310

LADY WOODVILL

    He's so good a man that were you not engaged—

LADY TOWNLEY

    You'll have but little night to sleep in.

LADY WOODVILL

    Lord! 'tis perfect day—

DORIMANT (*Aside*)

    The hour is almost come I appointed Bellinda, and I am not so
    foppishly in love here to forget. I am flesh and blood yet.   315

LADY TOWNLEY

    I am very sensible, madam.

LADY WOODVILL

    Lord, madam—

HARRIET

    Look, in what a struggle is my poor mother yonder!

YOUNG BELLAIR

    She has much ado to bring out the compliment.

DORIMANT

    She strains hard for it.   320

HARRIET

    See, see—her head tottering, her eyes staring, and her underlip
    trembling.

DORIMANT

    Now, now she's in the very convulsions of her civility. (*Aside*)—
    'Sdeath, I shall lose Bellinda! I must fright her hence. She'll be
    an hour in this fit of good manners else. (*To* LADY WOODVILL)   325
    Do you not know Sir Fopling, madam?

LADY WOODVILL

    I have seen that face. Oh heaven!—'tis the same we met in the
    Mall! How came he here?

DORIMANT

    A fiddle in this town is a kind of fop-call. No sooner it strikes
    up, but the house is besieged with an army of masquerades   330
    straight.

309 *forms* see note to I, 114–15.
313 *perfect day* i.e., broad daylight
316 *sensible* aware of (your courtesy)

LADY WOODVILL

Lord, I tremble, Mr Courtage! For certain Dorimant is in the company.

DORIMANT

I cannot confidently say he is not. You had best begone; I will wait upon you. Your daughter is in the hands of Mr Bellair.　335

LADY WOODVILL

I'll see her before me.—Harriet, come away!

[Exeunt LADY WOODVILL *and* HARRIET]

YOUNG BELLAIR

Lights, lights!

LADY TOWNLEY

Light, down there!

OLD BELLAIR

Adod, it needs not—

[Exeunt LADY TOWNLEY, EMILIA *and* YOUNG BELLAIR]

DORIMANT [*Calling to the servants outside*]

Call my Lady Woodvill's coach to the door, quickly.　340

[*Exit* DORIMANT]

OLD BELLAIR

Stay, Mr Medley, let the young fellows do that duty. We will drink a glass of wine together. 'Tis good after dancing. [*Looks at* SIR FOPLING]—What mumming spark is that?

MEDLEY

He is not to be comprehended in few words.

SIR FOPLING

Hey, La Tour!　345

MEDLEY

Whither away, Sir Fopling?

SIR FOPLING

I have business with Courtage.

MEDLEY

He'll but put the ladies into their coach and come up again.

OLD BELLAIR

In the meantime I'll call for a bottle　[*Exit* OLD BELLAIR]

Enter YOUNG BELLAIR

MEDLEY

Where's Dorimant?　350

345　*Tour* V, CA (Towèr Q1)

YOUNG BELLAIR

Stolen home. He has had business waiting for him there all this
night, I believe, by an impatience I observed in him.

MEDLEY

Very likely. 'Tis but dissembling drunkenness, railing at his
friends, and the kind soul will embrace the blessing and forget
the tedious expectation.   355

SIR FOPLING

I must speak with him before I sleep.

YOUNG BELLAIR [*To* MEDLEY]

Emilia and I are resolved on that business.

MEDLEY

Peace, here's your father.

Enter OLD BELLAIR *and butler with a bottle of wine*

OLD BELLAIR

The women are all gone to bed.—Fill, boy!—Mr Medley, begin
a health.   360

MEDLEY (*Whispers*)

To Emilia

OLD BELLAIR

Out a pize! She's a rogue, and I'll not pledge you.

MEDLEY

I know you will.

OLD BELLAIR

Adod, drink it, then!

SIR FOPLING

Let us have the new *bachique*.   365

OLD BELLAIR

Adod, that is a hard word! What does it mean, sir?

MEDLEY

A catch or drinking song.

OLD BELLAIR

Let us have it, then.

---

363 *will* V, B, CA (well Q1)
365 *bachique* drinking song, as Medley explains. *OED* cites this as its single example (cf. Fr.
     chanson bachique). Although it occurs as an adjective from 1669 to 1699, this is prob-
     ably another example of Sir Fopling's French, not the isolated occurrence of an English
     word.

SIR FOPLING
  Fill the glasses round, and draw up in a body.—Hey, music!

They sing

The pleasures of love and the joys of good wine,   370
To perfect our happiness wisely we join.
    We to beauty all day
    Give the sovereign sway
And her favourite nymphs devoutly obey.
At the plays we are constantly making our court,   375
And when they are ended, we follow the sport
    To the Mall and the Park,
    Where we love till 'tis dark.
    Then sparkling champagne
    Puts an end to their reign: 380
    It quickly recovers
    Poor languishing lovers,
Makes us frolic and gay, and drowns all our sorrow;
But alas, we relapse again on the morrow.
    Let every man stand   385
    With his glass in his hand,
And briskly discharge at the word of command.
    Here's a health to all those
    Whom tonight we depose.
Wine and beauty by turns great souls should inspire;   390
Present all together—and now, boys, give fire!

[They drink]

370–91 *The pleasures . . . fire* Thorpe, p. 103, records several subsequent printed appearances
  of this song, and notes Etherege's own preference for women over heavy drinking; as
  Dryden said, 'For wine to leave a whore or play/Was ne'ere Your Excellence's way'
  ('Letter to Sir Etherege', [1686], ll. 53–4, *Works*, III, p. 224). Carnochan cites lines from
  two songs in Shadwell's *Psyche* (1675) which deal with the *topoi* of the first two lines of
  Etherege's song.
379 *champagne* a new word (and drink) from the French. First example in *OED* is from
  Hudibras, 1664. The modern technique for making champagne is the invention of Dom
  Pérignon, cellarer at the Abbey of Hautvillers from 1668 to 1715, though champagne
  was available prior to his discoveries.
390 *should* Q1 (shall Q2–3)
391 *Present all together* i.e., raise your drinks and aim. The military metaphor runs through
  the song's last seven lines.

OLD BELLAIR

    Adod, a pretty business and very merry!

SIR FOPLING

    Hark you, Medley, let you and I take the fiddles and go waken
    Dorimant.

MEDLEY

    We shall do him a courtesy, if it be as I guess. For after the   395
    fatigue of this night, he'll quickly have his belly full and be glad
    of an occasion to cry, 'Take away, Handy!'

YOUNG BELLAIR

    I'll go with you; and there we'll consult about affairs, Medley.

OLD BELLAIR

    Adod, 'tis six o'clock!

SIR FOPLING

    Let's away, then.   400

OLD BELLAIR

    Mr Medley, my sister tells me you are an honest man. And,
    adod, I love you.—Few words and hearty, that's the way with
    old Harry, old Harry.

SIR FOPLING [*To his servants*]

    Light your flambeaux! Hey!

OLD BELLAIR

    What does the man mean?   405

MEDLEY

    'Tis day, Sir Fopling.

SIR FOPLING

    No matter; our serenade will look the greater.

                                            Exeunt omnes

404 *flambeaux* torches, esp. ones made from several thick wicks dipped in wax
407 *serenade* See note to II.i, 115–16.

ACT IV, SCENE II

DORIMANT's *lodging; a table, a candle, a toilet, etc.* HANDY *tying up linen*

Enter DORIMANT *in his gown, and* BELLINDA

DORIMANT
Why will you be gone so soon?

BELLINDA
Why did you stay out so late?

DORIMANT
Call a chair, Handy.

[*Exit* HANDY]

—What makes you tremble so?

BELLINDA
I have a thousand fears about me. Have I not been seen, think   5
you?

DORIMANT
By nobody but myself and trusty Handy.

BELINDA
Where are all your people?

DORIMANT
I have dispersed 'em on sleeveless errands. What does that sigh
mean?   10

BELLINDA
Can you be so unkind to ask me? Well—(*Sighs*)—were it to do
again—

DORIMANT
We should do it, should we not?

BELLINDA
I think we should: the wickeder man you, to make me love so
well. Will you be discreet now?   15

DORIMANT
I will.

BELLINDA
You cannot.

---

9   *sleeveless* trifling

112

DORIMANT

Never doubt it.

BELLINDA

I will not expect it.

DORIMANT

You do me wrong.   20

BELLINDA

You have no more power to keep the secret than I had not to trust you with it.

DORIMANT

By all the joys I have had, and those you keep in store—

BELLINDA

—You'll do for my sake what you never did before.

DORIMANT

By that truth thou hast spoken, a wife shall sooner betray   25
herself to her husband.

BELLINDA

Yet I had rather you should be false in this than in another thing you promised me.

DORIMANT

What's that?

BELLINDA

That you would never see Loveit more but in public places—in   30
the Park, at court and plays.

DORIMANT

'Tis not likely a man should be fond of seeing a damned old play when there is a new one acted.

BELLINDA

I dare not trust your promise.

DORIMANT

You may.   35

BELLINDA

This does not satisfy me. You shall swear you never will see her more.

DORIMANT

I will, a thousand oaths! By all—

BELLINDA

Hold! You shall not, now I think on't better.

23–4 *By . . . before* Dorimant's speech begins to fall into an Alexandrine, but Bellinda 'is quick to interrupt his heroics with her rhyming reply' (Brett-Smith).

DORIMANT

    I will swear! 40

BELLINDA

    I shall grow jealous of the oath and think I owe your truth to that, not to your love.

DORIMANT

    Then, by my love! No other oath I'll swear.

Enter HANDY

HANDY

    Here's a chair.

BELLINDA

    Let me go. 45

DORIMANT

    I cannot.

BELLINDA

    Too willingly, I fear.

DORIMANT

    Too unkindly feared. When will you promise me again?

BELLINDA

    Not this fortnight.

DORIMANT

    You will be better than your word. 50

BELLINDA

    I think I shall. Will it not make you love me less?

                                     Fiddles without

    (*Starting*) Hark, what fiddles are these?

DORIMANT

    Look out, Handy.   *Exit* HANDY *and returns*

HANDY

    Mr Medley, Mr Bellair, and Sir Fopling. They are coming up.

DORIMANT

    How got they in? 55

HANDY

    The door was open for the chair.

BELLINDA

    Lord, let me fly!

DORIMANT

    Here, here, down the back stairs. I'll see you into your chair.

BELLINDA

    No, no! Stay and receive 'em. And be sure you keep your

word and never see Loveit more. Let it be a proof of your   60
kindness.

DORIMANT
It shall.—Handy, direct her.—(*Kissing her hand*) Everlasting
love go along with thee.

Exeunt BELLINDA *and* HANDY

Enter YOUNG BELLAIR, MEDLEY, *and* SIR FOPLING [*with his* PAGE]

YOUNG BELLAIR
Not abed yet?

MEDLEY
You have had an irregular fit, Dorimant.   65

DORIMANT
I have.

YOUNG BELLAIR
And is it off already?

DORIMANT
Nature has done her part, gentlemen. When she falls kindly to
work, great cures are effected in little time, you know.

SIR FOPLING
We thought there was a wench in the case, by the chair that   70
waited. Prithee, make us a *confidence.*

DORIMANT
Excuse me.

SIR FOPLING
Le sage Dorimant. Was she pretty?

DORIMANT
So pretty she may come to keep her coach and pay parish
duties, if the good humour of the age continue.   75

MEDLEY
And be of the number of the ladies kept by public-spirited men
for the good of the whole town.

SIR FOPLING
Well said, Medley.   SIR FOPLING *dancing by himself*

---

65 *irregular fit* unexpected bout of illness. Presumably Medley overhears Dorimant at IV.i,
141.
73 *Le sage* judicious, discreet
74–5 *So . . . continue* 'an instance of Dorimant's discretion. The description could hardly apply
to Bellinda, who is not mercenary' (Conaghan).

YOUNG BELLAIR

See Sir Fopling dancing.

DORIMANT

You are practising and have a mind to recover, I see.   80

SIR FOPLING

Prithee, Dorimant, why hast not thou a glass hung up here? A
room is the dullest thing without one!

YOUNG BELLAIR

Here is company to entertain you.

SIR FOPLING

But I mean in case of being alone. In a glass a man may
entertain himself—   85

DORIMANT

The shadow of himself, indeed.

SIR FOPLING

—Correct the errors of his motions and his dress.

MEDLEY

I find, Sir Fopling, in your solitude you remember the saying of
the wise man, and study yourself.

SIR FOPLING

'Tis the best diversion in our retirements. Dorimant, thou art a   90
pretty fellow and wearest thy clothes well, but I never saw thee
have a handsome cravat. Were they made up like mine, they'd
give another air to thy face. Prithee, let me send my man to dress
thee but one day. By heavens, an Englishman cannot tie a ribbon!

DORIMANT

They are something clumsy-fisted.   95

SIR FOPLING

I have brought over the prettiest fellow that ever spread a toilet.
He served some time under Mérille, the greatest *génie* in the
world for a *valet de chambre*.

97 *Mérille* Mérille had been in service with the Duc de Candale, and was his 'principal
confident' (*Memoires de Roger de Rabutin Comte Bussy* . . ., ed. L. Lalanne, II, p. 322).
After de Candale's death Mérille was in service with the Duc d'Orléans and by 1677 was
his 'premier valet de chambre' (*Correspondance de Roger de Rabutin* . . ., ed. L. Lalanne, 3
vols., 1858, III, p. 240n).
génie man of genius (cf. Fr. *homme de génie*). OED gives only three instances, of which
this is the first, between 1676 and 1687. It is best regarded as a French word.

98 *valet de chambre* although OED records this as English from 1646 onwards, and Handy is
so described in the Dramatis Personæ, Sir Fopling looks to the French (as Q1's spelling,
'Valet d'Chambré', indicates).

DORIMANT

    What, he who formerly belonged to the Duke of Candale?

SIR FOPLING

    The same, and got him his immortal reputation.   100

DORIMANT

    You've a very fine brandenburgh on, Sir Fopling.

SIR FOPLING

    It serves to wrap me up, after the fatigue of a ball.

MEDLEY

    I see you often in it, with your periwig tied up.

SIR FOPLING

    We should not always be in a set dress. 'Tis more *en cavalier to*
    appear now and then in a *déshabillé*.   105

MEDLEY

    Pray, how goes your business with Loveit?

SIR FOPLING

    You might have answered yourself in the Mall last night.—
    Dorimant, did you not see the advances she made me? I have
    been endeavouring at a song.

DORIMANT

    Already?   110

---

99 *Duke of Candale* Louis-Charles Gaston de Nogaret de Foix, Duc de Candale (1627–58)
    French general. Bussy reports, 'Sa taille étoit admirable. Il s'habilloit bien, et les plus
    proches tâchoient de l'imiter', but attributed this not to his valet but his mistress: Mlle
    de la Roche-Posay 'avoit pris tant de soin de le dresser, et lui de plaire à cette belle, que
    l'art avoit passé le nature, et qu'il étoit beaucoup plus honnête homme que mille gens
    qui avoient plus d'esprit que lui' (*Histoire Amoureuse . . .*, ed. Poitevin, 1857–8, I, pp.
    69–70).

101 *brandenburgh* morning gown (names after the Prussian city famous for its woollen
    goods). *OED* cites Etherege's use as its first occurrence. Conaghan further cites the
    Epilogue, ll. 14-15, to Lee's *Gloriana*, 1676: 'Huge *Brandenburgh* had so disguis'd each
    one,/ That from your Coachman you could scarce be known', and it is also used in
    Wycherley's *The Plain-Dealer*, 1677 (first acted 1676) (*Plays*, ed. cit., II.i, 519).

103 *periwig tied up* i.e., to save combing.

104 *en cavalier* jaunty, dashing

105 *déshabillé* V, CA (dissabillé Q1) casually dressed, Q1's spelling appears to be a phonetic
    rendering of the French. Compare with II.ii, 76 and textual note. The audience may
    have felt a pun.

108 *advances . . . made* see note to IV.i, 158–9.

SIR FOPLING

'Tis my *coup d'essai* in English. I would fain have thy opinion
of it.

DORIMANT

Let's see it.

SIR FOPLING

Hey, page, give me my song.—Bellair, here. Thou hast a pretty
voice, sing it.   115

YOUNG BELLAIR

Sing it yourself, Sir Fopling.

SIR FOPLING

Excuse me.

YOUNG BELLAIR

You learnt to sing in Paris.

SIR FOPLING

I did—of Lambert, the greatest master in the world; but I have
his own fault, a weak voice, and care not to sing out of a ruelle.   120

DORIMANT

A ruelle is a pretty cage for a singing fop, indeed.

YOUNG BELLAIR (*Reads the song*)

> How charming Phillis is, how fair!
>   Ah, that she were as willing
> To ease my wounded heart of care,
>   And make her eyes less killing.   125
> I sigh! I sigh! I languish now,
>   And love will not let me rest;
> I drive about the Park and bow,
>   Still as I meet my dearest.

111 *coup d'essai* trial shot, first attempt
119 *Lambert* Michel Lambert (1610–96), French lutenist and singer. He was made master of
      the royal chamber music by Cardinal Richelieu, and was a popular teacher in Louis
      XIV's Court.
120, 121 *ruelle* 'a bedroom, where ladies of fashion, in the seventeenth and eighteenth
      centuries, esp. in France, held a morning reception of persons of distinction; hence, a
      reception of this kind' (*OED*, which gives this as its first example). As Brett-Smith
      points out, Littré's *Dictionnaire*, 1863–72, shows the peculiar aptness to Sir Fopling bet-
      ter—'se disait particulièrement des chambres à coucher sous Louis XIV, des alcôves de
      certaines dames de qualité, servant de salon de conversation et où régnait souvent le ton
      précieux'.
122–9 *How . . . dearest* Thorpe (p. 104) gives later printings, those from 1707 onwards having
      music by Ramonden, though its satirical intent is lost in the context of the songbooks.
129 *Still as* Whenever

SIR FOPLING

Sing it, sing it, man! It goes to a pretty new tune which I am   130
confident was made by Baptiste.

MEDLEY

Sing it yourself, Sir Fopling. He does not know the tune.

SIR FOPLING

I'll venture.   SIR FOPLING *sings*

DORIMANT

Ay, marry, now 'tis something. I shall not flatter you, Sir
Fopling: there is not much thought in 't, but 'tis passionate and   135
well-turned

MEDLEY

After the French way.

SIR FOPLING

That I aimed at. Does it not give you a lively image of the thing?
Slap, down goes the glass, and thus we are at it.

DORIMANT

It does indeed. I perceive, Sir Fopling, you'll be the very head of   140
the sparks who are lucky in compositions of this nature.

Enter Sir Fopling's FOOTMAN

SIR FOPLING

La Tour, is the bath ready?

FOOTMAN

Yes, sir.

SIR FOPLING

Adieu donc, mes chers.

Exit SIR FOPLING [*with* FOOTMAN *and* PAGE]

MEDLEY

When have you your revenge on Loveit, Dorimant?   145

---

131 *Baptiste* probably Jean-Baptiste Lully (1632–87), Louis XIV's master of court music,
     composer, and credited with the founding of French opera. Called by Pepys (18 June
     1666) 'the present great composer'. But, as Conaghan says, 'Baptist' at this time often
     refers to Giovanni Battista Draghi (c. 1640–c. 1710), an Italian harpsichordist and
     composer, who had settled in England after the Restoration. He composed the operatic
     music for Shadwell's adaptation of *The Tempest*, 1674, as well as for his *Psyche*, 1675.

139 *glass* Carnochan suggests 'coach-window', but looking-glass seems more likely from the
     context.

142 *Tour* V, CA (Tower Q1)

144 *Adieu donc, mes chers* goodbye then, my friends

DORIMANT

I will but change my linen and about it.

MEDLEY

The powerful considerations which hindered have been removed then?

DORIMANT

Most luckily, this morning. You must go along with me; my reputation lies at stake there.   150

MEDLEY

I am engaged to Bellair.

DORIMANT

What's your business?

MEDLEY

Ma-tri-mony, an't like you.

DORIMANT

It does not, sir.

YOUNG BELLAIR

It may in time, Dorimant. What think you of Mrs Harriet?   155

DORIMANT

What does she think of me?

YOUNG BELLAIR

I am confident she loves you.

DORIMANT

How does it appear?

YOUNG BELLAIR

Why, she's never well but when she's talking of you, but then she finds all the faults in you she can. She laughs at all who   160 commend you; but then she speaks ill of all who do not.

DORIMANT

Women of her temper betray themselves by their over-cunning. I had once a growing love with a lady who would always quarrel with me when I came to see her, and yet was never quiet if I stayed a day from her.   165

YOUNG BELLAIR

My father is in love with Emilia.

DORIMANT

That is a good warrant for your proceedings. Go on and prosper—I must to Loveit. Medley, I am sorry you cannot be a witness.

153 *Ma-tri-mony an't like you* i.e., 'Medley mimics tradesmen's speech, in response to Dorimant's "business" ' (Conaghan).

MEDLEY

    Make her meet Sir Fopling again in the same place and use him   170
ill before me.

DORIMANT

    That may be brought about, I think.—I'll be at your aunt's
anon and give you joy, Mr Bellair.

YOUNG BELLAIR

    You had not best think of Mrs Harriet too much. Without
church security, there's no taking up there.   175

DORIMANT

    I may fall into the snare, too. But,

> The wise will find a difference in our fate:
> You wed a woman, I a good estate.

Exeunt

---

173 *give you* joy congratulate you
174 *not best* Q1 (best not CA)
175 *taking up* hire, buy up wholesale, borrow at interest (extending the metaphor estab-
     lished in 'church security').

ACT IV, SCENE III

[*Outside* MRS LOVEIT's]

Enter the chair with BELLINDA; *the men set it down and open it.*
BELLINDA *starting*

BELLINDA (*Surprised*)
Lord, where am I? In the Mall! Whither have you brought me?
FIRST CHAIRMAN
You gave us no directions, madam.
BELLINDA (*Aside*)
The fright I was in made me forget it.
FIRST CHAIRMAN
We use to carry a lady from the squire's hither.
BELLINDA (*Aside*)
This is Loveit! I am undone if she sees me.—Quickly, carry me   5
away!
FIRST CHAIRMAN
Whither, an't like your honour?
BELLINDA
Ask no questions!

Enter Mrs Loveit's FOOTMAN

FOOTMAN
Have you seen my lady, madam?
BELLINDA
I am just come to wait upon her.   10
FOOTMAN
She will be glad to see you, madam. She sent me to you this
morning to desire your company, and I was told you went out
by five o'clock.
BELLINDA (*Aside*)
More and more unlucky!
FOOTMAN
Will you walk in, madam?   15
BELLINDA
I'll discharge my chair and follow. Tell your mistress I am here.
[*Exit* FOOTMAN]

Take this! ([BELLINDA] *gives the* CHAIRMEN *money*)—and if ever
you should be examined, be sure you say you took me up in the
Strand, over against the Exchange—as you will answer it to Mr
Dorimant.   20

CHAIRMEN

We will, an't like your honour.   [*Exeunt* CHAIRMEN]

BELLINDA

Now to come off, I must on:

> In confidence and lies some hope is left;
> 'Twere hard to be found out in the first theft.   *Exit*

ACT V, SCENE I

Enter MRS LOVEIT *and* PERT, *her woman*

PERT
Well! In my eyes, Sir Fopling is no such despicable person.

MRS LOVEIT
You are an excellent judge.

PERT
He's as handsome a man as Mr Dorimant, and as great a gallant.

MRS LOVEIT
Intolerable! Is 't not enough I submit to his impertinences, but   5
must I be plagued with yours too?

PERT
Indeed, madam—

MRS LOVEIT
'Tis false, mercenary malice—

Enter her FOOTMAN

FOOTMAN
Mrs Bellinda, madam.

MRS LOVEIT
What of her?   10

FOOTMAN
She's below.

MRS LOVEIT
How came she?

FOOTMAN
In a chair—Ambling Harry brought her.

MRS LOVEIT
He bring her! His chair stands near Dorimant's door and always brings me from thence.—Run and ask him where he took her   15
up. Go!   [*Exit* FOOTMAN]
There is no truth in friendship neither. Women as well as men, all are false—or all are so to me at least.

124

PERT

You are jealous of her too?

MRS LOVEIT

You had best tell her I am. 'Twill become the liberty you take of   20
late. [*Aside*] This fellow's bringing of her, her going out by five
o'clock—I know not what to think.

Enter BELLINDA

Bellinda, you are grown an early riser, I hear!

BELLINDA

Do you not wonder, my dear, what made me abroad so
soon?   25

MRS LOVEIT

You do not use to be so.

BELLINDA

The country gentlewomen I told you of—Lord, they have the
oddest diversions!—would never let me rest till I promised to
go with them to the markets this morning to eat fruit and buy
nosegays.   30

MRS LOVEIT

Are they so fond of a filthy nosegay?

BELLINDA

They complain of the stinks of the town and are never well but
when they have their noses in one.

MRS LOVEIT

There are essences and sweet waters.

BELLINDA

Oh, they cry out upon perfumes, they are unwholesome. One of   35
'em was falling into a fit with the smell of these nerolii.

MRS LOVEIT

Methinks, in complaisance you should have had a nosegay too.

BELLINDA

Do you think, my dear, I could be so loathsome to trick myself

---

36 *nerolii* presumably the plural of 'neroli', which normally meant the essential oil distilled
from the flowers of the bitter orange and used for scenting gloves. (Named after the
Italian princess to whom its discovery is attributed.) Here it seems to refer to the gloves
worn by Bellinda (see 1. 40). For the popularity of essence of orange, see note to III.ii,
209.

37 *complaisance* See note to I, 382 and Introduction, pp. xxx-xxxii.

up with carnations and stock-gilly flowers? I begged their
pardon and told them I never wore anything but orange-flowers   40
and tuberose. That which made me willing to go was a strange
desire I had to eat some fresh nectarines.

MRS LOVEIT

And had you any?

BELLINDA

The best I ever tasted.

MRS LOVEIT

Whence came you now?   45

BELLINDA

From their lodgings, where I crowded out of a coach and took a
chair to come and see you, my dear.

MRS LOVEIT

Whither did you send for that chair?

BELLINDA

'Twas going by empty.

MRS LOVEIT

Where do these country gentlewomen lodge, I pray?   50

BELLINDA

In the Strand, over against the Exchange.

PERT

That place is never without a nest of 'em. They are always, as
one goes by, fleering in balconies or staring out of windows.

Enter FOOTMAN

MRS LOVEIT (*To the* FOOTMAN)

Come hither.   *Whispers*

BELLINDA (*Aside*)

This fellow by her order has been questioning the chairmen. I   55

---

39 *stock-gilly flower* white stock (*matthiola incana*). So-called both because of its clove-like
   smell and because it blooms in July.
41 *tuberose* liliaceous flower, with creamy white, funnel-shaped, fragrant flowers and a
   tuberous root. Like the orange-flower this was an exotic having only recently reached
   England (Evelyn mentions it in 1664 and the *London Gazette*, No. 2654/4 (1691), reports,
   'There are lately brought from Italy . . . Onions of Tubereuse'). In the language of flowers,
   tuberose signifies dangerous pleasures.
50–3 *Where . . . windows* See note to I, 55.
53 *fleering* jeering

threatened 'em with the name of Dorimant. If they should have
told truth, I am lost forever.

MRS LOVEIT

In the Strand, said you?

FOOTMAN

Yes, madam, over against the Exchange.   [*Exit* FOOTMAN]

MRS LOVEIT

She's innocent, and I am much to blame.   60

BELLINDA (*Aside*)

I am so frightened my countenance will betray me.

MRS LOVEIT

Bellinda, what makes you look so pale?

BELLINDA

Want of my usual rest and jolting up and down so long in an
odious hackney.

FOOTMAN *returns*

FOOTMAN

Madam, Mr Dorimant   [*Exit* FOOTMAN]   65

MRS LOVEIT

What makes him here?

BELLINDA (*Aside*)

Then I am betrayed indeed. He has broke his word, and I love a
man that does not care for me.

MRS LOVEIT

Lord!—you faint, Bellinda.

BELLINDA

I think I shall—such an oppression here on the sudden.   70

PERT

She has eaten too much fruit, I warrant you.

MRS LOVEIT

Not unlikely.

PERT

'Tis that lies heavy on her stomach.

MRS LOVEIT

Have her into my chamber, give her some surfeit-water, and let
her lie down a little.   75

66 *What . . . here* What's brought him here?
74 *surfeit-water* medicinal drink made by diffusion or distillation

PERT

Come, madam. I was a strange devourer of fruit when I was young—so ravenous.

Exeunt BELLINDA *and* PERT, *leading her off*

MRS LOVEIT

Oh, that my love would be but calm awhile, that I might receive this man with all the scorn and indignation he deserves!

Enter DORIMANT

DORIMANT

Now for a touch of Sir Fopling to begin with.—Hey, Page! Give   80
positive order that none of my people stir. Let the *canaille*
wait, as they should do.—Since noise and nonsense have such
powerful charms,

'I, that I may successful prove,
Transform myself to what you love'.   85

MRS LOVEIT

If that would do, you need not change from what you are—you can be vain and loud enough.

DORIMANT

But not with so good a grace as Sir Fopling.—'Hey, Hampshire!'—Oh, that sound! That sound becomes the mouth of a man of quality.   90

MRS LOVEIT

Is there a thing so hateful as a senseless mimic?

DORIMANT

He's a great grievance, indeed, to all who—like yourself, madam—love to play the fool in quiet.

MRS LOVEIT

A ridiculous animal, who has more of the ape than the ape has of the man in him.   95

DORIMANT

I have as mean an opinion of a sheer mimic as yourself; yet were he all ape, I should prefer him to the gay, the giddy, brisk, insipid, noisy fool you dote on.

76 *strange* exceptional
81 *canaille* riff-raff
84–5 *I . . . love* Waller, 'To the Mutable Fair', ll. 5–6 (*Poems*, I, p. 106). Dorimant changes the first word from 'And' to 'I'.

MRS LOVEIT

Those noisy fools, however you despise 'em, have good qualities
which weigh more (or ought, at least) with us women than all   100
the pernicious wit you have to boast of.

DORIMANT

That I may hereafter have a just value for their merit, pray do
me the favour to name 'em.

MRS LOVEIT

You'll despise 'em as the dull effects of ignorance and vanity, yet
I care not if I mention some. First, they really admire us, while   105
you at best but flatter us well.

DORIMANT

Take heed!—fools can dissemble too.

MRS LOVEIT

They may—but not so artificially as you. There is no fear they
should deceive us. Then, they are assiduous, sir. They are ever
offering us their service and always waiting on our will.   110

DORIMANT

You owe that to their excessive idleness. They know not how to
entertain themselves at home, and find so little welcome
abroad, they are fain to fly to you who countenance 'em, as a
refuge against the solitude they would be otherwise condemned
to.   115

MRS LOVEIT

Their conversation, too, diverts us better.

DORIMANT

Playing with your fan, smelling to your gloves, commending
your hair, and taking notice how 'tis cut and shaded after the
new way—

MRS LOVEIT

Were it sillier than you can make it, you must allow 'tis   120
pleasanter to laugh at others than to be laughed at ourselves,
though never so wittily. Then, though they want skill to flatter
us, they flatter themselves so well, they save us the labour. We
need not take that care and pains to satisfy 'em of our love,
which we so often lose on you.   125

DORIMANT

They commonly, indeed, believe too well of themselves, and
always better of you than you deserve.

96–128 David Vieth (N&Q, 203 (Nov. 1958), 473–4) points out the parallel with Rochester's
'Letter from Artemiza . . . to Chloe', ?Nov. 1673–spring 1675, ll. 101–35.

MRS LOVEIT

You are in the right; they have an implicit faith in us, which
keeps 'em from prying narrowly into our secrets, and saves us
the vexatious trouble of clearing doubts which your subtle and   130
causeless jealousies every moment raise.

DORIMANT

There is an inbred falsehood in women which inclines 'em still
to them whom they may most easily deceive.

MRS LOVEIT

The man who loves above his quality does not suffer more from
the insolent impertinence of his mistress than the woman who   135
loves above her understanding does from the arrogant
presumptions of her friend.

DORIMANT

You mistake the use of fools: they are designed for properties
and not for friends. You have an indifferent stock of
reputation left yet. Lose it all like a frank gamester on the   140
square. 'Twill then be time enough to turn rook and cheat it
up again on a good, substantial bubble.

MRS LOVEIT

The old and the ill-favoured are only fit for properties, indeed,
but young and handsome fools have met with kinder fortunes.

DORIMANT

They have, to the shame of your sex be it spoken. 'Twas this, the   145
thought of this, made me by a timely jealousy endeavour to
prevent the good fortune you are providing for Sir Fopling. But
against a woman's frailty all our care is vain.

---

138 *properties* mere instruments, tools, cat's–paws

139 *indifferent* tolerable

140–1 *on the square* face to face, openly. The modern idiom makes sense here, and was in use
from 1611, but the phrase may have been a term in gaming. The sense, 'without deceit,
fraud, or trickery' occurs from 1667–8 onwards, and is frequently used of gaming.
Wheadle, the gamester in *The Comical Revenge; or, Love in a Tub*, 1664, says that he
could stay within the law if he could give up gaming—'Could I but leave this Ordinary
[notorious for late-night gaming], this Square . . .' (I.iii, 16). Brett-Smith is unable to
explain this, but taking the two passages together the 'square' may refer to the gaming-
table or board.

141 *rook* cheat, swindler (esp. in gaming)

142 *bubble* a dupe or gull, esp. in gaming. A Restoration word. The use of the verb by
Wheadle in *Love in a Tub*, 1664, II.iii, 67, precedes the first instance in *OED*, and
suggests that it began as gaming slang.

MRS LOVEIT

Had I not with a dear experience bought the knowledge of
your falsehood, you might have fooled me yet. This is not the   150
first jealousy you have feigned to make a quarrel with me, and
get a week to throw away on some such unknown,
inconsiderable slut as you have been lately lurking with at
plays.

DORIMANT

Women, when they would break off with a man, never want the   155
address to turn the fault on him.

MRS LOVEIT

You take a pride of late in using of me ill, that the town may
know the power you have over me, which now (as unreasonably
as yourself) expects that I, do me all the injuries you can, must
love you still.   160

DORIMANT

I am so far from expecting that you should, I begin to think you
never did love me.

MRS LOVEIT

Would the memory of it were so wholly worn out in me that I
did doubt it too. What made you come to disturb my growing
quiet?   165

DORIMANT

To give you joy of your growing infamy.

MRS LOVEIT

Insupportable! Insulting devil! This from you, the only author
of my shame! This from another had been but justice, but
from you, 'tis a hellish and inhuman outrage. What have I
done?   170

DORIMANT

A thing that puts you below my scorn and makes my anger as
ridiculous as you have made my love.

MRS LOVEIT

I walked last night with Sir Fopling.

DORIMANT

You did, madam; and you talked and laughed aloud, 'Ha, ha,
ha'. Oh, that laugh! That laugh becomes the confidence of a   175
woman of quality.

MRS LOVEIT

You, who have more pleasure in the ruin of a woman's

reputation than in the endearments of her love, reproach me
not with yourself—and I defy you to name the man can lay a
blemish on my fame. 180

DORIMANT

To be seen publicly so transported with the vain follies of that
notorious fop, to me is an infamy below the sin of prostitution
with another man.

MRS LOVEIT

Rail on! I am satisfied in the justice of what I did: you had
provoked me to it. 185

DORIMANT

What I did was the effect of a passion whose extravagancies you
have been willing to forgive.

MRS LOVEIT

And what I did was the effect of a passion you may forgive if
you think fit.

DORIMANT

Are you so indiferent grown? 190

MRS LOVEIT

I am.

DORIMANT

Nay, then 'tis time to part. I'll send you back your letters you
have so often asked for. [*Looks in his pockets*] I have two or three
of 'em about me.

MRS LOVEIT

Give 'em me. 195

DORIMANT

You snatch as if you thought I would not. [*Gives her the
letters*]—There. And may the perjuries in 'em be mine if e'er
I see you more. *Offers to go: she catches him*

MRS LOVEIT

Stay!

DORIMANT

I will not. 200

MRS LOVEIT

You shall!

DORIMANT

What have you to say?

MRS LOVEIT

I cannot speak it yet.

DORIMANT

Something more in commendation of the fool. Death, I want
patience! Let me go.   205

MRS LOVEIT

I cannot. (*Aside*) I can sooner part with the limbs that hold
him.—I hate that nauseous fool, you know I do.

DORIMANT

Was it the scandal you were fond of, then?

MRS LOVEIT

You had raised my anger equal to my love, a thing you ne'er
could do before; and in revenge I did—I know not what I did.   210
Would you would not think on't any more.

DORIMANT

Should I be willing to forget it, I shall be daily minded of it.
'Twill be a commonplace for all the town to laugh at me, and
Medley, when he is rhetorically drunk, will ever be declaiming
on it in my ears.   215

MRS LOVEIT

'Twill be believed a jealous spite! Come, forget it.

DORIMANT

Let me consult my reputation; you are too careless of it.
(*Pauses*) You shall meet Sir Fopling in the Mall again tonight.

MRS LOVEIT

What mean you?

DORIMANT

I have thought on it, and you must. 'Tis necessary to justify my   220
love to the world. You can handle a coxcomb as he deserves
when you are not out of humour, madam.

MRS LOVEIT

Public satisfaction for the wrong I have done you! This is some
new device to make me more ridiculous.

DORIMANT

Hear me.   225

MRS LOVEIT

I will not.

DORIMANT

You will be persuaded.

MRS LOVEIT

Never!

DORIMANT

Are you so obstinate?

MRS LOVEIT

Are you so base? 230

DORIMANT

You will not satisfy my love?

MRS LOVEIT

I would die to satisfy that; but I will not, to save you from a thousand racks, do a shameless thing to please your vanity.

DORIMANT

Farewell, false woman!

MRS LOVEIT

Do! Go! 235

DORIMANT

You will call me back again.

MRS LOVEIT

Exquisite fiend! I knew you came but to torment me.

Enter BELLINDA *and* PERT

DORIMANT (*Surprised*)

Bellinda here!

BELLINDA (*Aside*)

He starts and looks pale. The sight of me has touched his guilty soul. 240

PERT

'Twas but a qualm, as I said, a little indigestion. The surfeit-water did it, madam, mixed with a little mirabilis.

DORIMANT [*Aside*]

I am confounded, and cannot guess how she came hither.

MRS LOVEIT

'Tis your fortune, Bellinda, ever to be here when I am abused by this prodigy of ill nature. 245

BELLINDA

I am amazed to find him here. How has he the face to come near you?

DORIMANT (*Aside*)

Here is fine work towards! I never was at such a loss before.

---

242 *mirabilis* acqua mirabilis, a medicinal drink—'The wonderful water, prepared of cloves, galangols, cubebs, mace, cardomums, nutmegs, ginger, and spirits of wine, digested twenty-four hours' (Johnson).

BELLINDA

    One who makes a public profession of breach of faith and
ingratitude—I loathe the sight of him.   250

DORIMANT [*Aside*]

    There is no remedy. I must submit to their tongues now and
some other time bring myself off as well as I can.

BELLINDA

    Other men are wicked, but then they have some sense of shame.
He is never well but when he triumphs—nay, glories—to a
woman's face in his villainies.   255

MRS LOVEIT

    You are in the right, Bellinda; but methinks your kindness for
me makes you concern yourself too much with him.

BELLINDA

    It does indeed, my dear. His barbarous carriage to you
yesterday made me hope you ne'er would see him more, and the
very next day to find him here again provokes me strangely. But   260
because I know you love him, I have done.

DORIMANT

    You have reproached me handsomely, and I deserve it for
coming hither, but—

PERT

    You must expect it, sir! All women will hate you for my lady's
sake.   265

DORIMANT [*Aside*]

    Nay, if she begins too, 'tis time to fly. I shall be scolded to
death, else. (*Aside to* BELLINDA) I am to blame in some
circumstances, I confess; but as to the main, I am not so guilty
as you imagine. [*Aloud*] I shall seek a more convenient time to
clear myself.   270

MRS LOVEIT

    Do it now! What impediments are here?

DORIMANT

    I want time, and you want temper.

MRS LOVEIT

    These are weak pretences!

---

254 *glories* Hobbes, *Leviathan* . . ., 1651, defines 'glory' as '*Joy*, arising from imagination of a
    mans own power and ability, is that exultation of the mind which is called GLORYING
    . . .' (pp. 26–7)
258 *carriage* behaviour

DORIMANT

You were never more mistaken in your life—and so
farewell. DORIMANT *flings off* 275

MRS LOVEIT

Call a footman, Pert. Quickly! I will have him dogged.

PERT

I wish you would not, for my quiet and your own.

MRS LOVEIT

I'll find out the infamous causes of all our quarrels, pluck her
mask off, and expose her bare-faced to the world!

[*Exit* PERT]

BELLINDA (*Aside*)

Let me but escape this time, I'll never venture more. 280

MRS LOVEIT

Bellinda, you shall go with me.

BELLINDA

I have such a heaviness hangs on me with what I did this
morning, I would fain go home and sleep, my dear.

MRS LOVEIT

Death and eternal darkness! I shall never sleep again. Raging
fevers seize the world and make mankind as restless all as I 285
am! *Exit* MRS LOVEIT

BELLINDA

I knew him false and helped to make him so. Was not her ruin
enough to fright me from the danger? It should have been, but
love can take no warning. *Exit* BELLINDA

---

282 *heaviness* torpor, dullness

ACT V, SCENE II

LADY TOWNLEY's *house*

Enter MEDLEY, YOUNG BELLAIR, LADY TOWNLEY, EMILIA, *and*
[SMIRK, *a*] *chaplain*

MEDLEY
Bear up, Bellair, and do not let us see that repentance in thine
we daily do in married faces.

LADY TOWNLEY
This wedding will strangely surprise my brother when he knows
it.

MEDLEY
Your nephew ought to conceal it for a time, madam. Since   5
marriage has lost its good name, prudent men seldom
expose their own reputations till 'tis convenient to justify their
wives'.

OLD BELLAIR (*Without*)
Where are you all there? Out, adod, will nobody hear?

LADY TOWNLEY
My brother! Quickly, Mr Smirk, into this closet. You must not   10
be seen yet.

[SMIRK] *goes into the closet*

Enter OLD BELLAIR *and Lady Townley's* PAGE

OLD BELLAIR [*To* PAGE]
Desire Mr Fourbe to walk into the lower parlour. I will be with
him presently.   [*Exit* PAGE]
(*To* YOUNG BELLAIR) Where have you been, sir, you could not
wait on me today?   15

YOUNG BELLAIR
About a business.

OLD BELLAIR
Are you so good at business? Adod, I have a business too you

---

10 *closet* small inner room for privacy
12 *Mr Fourbe* See note to II.i, 38.

137

shall dispatch out of hand, sir.—Send for a parson, sister. My
Lady Woodvill and her daughter are coming.

LADY TOWNLEY

What need you huddle up things thus?   20

OLD BELLAIR

Out a pize! Youth is apt to play the fool, and 'tis not good it
should be in their power.

LADY TOWNLEY

You need not fear your son.

OLD BELLAIR

He has been idling this morning, and adod, I do not like him.
(*To* EMILIA)—How dost thou do, sweetheart?   25

EMILIA

You are very severe, sir. Married in such haste!

OLD BELLAIR

Go to, thou'rt a rogue, and I will talk with thee anon. Here's
my Lady Woodvill come.

Enter LADY WOODVILL, HARRIET, *and* BUSY

Welcome, madam. Mr Fourbe's below with the writings.

LADY WOODVILL

Let us down and make an end, then.   30

OLD BELLAIR

Sister, show the way. (*To* YOUNG BELLAIR, *who is talking to*
HARRIET)—Harry, your business lies not there yet!—Excuse
him till we have done, lady, and then, adod, he shall be for
thee.—Mr Medley, we must trouble you to be a witness.

MEDLEY

I luckily came for that purpose, sir.   35

Exeunt OLD BELLAIR, MEDLEY, YOUNG BELLAIR, LADY TOWNLEY,
and LADY WOODVILL

BUSY [*To* HARRIET]

What will you do, madam?

HARRIET

Be carried back and mewed up in the country again, run away

27 *Go to* 'Come along!'
    to V, CA (too Q1)
29 *writings* i.e., the legal documents for the marriage settlement
37 *mewed up* shut up, cooped up

here—anything rather than be married to a man I do not care
for.—Dear Emilia, do thou advise me.

EMILIA

Mr Bellair is engaged, you know. 40

HARRIET

I do, but know not what the fear of losing an estate may fright
him to.

EMILIA

In the desperate condition you are in, you should consult with
some judicious man. What think you of Mr Dorimant?

HARRIET

I do not think of him at all. 45

BUSY [*Aside*]

She thinks of nothing else, I am sure.

EMILIA

How fond your mother was of Mr Courtage.

HARRIET

Because I contrived the mistake to make a little mirth, you
believe I like the man.

EMILIA

Mr Bellair believes you love him. 50

HARRIET

Men are seldom in the right when they guess at a woman's
mind. Would she whom he loves loved him no better!

BUSY (*Aside*)

That's e'en well enough, on all conscience.

EMILIA

Mr Dorimant has a great deal of wit.

HARRIET

And takes a great deal of pains to show it. 55

EMILIA

He's extremely well-fashioned.

HARRIET

Affectedly grave, or ridiculously wild and apish.

BUSY

You defend him still against your mother.

---

57 *wild and apish* for 'wild' see Introduction, pp. xxvi–viii. 'Apish' meant either ape-like, or
foolishly imitative like an ape.

HARRIET

I would not, were he justly rallied; but I cannot hear anyone
undeservedly railed at.   60

EMILIA

Has your woman learnt the song you were so taken with?

HARRIET

I was fond of a new thing. 'Tis dull at second hearing.

EMILIA

Mr Dorimant made it.

BUSY

She knows it, madam, and has made me sing it at least a dozen
times this morning.   65

HARRIET

Thy tongue is as impertinent as thy fingers.

EMILIA [*To* BUSY]

You have provoked her.

BUSY

'Tis but singing the song and I shall appease her.

EMILIA

Prithee, do.

HARRIET

She has a voice will grate your ears worse than a catcall, and   70
dresses so ill she's scarce fit to trick up a yeoman's daughter on
a holiday.

BUSY *sings*

Song, by Sir C. S.

As Amoret with Phillis sat
    One evening on the plain,
And saw the charming Strephon wait   75
    To tell the nymph his pain,

---

70 *catcall* a kind of whistle. On 7 March 1660 Pepys went to Pope's Head Alley and 'bought a
    catcall there, it cost me two groats'. It was used later in the century and in the eighteenth-
    century theatre to demonstrate an audience's disapproval of a play. See Leo Hughes, *The
    Drama's Patrons: A Study of the Eighteenth-Century London Audience*, 1971, pp. 35–43.

72 s.d. *Sir C.S.* almost certainly by Sir Car Scroope who wrote the Prologue, rather than Sir
    Charles Sedley to whom it was attributed in 1722. Brett-Smith supplies the lines from an
    elegy by Comtesse de la Suze in the *Recueil des Pièces Gallantes* which Scroope imitated. It
    was an unusually popular song, and appears in several manuscripts, musical broadsides,
    and songbooks (Thorpe, p. 144).

The threat'ning danger to remove,
　　She whispered in her ear,
'Ah, Phillis, if you would not love,
　　This shepherd do not hear:　　　　　　　　　　　　80

None ever had so strange an art,
　　His passion to convey
Into a list'ning virgin's heart
　　And steal her soul away.

Fly, fly betimes, for fear you give　　　　　　　　　　85
　　Occasion for your fate'.
'In vain', said she, 'in vain I strive.
　　Alas, 'tis now too late'.

Enter DORIMANT

DORIMANT
　　　　'Music so softens and disarms the mind—'
HARRIET
　　　　'That not one arrow does resistance find'.　　　　90
DORIMANT
　　Let us make use of the lucky minute, then.
HARRIET (*Aside, turning from* DORIMANT)
　　My love springs with my blood into my face. I dare not look
　　upon him yet.
DORIMANT
　　What have we here—the picture of a celebrated beauty giving
　　audience in public to a declared lover?　　　　　　　　95
HARRIET
　　Play the dying fop and make the piece complete, sir.
DORIMANT
　　What think you if the hint were well improved—the whole
　　mystery of making love pleasantly designed and wrought in a
　　suit of hangings?

85 *betimes* in good time
89–90 *Music . . . find* Waller, 'Of my Lady Isabella Playing on the Lute, ll. 11–12 (*Poems*, I,
　　p. 90), but with 'one' substituted for 'an'.
94 *a celebrated* B, CA, CO (celebrated Q1; Brett-Smith believes 'a' was accidentally omitted
　　and notes the parallelism with 'a declared lover' in l. 95)
99 *suit of hangings* set of tapestry wall-hangings

HARRIET

'Twere needless to execute fools in effigy who suffer daily in   100
their own persons.

DORIMANT (*To* EMILIA, *aside*)

Mistress Bride, for such I know this happy day has made
you—

EMILIA

Defer the formal joy you are to give me, and mind your business
with her. (*Aloud*)—Here are dreadful preparations, Mr   105
Dorimant—writings sealing, and a parson sent for.

DORIMANT

To marry this lady?

BUSY

Condemned she is; and what will become of her I know not,
without you generously engage in a rescue.

DORIMANT

In this sad condition, madam, I can do no less than offer you   110
my service.

HARRIET

The obligation is not great; you are the common sanctuary for
all young women who run from their relations.

DORIMANT

I have always my arms open to receive the distressed. But I will
open my heart and receive you where none yet did ever enter.   115
You have filled it with a secret, might I but let you know it—

HARRIET

Do not speak it if you would have me believe it. Your tongue is
so famed for falsehood, 'twill do the truth an injury.

Turns away her head

DORIMANT

Turn not away, then, but look on me and guess it.

HARRIET

Did you not tell me there was no credit to be given to faces—   120
that women nowadays have their passions as much at will as
they have their complexions, and put on joy and sadness, scorn
and kindness, with the same ease they do their paint and
patches? Are they the only counterfeits?

DORIMANT

You wrong your own while you suspect my eyes. By all the hope   125

102 *Mistress* ed. (Mrs. Q1)

I have in you, the inimitable colour in your cheeks is not more free from art than are the sighs I offer.

HARRIET

In men who have been long hardened in sin, we have reason to mistrust the first signs of repentance.

DORIMANT

The prospect of such a heaven will make me persevere and give 130
you marks that are infallible.

HARRIET

What are those?

DORIMANT

I will renounce all the joys I have in friendship and wine, sacrifice to you all the interest I have in other women—

HARRIET

Hold! Though I wish you devout, I would not have you turn 135
fanatic. Could you neglect these a while and make a journey into the country?

DORIMANT

To be with you, I could live there and never send one thought to London.

HARRIET

Whate'er you say, I know all beyond Hyde Park's a desert to 140
you, and that no gallantry can draw you farther.

DORIMANT

That has been the utmost limit of my love; but now my passion knows no bounds, and there's no measure to be taken of what I'll do for you from anything I ever did before.

HARRIET

When I hear you talk thus in Hampshire, I shall begin to think 145
there may be some little truth enlarged upon.

DORIMANT

Is this all? Will you not promise me—

HARRIET

I hate to promise! What we do then is expected from us and wants much of the welcome it finds when it surprises.

DORIMANT

May I not hope? 150

146 *little* Q1^c (omitted Q1^u, W, V)

143

HARRIET

That depends on you and not on me; and 'tis to no purpose to
forbid it. *Turns to* BUSY

BUSY

Faith, madam, now I perceive the gentleman loves you too. E'en
let him know your mind, and torment yourselves no longer.

HARRIET

Dost think I have no sense of modesty? 155

BUSY

Think, if you lose this, you may never have another
opportunity.

HARRIET

May he hate me—a curse that frights me when I speak it!—if
ever I do a thing against the rules of decency and honour.

DORIMANT (*To* EMILIA)

I am beholding to you for your good intentions, madam. 160

EMILIA

I thought the concealing of our marriage from her might have
done you better service.

DORIMANT

Try her again.

EMILIA [*To* HARRIET]

What have you resolved, madam? The time draws near.

HARRIET

To be obstinate and protest against this marriage. 165

Enter LADY TOWNLEY *in haste*

LADY TOWNLEY (*To* EMILIA)

Quickly, quickly, let Mr Smirk out of the closet!

SMIRK *comes out of the closet*

HARRIET

A parson! [*To* DORIMANT]—Had you laid him in here?

DORIMANT

I knew nothing of him.

HARRIET

Should it appear you did, your opinion of my easiness may
cost you dear. 170

169 *easiness* See note to I, 123.

Enter OLD BELLAIR, YOUNG BELLAIR, MEDLEY *and* LADY
WOODVILL

OLD BELLAIR

Out a pize, the canonical hour is almost past! Sister, is the man
of God come?

LADY TOWNLEY [*Indicating* SMIRK]

He waits your leisure.

OLD BELLAIR [*To* SMIRK]

By your favour, sir—Adod, a pretty spruce fellow! What may we
call him?   175

LADY TOWNLEY

Mr Smirk—my Lady Biggot's chaplain.

OLD BELLAIR

A wise woman, adod she is! The man will serve for the flesh as
well as the spirit.—Please you, sir, to commission a young
couple to go to bed together a God's name?—Harry!

YOUNG BELLAIR

Here, sir.   180

OLD BELLAIR

Out a pize! Without your mistress in your hand?

SMIRK

Is this the gentleman?

OLD BELLAIR

Yes, sir.

SMIRK

Are you not mistaken, sir?

OLD BELLAIR

Adod, I think not, sir!   185

SMIRK

Sure you are, sir.

OLD BELLAIR

You look as if you would forbid the banns, Mr Smirk. I hope
you have no pretension to the lady!

SMIRK

Wish him joy, sir! I have done him the good office today already.

---

171 *canonical hour* the hours in which marriage could take place legally (8–12 a.m.).
179 *a* Q1 (i' V)

OLD BELLAIR

    Out a pize! What do I hear?   190

LADY TOWNLEY

    Never storm, brother. The truth is out.

OLD BELLAIR

    How say you, sir? Is this your wedding day?

YOUNG BELLAIR

    It is, sir.

OLD BELLAIR

    And, adod, it shall be mine too. (*To* EMILIA) Give me thy hand,
    sweetheart. [*She refuses*] What dost thou mean? Give me thy   195
    hand, I say!   EMILIA *kneels, and* YOUNG BELLAIR

LADY TOWNLEY

    Come, come, give her your blessing. This is the woman your son
    loved and is married to.

OLD BELLAIR

    Ha! Cheated! Cozened! And by your contrivance, sister!

LADY TOWNLEY

    What would you do with her? She's a rogue, and you can't abide   200
    her.

MEDLEY

    Shall I hit her a pat for you, sir?

OLD BELLAIR

    Adod, you are all rogues, and I never will forgive you.
                                          [*Flings away, as if to exit*]

LADY TOWNLEY

    Whither? Whither away?

MEDLEY

    Let him go and cool awhile.   205

LADY WOODVILL (*To* DORIMANT)

    Here's a business broke out now, Mr Courtage. I am made a fine
    fool of.

DORIMANT

    You see the old gentleman knew nothing of it.

LADY WOODVILL

    I find he did not. I shall have some trick put upon me, if I stay in
    this wicked town any longer.—Harriet, dear child, where art   210
    thou? I'll into the country straight.

---

199 *Cozened* defrauded, duped

OLD BELLAIR

    Adod, madam, you shall hear me first—

             Enter MRS LOVEIT *and* BELLINDA

MRS LOVEIT

    Hither my man dogged him.

BELLINDA

    Yonder he stands, my dear.

MRS LOVEIT

    I see him, (*Aside*) and with him the face that has undone me.   215
    Oh, that I were but where I might throw out the anguish of my
    heart! Here it must rage within and break it.

LADY TOWNLEY

    Mrs Loveit! Are you afraid to come forward?

MRS LOVEIT

    I was amazed to see so much company here in a morning. The
    occasion sure is extraordinary.   220

DORIMANT (*Aside*)

    Loveit and Bellinda! The devil owes me a shame today, and I
    think never will have done paying it.

MRS LOVEIT

    Married! Dear Emilia, how am I transported with the news!

HARRIET (*To* DORIMANT)

    I little thought Emilia was the woman Mr Bellair was in love
    with. I'll chide her for not trusting me with the secret.   225

DORIMANT

    How do you like Mrs Loveit?

HARRIET

    She's a famed mistress of yours, I hear.

DORIMANT

    She has been, on occasion.

OLD BELLAIR (*To* LADY WOODVILL)

    Adod, madam, I cannot help it.

LADY WOODVILL

    You need make no more apologies, sir.   230

221–2 *The devil . . . it* Carnochan points out that Dorimant varies the proverb, 'the devil
    owed (one) a shame and now has paid it' (Tilley, op. cit., D261). See also Sir Frederick
    Frollick's 'The Devil ows some men a shame . . .' (*The Comical Revenge; or, Love in a
    Tub*, 1664, II.ii, 107).
227 *mistress* V, CA (Mrs. Q1)

EMILIA (*To* MRS LOVEIT)

The old gentleman's excusing himself to my Lady Woodvill.

MRS LOVEIT

Ha, ha, ha! I never heard of anything so pleasant.

HARRIET (*To* DORIMANT)

She's extremely overjoyed at something.

DORIMANT

At nothing. She is one of those hoiting ladies who gaily fling themselves about and force a laugh when their aching hearts are full of discontent and malice.   235

MRS LOVEIT

Oh heaven! I was never so near killing myself with laughing.— Mr Dorimant, are you a brideman?

LADY WOODVILL

Mr Dorimant! Is this Mr Dorimant, madam?

MRS LOVEIT

If you doubt it, your daughter can resolve you, I suppose.   240

LADY WOODVILL

I am cheated too, basely cheated!

OLD BELLAIR

Out a pize, what's here? More knavery yet?

LADY WOODVILL

Harriet! On my blessing, come away, I charge, you.

HARRIET

Dear mother, do but stay and hear me.

LADY WOODVILL

I am betrayed, and thou art undone, I fear.   245

HARRIET

Do not fear it. I have not, nor never will, do anything against my duty. Believe me, dear mother, do!

DORIMANT (*To* MRS LOVEIT)

I had trusted you with this secret but that I knew the violence of your nature would ruin my fortune—as now unluckily it has. I thank you, madam.   250

MRS LOVEIT

She's an heiress, I know, and very rich.

DORIMANT

To satisfy you, I must give up my interest wholly to my love.

---

234 *hoiting* involved in riotous and noisy mirth, acting the hoyden

Had you been a reasonable woman, I might have secured 'em
both and been happy.

MRS LOVEIT

You might have trusted me with anything of this kind, you   255
know you might. Why did you go under a wrong name?

DORIMANT

The story is too long to tell you now. Be satisfied; this is the
business, this is the mask has kept me from you.

BELLINDA (*Aside*)

He's tender of my honour, though he's cruel to my love.

MRS LOVEIT

Was it no idle mistress, then?   260

DORIMANT

Believe me—a wife, to repair the ruins of my estate that needs
it.

MRS LOVEIT

The knowledge of this makes my grief hang lighter on my soul,
but I shall never more be happy.

DORIMANT

Bellinda—   265

BELLINDA

Do not think of clearing yourself with me. It is impossible. Do
all men break their words thus?

DORIMANT

Th' extravagant words they speak in love. 'Tis as unreasonable
to expect we should perform all we promise then, as do all we
threaten when we are angry. When I see you next—   270

BELLINDA

Take no notice of me, and I shall not hate you.

DORIMANT

How came you to Mrs Loveit?

BELLINDA

By a mistake the chairmen made for want of my giving them
directions.

DORIMANT

'Twas a pleasant one. We must meet again.   275

BELLINDA

Never.

DORIMANT

Never?

277 *Never?* V, CA (Never! Q1)

149

BELLINDA

When we do, may I be as infamous as you are false.

LADY TOWNLEY

Men of Mr Dorimant's character always suffer in the general
opinion of the world.   280

MEDLEY

You can make no judgment of a witty man from common fame,
considering the prevailing faction, madam.

OLD BELLAIR

Adod, he's in the right.

MEDLEY

Besides, 'tis a common error among women to believe too well
of them they know and too ill of them they don't.   285

OLD BELLAIR

Adod, he observes well.

LADY TOWNLEY

Believe me, madam, you will find Mr Dorimant as civil a
gentleman as you thought Mr Courtage.

HARRIET

If you would but know him better—

LADY WOODVILL

You have a mind to know him better? Come away! You shall   290
never see him more.

HARRIET

Dear mother, stay!

LADY WOODVILL

I won't be consenting to your ruin.

HARRIET

Were my fortune in your power—

LADY WOODVILL

Your person is.   295

---

282 *prevailing faction* antipathy to the Wits, and the Wits' defensive reaction, is evident in
Dryden's dedication of *The Assignation*, 1673, to Sir Charles Sedley, which speaks of 'the
ignorant and ridiculous Descriptions which some Pedants have given of the Wits (as
they are pleas'd to call them) ... those wretches Paint leudness, Atheism, Folly, ill-
Reasoning, and all manner of Extravagances amongst us, for want of understanding
what we are' (*Works*, XI, p. 321). (Cited by Conaghan.)

HARRIET

Could I be disobedient, I might take it out of yours and put it into his.

LADY WOODVILL

'Tis that you would be at! You would marry this Dorimant!

HARRIET

I cannot deny it. I would, and never will marry any other man.

LADY WOODVILL

Is this the duty that you promised?   300

HARRIET

But I will never marry him against your will.

LADY WOODVILL (*Aside*)

She knows the way to melt my heart. (*To* HARRIET)—Upon yourself light your undoing.

MEDLEY (*To* OLD BELLAIR)

Come, sir, you have not the heart any longer to refuse your blessing.   305

OLD BELLAIR

Adod, I ha' not.—Rise, and God bless you both! Make much of her, Harry; she deserves thy kindness. (*To* EMILIA) Adod, sirrah, I did not think it had been in thee.

Enter SIR FOPLING *and his* PAGE

SIR FOPLING

'Tis a damned windy day. Hey, page! Is my periwig right?

PAGE

A little out of order, sir.   310

SIR FOPLING

Pox o' this apartment! It wants an antechamber to adjust one's self in. (*To* MRS LOVEIT)—Madam, I came from your house, and your servants directed me hither.

MRS LOVEIT

I will give order hereafter they shall direct you better.

SIR FOPLING

The great satisfaction I had in the Mall last night has given me   315
much disquiet since.

311–12 *one's self* ed. (ones self Q1; oneself V, CA)

MRS LOVEIT

'Tis likely to give me more than I desire.

SIR FOPLING [*Aside*]

What the devil makes her so reserved?—Am I guilty of an indiscretion, madam?

MRS LOVEIT

You will be of a great one, if you continue your mistake, sir.   320

SIR FOPLING

Something puts you out of humour.

MRS LOVEIT

The most foolish, inconsiderable thing that ever did.

SIR FOPLING

Is it in my power?

MRS LOVEIT

To hang or drown it. Do one of 'em, and trouble me no more.

SIR FOPLING

So *fière? Serviteur*, madam!—Medley, where's Dorimant?   325

MEDLEY

Methinks the lady has not made you those advances today she did last night, Sir Fopling.

SIR FOPLING

Prithee, do not talk of her.

MEDLEY

She would be a *bonne fortune*.

SIR FOPLING

Not to me at present.   330

MEDLEY

How so?

SIR FOPLING

An intrigue now would be but a temptation to me to throw away that vigour on one which I mean shall shortly make my court to the whole sex in a ballet.

MEDLEY

Wisely considered, Sir Fopling.   335

SIR FOPLING

No one woman is worth the loss of a cut in a caper.

325 *fière* proud, haughty;
   Serviteur your servant Arthur Sherbo thinks Sir Fopling's response echoes Molière's *Les Précieuses ridicules*, Sc. 16 (*MLN*, 64 (1949), 343–5).
336 *cut* a step in dancing (*OED* gives this as its first example). From the verb 'cut', to spring into the air and kick the feet with great rapidity (current from 1603).

MEDLEY

Not when 'tis so universally designed.

LADY WOODVILL

Mr Dorimant, everyone has spoke so much in your behalf that I
can no longer doubt but I was in the wrong.

MRS LOVEIT (*To* BELLINDA)

There's nothing but falsehood and impertinence in this world.   340
All men are villains or fools. Take example from my
misfortunes. Bellinda, if thou wouldst be happy, give thyself
wholly up to goodness.

HARRIET (*To* MRS LOVEIT)

Mr Dorimant has been your God Almighty long enough. 'Tis
time to think of another.   345

MRS LOVEIT [*To* BELLINDA]

Jeered by her! I will lock myself up in my house and never see
the world again.

HARRIET

A nunnery is the more fashionable place for such a retreat and
has been the fatal consequence of many a *belle passion*.

MRS LOVEIT [*Aside*]

Hold, heart, till I get home! Should I answer, 'twould make her   350
triumph greater.   *Is going out*

DORIMANT

Your hand, Sir Fopling—

SIR FOPLING

Shall I wait upon you, madam?

MRS LOVEIT

Legion of fools, as many devils take thee!   *Exit* MRS LOVEIT

MEDLEY

Dorimant! I pronounce thy reputation clear, and henceforward,   355
when I would know anything of woman, I will consult no other
oracle.

SIR FOPLING

Stark mad, by all that's handsome!—Dorimant, thou hast
engaged me in a pretty business.

342 *misfortunes. Bellinda*, Q1 (misfortunes, Bellinda; V, B)
349 *belle passion* violent passion
354 *Legion* innumerable hosts, with an echo of Mark v. 9, 'My name is Legion for we are
     many'. Cf. Epilogue, 1. 18.

DORIMANT

I have not leisure now to talk about it.   360

OLD BELLAIR

Out a pize, what does this man of mode do here again?

LADY TOWNLEY

He'll be an excellent entertainment within, brother, and is
luckily come to raise the mirth of the company.

LADY WOODVILL

Madam, I take my leave of you.

LADY TOWNLEY

What do you mean, madam?   365

LADY WOODVILL

To go this afternoon part of my way to Hartley—

OLD BELLAIR

Adod, you shall stay and dine first! Come, we will all be good
friends, and you shall give Mr Dorimant leave to wait upon you
and your daughter in the country.

LADY WOODVILL

If his occasions bring him that way, I have now so good an   370
opinion of him, he shall be welcome.

HARRIET

To a great, rambling, lone house that looks as it were not
inhabited, the family's so small. There you'll find my mother, an
old lame aunt, and myself, sir, perched up on chairs at a
distance in a large parlour, sitting moping like three or four   375
melancholy birds in a spacious volary. Does not this stagger
your resolution?

DORIMANT

Not at all, madam. The first time I saw you, you left me with the
pangs of love upon me, and this day my soul has quite given up
her liberty.   380

HARRIET

This is more dismal than the country.—Emilia, pity me who am
going to that sad place. Methinks I hear the hateful noise of

---

366 *Hartley* there are a Hartley Wespall, a Hartley Mauditt, and a Hartley Wintney in
Hampshire.

370 *occasions* 1) needs, requirements, 2) affairs, business

376 *volary* a large bird-cage; an aviary. Introduced from the French *volière* in the seventeenth century. *OED* cites first instance from Jonson's *New Inn*, 1630, V.i.

rooks already—kaw, kaw, kaw. There's music in the worst cry in
London—'My dill and cucumbers to pickle'.

OLD BELLAIR

Sister, knowing of this matter, I hope you have provided us   385
some good cheer.

LADY TOWNLEY

I have, brother, and the fiddles too.

OLD BELLAIR

Let 'em strike up then. The young lady shall have a dance before
she departs.

Dance

(*After the dance*) So now we'll in, and make this an arrant   390
wedding day.
(*To the pit*)

> And if these honest gentlemen rejoice,
> Adod, the boy has made a happy choice.

Exeunt omnes

---

384 *My dill . . . pickle* Addison, writing on the cries of London street-traders, says, 'I am
always pleased with that particular Time of the Year which is proper for the pickling of
Dill and Cucumbers; but alas this Cry, like the Song of the Nightingales, is not heard
above two Months' (*Spectator*, No. 251 (18 Dec. 1711)).

THE EPILOGUE

By Mr Dryden

Most modern wits such monstrous fools have shown,
They seemed not of heav'n's making, but their own.
Those nauseous harlequins in farce may pass,
But there goes more to a substantial ass!
Something of man must be exposed to view,   5
That, gallants, they may more resemble you.
Sir Fopling is a fool so nicely writ,
The ladies would mistake him for a wit,
And when he sings, talks loud, and cocks, would cry:
'I vow, methinks, he's pretty company –   10
So brisk, so gay, so travelled, so refined!'
As he took pains to graft upon his kind,
True fops help nature's work, and go to school
To file and finish God A'mighty's fool.
Yet none Sir Fopling him, or him, can call –   15
He's knight o' the shire and represents ye all.
From each he meets, he culls whate'er he can:

Most probably spoken by the actress playing Harriet. See Barnard, art. cit., pp. 305–6.

3 *harlequins* Harlequin is the traditional figure in French and Italian *commedia dell'arte*. Travelling companies from the continent had been well received in England, but were disapproved of by Dryden (and later Pope) as a vulgar, 'low' form.

6 *they* Q1 (it B, CA; B adopts the reading of the Bodleian ms.: see Note on the Text)

9 *cocks* struts, brags, or crows over

10 *I vow* Q1 (I now B: Aye now CA; both readings follow mss. texts)

11 *refined!* ed. (refin'd! Q1: refined, CA; V, however, regards l. 11 as the only line cried out by the ladies)

12–14 Sloane ms. adds an extra couplet after l. 12: 'Labouring to put in more as Mr. Bayes/ Thrums in Additions to his ten years plays'. Bodlein ms. Places the couplet, with slight variants, after l. 14. (Further, see Note on Text). Dryden's additional couplet 'turns the tables on George Villiers, Duke of Buckingham, for his satiric portrait of Dryden as Bayes in *The Rehearsal*; Buckingham's play was several years in the making before its first appearance in 1671 and was often amended afterward' (Carnochan).

12 *upon . . . kind* upon what nature gave him
   kind, ed. (kind. Q1; kind.' CA)

13–14 See note to I, 343–6.

16 *knight o' the shire* parliamentary representative of a shire (or country)

Legion's his name, a people in a man.
His bulky folly gathers as it goes,
And, rolling o'er you, like a snowball grows.   20
His various modes from various fathers follow;
One taught the toss, and one the new French wallow.
His sword-knot, this, his cravat, this designed –
And this, the yard-long snake he twirls behind.
From one, the sacred periwig he gained,   25
Which wind ne'er blew, nor touch of hat profaned;
Another's diving bow he did adore,
Which with a shog casts all the hair before,
Till he with full decorum brings it back
And rises with a water spaniel shake.   30
As for his songs (the ladies' dear delight),
Those sure he took from most of you who write.
Yet every man is safe from what he feared,
For no one fool is hunted from the herd.

18 *Legion* See note to V.ii, 354.
21 *modes* See note to II. ii, 29.
22 *toss* i.e., of the head. *OED* gives as first example of this usage.
    wallow rolling walk or gait. *OED* gies this sole example.
24 *snake* long curl or tail attached to a wig. *OED* gives this example, and one from Swift
    (1728).
26 *nor . . . profaned* for the fashion of carrying the hat (to avoid disordering the wig), cf.
    Dryden's 'Epilogue Spoken at the Opening of the New House' [1674], 1.13, 'So may your
    Hats your Foretops never press . . .' *Works*, I, p. 150).
28 *shog* shake, jerk. Cotgrave (1611) gives 'shake, shog, or shocke' as synonyms.
33–4 *Yet . . . herd* a conventional claim, but although identifications were quickly made,
    Dryden's claim is probably correct (see Introduction, pp. xlix–l and n. 59).

APPENDIX A

Dr Staggins's Settings of Dorimant's Song and Sir Car Scroope's Song

These two settings of Dorimant's song ('When first Amintas charmed my heart') in Act III, Scene i, and Sir Car Scroope's song ('As Amoret with Phillis sat') in Act V, Scene ii, are the nearest contemporary settings known. Dr Nicholas Staggins (1650?–1700) was made master of 'his Majesty's Music' in 1675, but he published few of his compositions.

The nearest contemporary setting of Sir Fopling's song (Act IV, Scene ii) dates from 1707, and is by Ramonden (see Thorpe, pp. 103–104).

Mr Philip Wilby has kindly made these modern realizations from the original printed music. The part for the piano, which would have been improvised at will, has been added by Mr Wilby.

Staggins's setting of Dorimant's song is printed in John Playford's *Choice Ayres and Songs to sing to the Theorbo-Lute, or Bass-Viol: being most of the Newest Ayres and Songs Sung at Court, And at the Publick Theatres. Composed by Several Gentlemen of His Majesty's Music, and Others . . . The Fifth Book* (1684), p. 38. Ramonden's setting, dating from 1707, is also extant. For a record of other printings of the song, and reprintings of Staggins's music, see Thorpe, p. 102.

Staggins's setting of Sir Car Scroope's song is printed in Playford's *Choice Ayres . . . The Second Book* (1679), p. 5. It was an unusually popular song. Thorpe (p. 144) records manuscript copies, various printings, and further notes that its popularity continued into the early eighteenth century.

'When First Amintas Charmed My Heart'

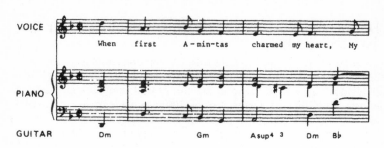

When first A-min-tas charmed my heart, My

heed-less sheep be-gan to_stray; The wolves soon stole the

great-est part, And all will now be_made a prey.

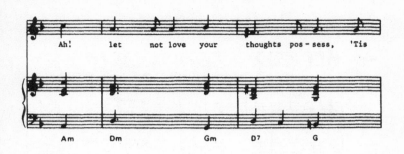

'As Amoret with Phillis Sat'

As A - mor-et with Phil - lis sat, One

Gm   Gm   Eb Cm̊   D

even - ing on the plain, And saw the charm-ing

C(m)   Gm Cm   D7   Gm   Cm   F7

Stre - phon wait to tell the nymph his pain, The

Bb   F   Eb   F7   Bb

APPENDIX B

The Bullies' Song

The scraps of the song directed by the bullies at Sir Fopling, Mrs Loveit, and Bellinda in Act III, Scene iii, 205, 214 have been identified by W. B. Carnochan as being from an anonymous ballad in *A New Collection of the Choicest Songs. Now in Esteem in Town or Court* (1676), sig. B6ᵛ. The volume also contains Dorimant's song ('When first Amintas'), mistakenly attributed to Sir Fopling, the drinking-song from Act IV, Scene i, and Sir Car Scroope's song. The song sung by the bullies became the basis for a ballad, 'Love al-a-Mode, or, the Modish Mistris' (Pepys Collection, iii. 102; Pepysian Library, Magdalene College, Cambridge). The text in *A New Collection*, which has no musical setting, is as follows:

> Tell me no more you love,
>   Unless you will grant my desire,
> Ev'rything else will prove,
>   But fuel to my fire.
>
> 'Tis not for kisses alone,
>   So long I have made my address,
> There's some thing else to be done,
>   Which you cannot chuse but guess.
>
> 'Tis not a charming smile,
>   That brings me the perfect Joys,
> Nor can you me beguile,
>   With sighs and with languishing eyes:
>
> There is an essence within,
>   Kind Nature hath clear'd the doubt,
> Such bliss can never be sin,
>   And therefore i'le find it out.